MISSION AND LITURGY

Contest, Convergence and Congruence
with special reference to the
Malankara Mar Thoma Syrian Church

Dr. Jameson K. Pallikunnil

authorHOUSE®

AuthorHouse™ UK
1663 Liberty Drive
Bloomington, IN 47403 USA
www.authorhouse.co.uk
Phone: 0800.197.4150

© 2018 Dr. Jameson K. Pallikunnil. All rights reserved.
Cover design – Rev. Abraham Varghese

No part of this book may be reproduced, stored in a retrieval system, or transmitted by any means without the written permission of the author.

Published by AuthorHouse 06/14/2018

ISBN: 978-1-5462-9373-6 (sc)
ISBN: 978-1-5462-9374-3 (e)

Print information available on the last page.

Any people depicted in stock imagery provided by Getty Images are models, and such images are being used for illustrative purposes only. Certain stock imagery © Getty Images.

This book is printed on acid-free paper.

Because of the dynamic nature of the Internet, any web addresses or links contained in this book may have changed since publication and may no longer be valid. The views expressed in this work are solely those of the author and do not necessarily reflect the views of the publisher, and the publisher hereby disclaims any responsibility for them.

Foreword

Rev. Dr. Jameson K. Pallikunnil is publishing this book with the title, "Mission and Liturgy: Contest, Convergence and Congruence with special reference to the Malankara Mar Thoma Syrian Church." I am happy to write a Foreword for this book since it is a fruitful product of his doctoral research in the field of Liturgical Theology. This is a unique book referring to the Mission and Liturgy of the Mar Thoma Church. I commend the author for his systematic way of exploration in the field of liturgy and the hard work behind this venture.

The Mar Thoma Syrian Church of Malabar traces its origin to the ministry of St. Thomas, one of the disciples of Christ, in India around 52 CE. The inception of the Church in India is the result of this apostolic mission. As Emil Brunner says: "Church exists by her mission as the fire exists by burning." If the trajectories of the growth of this Church are traced through the centuries, the nature and content of the mission of the Church as well as the Liturgy it held as dear and good will be revealed. It is learned that these were also subject to change from time to time. Community formation and community living being integral to the nature of any Church as its mission and ministry, one cannot escape the liturgy it used through the years to enrich the life of the community.

The World Council of Churches (W.C.C.) recognizes Mar Thoma Church as a 'special family' among the global churches with special features such as: (a) Heritage of the St. Thomas Christians that is autonomous, indigenous and at the same time inclusive or welcoming, (b) liturgical footing in the Eastern Oriental Traditional and (c) theological reflections in the European Protestant doctrines, where the Holy Bible is held as the ground of all doctrines.

The Mar Thoma Church is a reformed Church, with the major reformation which took place in 1836. This nature of reformation still continues in the church. A community that gathered together first in

Malankara (Kerala, India) has now become a global Church. It continues to live and spread by reaffirming its reformed ideas and considering seriously her multi-cultural and multi ethnic identity. The Church is plural, diverse and multiple in her functions. The multitude, migrants and the margins understand the Church as the body of Christ with great expectation and hope. The need of inter subjectivity and inter connectivity within the one body of Christ enables the Church to be inclusive in nature. This inclusiveness equips the Church to be an 'open community', ready to share the pain and pathos of the wounded world and to embrace them to the fellowship of the Church. This is a sacramental living.

Worship is the epitome activity of the members of the Church, giving glory to God. Worship is not a mere, ritualistic act, rather it is an experience of one's dynamic relationship with the Risen Lord. It is through worship that the Church finds her identity and growth. It is the worship that illuminates the Church's service and enables the Church to remain as a witness to the larger society. Liturgy plays a vital part in the life of the Church. The regular worship gathers the members together. It enables the members to come together frequently. Liturgy, therefore, keeps the Church alive and dynamic. Liturgy is to be understood as an axis that gives the Christian life its purpose, shape and meaning in a given context. The Holy Qurbana is the central expression of the Church and remains as a mark of one's Christian identity. The liturgical celebration of Holy Qurbana strengthens the members in their relationship with God and with one another. Thus, it creates a sacramental living in the world. The Church, the faith-community becomes a witnessing community, carrying out an outreach ministry which is her mission. This book explores how the Church holds the scripture and Liturgy together in her spiritual journey and mission.

The mission of the Church is the Mission of God itself revealed ultimately in Jesus Christ, guided by Holy Spirit, making transformation to the entire creation. Mission is thus from everywhere to everywhere. This book clearly states: "The Eucharist Liturgy affirms that the community gathered for worship must be dispersed for mission. It orients the believing community towards new responsibilities such as the preservation of creation, witness to Jesus Christ and service to society." This book includes some liturgical proposals of the author that are pertinent in the onward journey of the Church. This book intensely analyses the mission and liturgy of the Mar Thoma Church and its intrinsic relation. It speaks about how these were contested historically, how convergence developed gradually in the life of the Church and how congruence gives the Mar Thoma Church a significant place in the Christendom. I present this book to the readers to rediscover the quintessence of the spiritual life of an ancient church with modern outlook by re-reading the mission and liturgy of the Malankara Mar Thoma Church.

May, 2018.   **Rt. Rev. Dr. Geevarghese Mar Theodosius**
Bishop of the Diocese of Mumbai,
Malankara Mar Thoma Syrian Church
Vashi, Navi Mumbai.

Preface

It seems not that long ago that the young author and I sat down together to reflect. At that modest wooden table we found ourselves at a kind of crossroads. Obviously a crossroads between youth and age. But also between East and West; he the promising son of the Malankara Mar Thoma Church; myself a Catholic, but one also quite immersed in the Russian Byzantine tradition. The meeting proved an enrichment and bond of friendship for both travellers.

The discussions had to do principally with the wedding of two fundamentals of Christian life, Liturgy and Mission, or, if you would, the meeting between community worship and outgoing activity, the vertical of prayer igniting the horizontal of outreach and embrace. Clearly, here, too, a crossroads.

At that table two individuals had necessarily to gaze backwards to their respective origins. After all, liturgical rites come to flower in the soil bed of community life, self-awareness and prayer. In his eloquent Greek John Chrysostom once reminded his flock that Our Lord was also worshipped elsewhere and in other languages. Liturgy directs our gaze to a precious past. Moreover, in their origin the Rites also bespeak geographical localization: Ethiopia, Egypt, Armenia, Syria, Persia, India, Byzantium, ancient Rus, North Africa and the Christian West. Mission, on the other hand, makes us look forward into the future. It is a movement that spills outward beyond boundaries. Is this not also crossroads?

At the encounter between past and future, between tradition and adaptation, between ancestral Rite and cultural insertions, is there not perhaps inherent strain? Today the children of Kerala have taken root throughout the Diaspora, not unlike the children of Israel. How then to pass on their sacred past to succeeding generations? This is one of the issues our author seeks to address. In the spirit of mission and positivity he would replace the term "strain" with that of "challenge." He has delved into the past in search of tradition's essentials which, <u>mutatis mutandis</u>, ever lend themselves excitingly to new environments. The sons and daughters of Mar Thoma have much to contribute to a new world. If I have understood the author correctly, he is attempting to initiate a "compass" that would guide his brothers and sisters, and indeed their children's children, so that they may remain essentially faithful to their past while orientating and contributing to the future. His is a vision, a first step, and an invitation to apostolic co-workers to come together to formulate a "compass" for mission. He himself believes the dynamics of such a compass are to be imbedded in liturgy. Accordingly, his hope is that the reader might examine, weigh up and contribute. This is properly a project for community.

Let me commend Rev. Dr. Jameson for his efforts and wish him all the best in his future endeavours. I wish the readers of this book to have a meaningful encounter with the liturgy and mission.

May, 2018   **Prof. Dr. Dennis P. Hainsworth**
                                                 Maynooth, Co. Kildare
                                                 Ireland.

Acknowledgements

It was an excellent opportunity and a wonderful experience to pursue my doctoral studies in the field of Liturgical Theology at St. Patrick's College, Maynooth, Ireland. This volume is a continuation of my first book, "The Eucharistic Liturgy: A Liturgical Foundation for Mission in the Malankara Mar Thoma Syrian Church," which is a revised version of my dissertation. Here, I would like to express my deep appreciation and heartfelt gratitude to all those who have helped out throughout my academic pursuit.

At this juncture, let me extend my wholehearted thanks to my thesis guide, Prof. Dr. Liam Tracey, OSM for his valuable advice, constructive criticism and unflagging support from the beginning till the end of this research.

I am indeed grateful to the Mar Thoma Metropolitan His Grace the Most. Rev, Dr. Joseph Mar Thoma who always remained as an inspirational and driving force in my theological journey and ministry. I thankfully remember the encouragement and valued support provided by the Diocesan Bishops, Rt. Rev. Dr. Geevarghese Mar Theodosius and Rt. Rev. Dr. Isaac Mar Philaxinos. I am much indebted to the Hon. Episcopal Synod of the Malankara Mar Thoma Church for the permission to pursue my higher studies in Ireland.

My gratitude also goes to the administrative staff of the Pontifical University of Ireland, St. Patrick's College - Maynooth, Library Staff at the National University of Ireland, the National Centre for Liturgy, the Cadbury Research Centre - Birmingham, the Basel Mission Centre - Switzerland, the Princeton Theological Seminary - Pennsylvania, the St. Ephrem Ecumenical Research Centre - Kottayam, the Mar Thoma Theological Seminary - Kottayam, and the United Theological College - Bengaluru.

I am indebted to numerous persons during this research programme. Let me acknowledge the support of Bishop Dr. John Fenwick, Bishop

Peter Eaton, Rev. Dr. Phillip Tovey, His Grace Mathews Mar Aprem, Prof. Dr. Michael Mullaney, Fr. Patrick Jones, Rev. Dr. Paul Kenny, Sr. Moira Bergin, Rev. Dr. M.J. Joseph, Rev. Dr. George Mathew Kuttiyil, Rev. Abraham Varghese and Rev. Eapen Varghese. Let me record my sincere thankfulness to Dr. Dennis Hainsworth and Mr. C. P. Mathew for proof reading and necessary corrections. Special words of gratitude goes to all my friends and well-wishers for their valuable support and prayers.

The encouragement, concern and prayers of my beloved parents, Oommen Kunjukunju and Thankamma Kunjukunju, loving siblings and their families are much appreciated. The love, patience and constant support of my wife Honey Rajan, children: Haaran, Darshan and Mahal are beyond words.

Above all,

Let me praise and glorify the name of God Almighty, the one who has called, sustained and guided throughout my faith journey.

Rev. Dr. Jameson. K. Pallikunnil

Contents

Introduction xvii

Chapter. 1
Discourse on Mission: Scripture, Ecclesia and Academia 1

1	Contesting Mission: Global Ecclesial Scenario 2
1.1	Conceptualizing Mission: Hermeneutical Paradigms 3
2	Mission: Ecclesiastic Traditions 5
2.1	Mission: In Orthodox Tradition 6
2.2	Mission: In Protestant Traditions 12

Chapter. 2
Mission in the Malankara Mar Thoma Syrian Church:
A Historical and Liturgical Overview 18

1	Mission Patterns of the Mar Thoma Church and its Liturgical Influence 18
2	Mission: A Historical Survey 22
3	Models of Mission 26
3.1	The Church Model of Mission 27
3.2	The Kingdom Model of Mission 29
3.3	An Incarnational Model of Mission 30
3.4	An Institutional Model of Mission 30
3.5	A Charity and Developmental Model 33
3.6	A Dialogue Model of Mission 36
3.7	Sacramental Model of Mission 37
4	Models of Mission: A Critical Assessment 39

Chapter. 3
Liturgy and Community Formation: Missional Significance in
the Mar Thoma Church 45

1	The Liturgy and Community Formation	46
1.1	The Characteristics of the Church as a Community	49
1.1.1	A Community of Word and Sacraments	50
1.1.2	A Eucharistic Community	52
1.1.3	A Missional Community	54
1.1.4	An Eschatological Community	55
2	The Sacrament of Baptism: An Invitation to the Eucharistic Community	57
2.1	Baptism: Call to Mission	62

Chapter. 4
Cultural Landscape of the Mar Thoma Community:
Liturgical Significance and Challenges 67

1	Culture: What is it?	69
1.1	Culture and Christianity	71
2	Cultural and Geographical Diversity	75
2.1	The Mar Thoma Diaspora: An Analysis	77
2.1.1	The Mar Thoma Diaspora: A Historical Glance	80
2.1.1.1	The Malaysian and Singapore	82
2.1.1.2	The Australian and New Zealand	84
2.1.1.3	Middle-East	85
2.1.1.4	African Continent	86
2.1.1.5	North America and Canada	86
2.1.1.6	Europe	88
2.1.2	Liturgical Life in the Diaspora: A Critical Observation	90
2.2	Mission Centers: An Overview	94
2.2.1	Liturgy in the Mission Field Milieu: An Analysis	95

2.2.2	Major Challenges in the Mission Field Context	98
2.2.3	Relevant Approaches to Mission in the Indian Mission Field Settings	103
2.2.4	Liturgical Orientation and Training	106
2.2.5	An Integration of Liturgy and Evangelism in the Church	107

Chapter. 5
Challenges in Mission: A Liturgical Review 112

| 1 | Challenges of the Mar Thoma Diaspora Community | 113 |
| 2 | Liturgical Challenges in the Mission centers | 117 |

Chapter. 6
Scope of Liturgical Renewal in the Mar Thoma Church 120

1	Liturgical Adaptation and Inculturation	121
2	Inculturation of Liturgy	125
2.1	Liturgical Inculturation in the Malankara Church	128
2.2	Liturgical Adaptation in the Mar Thoma Church	130
3	Contextual Liturgies and its Relevance	134

Chapter. 7
Scripture and Liturgy: Convergence and Congruence for Mission 137

1	Scripture and Liturgy in the Mar Thoma Church	138
1.1	The Orthodox and Protestant Approaches to Scripture	139
1.2	Integration of Scripture and the Liturgy	142
1.3	The Lectionary of the Mar Thoma Church	145
2	Characteristics of the Eucharistic Liturgy of the Mar Thoma Church	148
2.1	A Critical Reading on the Prospects of the Liturgy	152

Chapter. 8
Liturgical Proposals for Mission in the Mar Thoma Church................156

General Conclusion..173
Bibliography..179

Introduction

The Malankara Christians in Kerala attribute root of their spiritual heritage to St. Thomas and they claim their ecclesiastical existence right from the very first century. The arrival of missionaries from the West especially the ecclesial powers such as the Persians, the Portuguese, the Dutch, the French and the British made a great impact on the social and religious life of the people of Kerala from time to time. The immigration of a group of people from Persia under the leadership of the merchant Thomas of Cana in 345 CE paved the way for a connection between the Malankara Church and the Persian Church. Until the arrival of Portuguese in 1498 CE, the St. Thomas Christians were in connection with the Persian Church and they followed the prayers and practices of the East Syrian liturgical traditions. The arrival of Portuguese and the spreading of Catholicism among the Malankara Church (the Latinisation) that followed had caused a major division among the St. Thomas Christians. Subsequently, the relationship with the Syrian Orthodox Church in Antioch began together with an adoption of the West Syrian liturgy and customs. The colonisation and the rule of the British by the 17th century had made a great impact in the life of the Kerala society especially in the St. Thomas Christian community. The Church Missionary Society (CMS) from London arrived in India with the aim of revamping the St. Thomas Christians and it was yet another epoch making chapter in the history of the Malankara Church. The influence of the CMS missionaries caused a revival in the Malankara Church and thereby the formation of the Malankara Mar Thoma Syrian Church[1] (MTC), a reformed Church in the Malankara tradition. Being a reformed Church but at the same time, having

---

[1] The Malankara Mar Thoma Syrian Church is also known as the Mar Thoma Syrian Church of Malabar or simply the Mar Thoma Church. The name of the Church is hereafter referred to as the MTC. In order to understand the nature, identity, theology and liturgical background of this church, kindly refer the book "The Eucharistic Liturgy: A Liturgical Foundation for Mission in the Malankara Mar Thoma Syrian Church" by Jameson K. Pallikunnil. The first two chapters of this book is taken from the above mentioned book in a revised manner.

some elements of the cultural ethos of the Oriental Orthodox Church, the MTC uses the West Syrian liturgy and its theological position is in unison with the Anglican Church.

The translation of the Eucharistic liturgical texts from Syriac to Malayalam was the initial apparent attempt of the reformation process. Later, the availability of the Bible in the vernacular,[2] and the systematic study of Scripture, helped the reformers to revise the Eucharistic liturgy in line with Anglican theology. Since the reformation, the MTC uses the Liturgy of St. James in its revised form. A consequence of the reformation in the Malankara Church is the development of a mission paradigm, which gives equal importance to evangelization, social service, and the struggle for social justice and peace. Among Malankara Christians, the MTC is a pioneering Church that took the Word of God (Scripture) and Table (Eucharist) to the remote places where Gospel has not yet been preached and especially to the outcaste sections such as Dalits[3] and Tribal people in the Indian sub-continent by way of its missionary activities.

The mission of the Church is to participate in the mission of God. More precisely, the Church is commissioned with a mission that comes from God and that belongs to God. The mission is first and foremost, God's turning towards the world in creative love, redemptive healing and transforming power. The mission of Christ and thereby Church is for the entire creation. It can be understood as the work of a community (the Church), with a community (the holy Trinity), for a community (God's whole creation).

---

[2] The first attempt to translate the Bible into Malayalam was started by Rev. Claudius Buchanan, who persuaded Malankara church leaders to translate the holy text into Malayalam and gave guidance to local scholars. At that time Syriac was the liturgical language of Christians in Kerala. In 1811, Kayamkulam Philipose Ramban translated four Gospels from Syriac to Malayalam which is considered as the First version of the Bible that popularly known as "Ramban Bible." After Ramban Bible, it was Benjamin Bailey who continued the effort of translating Bible to Malayalam. He completed New Testament and published it in 1829. Bailey completed the translation of Old Testament and printed it in 1841. Hence, it was Benjamin Bailey who had translated the entire Bible to Malayalam language. Hermann Gundert updated Bailey's version and produced the first Malayalam-English dictionary (1872).

[3] Dalits are the most vulnerable group of people in Indian society who are marginalized and alienated from the main stream of Indian society because of their colour, occupation and social situations.

The Church is commissioned with the privilege and responsibility of participating in the mission of Jesus Christ by the power of the Holy Spirit.[4] A Christian community which actively participates in liturgical worship cannot remain thoughtlessly closed in on itself, but must progress in the practice of His mission. God's mission, as experienced in the Eucharist, embraces the entire human race and indeed all creation[5]. Through an active participation in the liturgy, the faithful experience communion and fellowship with the Triune God and with their fellow believers. Further, an active participation in the liturgy reminds the faithful of their responsibility to witness the salvific act of Christ both individually and collectively. It motivates the Church to impart a Eucharistic presence in the world and thereby accommodates others into a communion with the Triune God. The Eucharistic liturgy affirms that the community gathered for worship must be dispersed for mission. It orients the believing community towards new responsibilities such as the preservation of creation, witness to Jesus Christ and service to society. Wherever the Church is proclaiming the Gospel, the Eucharistic liturgy happens to be the directive and motive force for its life and mission.

Mission is, in fact, the life blood of the Church. Through its mission-work and revised liturgy, the MTC took a pioneer role in the formation and nurturing of new Christian communities in India and different parts of the world.[6] Accordingly, this research reflects on the role of liturgy and its influence on the missionary undertakings of the MTC especially in the context of the diaspora and the mission fields in India. It elucidates how the revised liturgy functions as a basis for mission and recounts how newly converted Christians, especially Dalits and Tribal people, embraced

---

[4] Vincent J. Nugent, "Theological Foundation for Mission Animation: A Study of the Church's Essence," *World Mission* 24, no.1 (Spring 1943): 7-18.

[5] Billy Swan, *The Eucharist, Communion and Formation: Proceedings of the International Symposium of Theology: The Ecclesiology of Communion Fifty Years after the Opening of Vatican II* (Dublin: Veritas, 2013), 575-576.

[6] The MTC has missionary works and outreach programs in more than twenty states including two union territories of India and other parts of the world such as Nepal (1945), Tibet (1972), and Malaysia (1980).

the richness of the Saint James Liturgy. It dwells on the necessity for an on-going revision of liturgy, inculturation with its possibilities and its prospects for new liturgies within the changing social scenario. This section concludes with pertinent liturgical proposals for the furtherance of mission in general. With a living experience and profound theological understanding, this ancient but reformed Church has something unique to offer to the whole Christendom.

Chapter categorization

The first two chapters mostly deal with the subject of Christian mission and its historical and liturgical overview in the MTC. The Bible and the revised liturgy of the Church act as foundations of mission in the MTC. Since this Church has both the Protestant and Oriental Orthodox traditions, theses chapters look at mission on the basis of these traditions. Further, it presents a historical survey of mission in the Church, and the various mission models employed by it. The reformation process (1836) in the Malankara Church has greatly influenced the early Marthomites to proliferate far and wide by their mission activities. The worldwide migration, social changes in Kerala and the evangelistic outreach has together made this Church very unique. It is now a multi-cultural, multi-lingual and multi-ethnic faith community. This global Church has encountered multi-cultural and multi-ethnic atmosphere and assimilated various cultural practices and faced faith confrontation in its own geographical regions. This confrontation has caused a renewed view of nature, identity and mission of the Church in a positive manner. Currently, the MTC is almost a worldwide Church, having an ecclesial presence in most of the regions of India and the major continents of the world as a result of evangelization process and constant migration. In this context, how does the liturgy penetrate into the life of the people at large? What is the role of the liturgy in its varied cultural and ethnic context, especially in the diaspora and mission-field regions? While considering the growth of the Church, it is important to ensure the relevance of the liturgy in general. While analysing the liturgy, it is imperative to examine major liturgical challenges the Church faces in its different contexts especially in the settings of diaspora and mission-fields. Without understanding the challenges and solutions pertaining to the Church in its mission, the Church cannot be a meaningful witnessing community in the present context. Hence the next four chapters largely studies the significance of the liturgy in various cultural and geographical contexts of the Church in which the mission field and in a diaspora settings are specifically stressed. It reflects how the liturgy motivates the faithful to gather as a worshipping community and various characteristics of the Church in general as a faith community. Here the importance of the Sacrament of Baptism is delineated. A detailed account of the historical development of the diaspora community and the influence of liturgy are examined. Further, the diverse mission centres of the Church and its cultural specialities, an integration of liturgy and evangelism, liturgical orientation and training, relevant approaches to mission in the Indian mission field settings are also dealt with in detail. Added to this, the various challenges of the Church in its mission fields and diaspora regions are studied in the framework of liturgy. Since the liturgy reflects the faith and theology of the Church as a reformed and reforming faith community, the scope of liturgical renewal is looked into where the liturgical adaptation and possibilities of contextual liturgies in the Church are studied.

The MTC exists as a "hybrid church" by blending the Eastern liturgical elements of the Oriental Orthodox Church and the evangelical ideas of the Protestant Reformation of the 16th century.[7] In the Oriental Eastern tradition, a theology of the Church is not articulated in the articles of faith but is embedded in the liturgy. Liturgy reflects the theology of the Church and active participation in the liturgical celebrations offer the faithful an inexplicable mystical experience of fellowship. But in the reformed tradition, Scripture is central to the Church's life, order and mission. Hence, as an ancient Church which stands as a bridge between the Oriental Orthodox tradition and the reformed tradition, it is essential to explore how the MTC holds Scripture and the liturgy together in its spiritual journey

---

[7] M. J. Joseph, ed., *Gleanings* (Madras: Printon, 1994), 24.

and mission. The seventh chapter scrutinizes how the Church keeps a balance with the liturgy and Scripture in its very life and mission. Further, this chapter evaluate the features of the present Eucharistic liturgy and its prospects. This study concludes with some of the pertinent liturgical proposals for the furtherance to sustain the life and mission of the Church.

One of the challenges that the MTC faces in the 21st century is to develop itself fully into a global Church by transcending local frontiers set by ethnicity and nationality. The Church is called to be a cross-cultural, inter-racial and inter-generational community responding to the needs of the hour. Responding creatively to the signs of the time marks the relevance of a Church. The Liturgy of the Church is designed in such a fashion as to bring God's life to the people. As an ancient Christian community, the MTC with its vibrant life of mission and sacraments for the extension of the Kingdom of God, has a pride of place in the Christendom. As a Church with modern outlook over against an ancient backdrop, this Church has a growing relevance in rediscovering the quintessence of its spiritual life by re-reading its historic liturgy.

Chapter. 1

Discourse on Mission: Scripture, Ecclesia and Academia

The Mar Thoma Church (MTC) is a mission-oriented Church. The reformation (1836) in the Malankara Church motivated them to carry out the mission of Christ seriously and it ignited them to move out from its caste scenario[8] of Kerala. The ecclesial identity and the mission theology of this Church were reshaped by its encounter with the CMS missionaries and also by the social and political changes that took place in Kerala during the first half of 18th century. An encounter with European Protestant Christianity encouraged them to accept evangelism, social service, and struggles for justice and peace as goals for the mission.[9] The mission of the MTC is significant because it is the pioneering Church among the Malankara Christians who initiated the first cross-cultural mission in the Indian sub-continent.[10] The translation and renewal of the Eucharistic liturgy on the basis of Scripture gave a strong impetus for the Church in its mission. Since, the Church holds a balanced position in between the

---

[8] The Malankara Christians in Kerala enjoyed a privileged position in the social terrain of Kerala with the privileges of the upper class. They were confined and found themselves comfortable in their own social set up. The Reformation process gave impetus to move out from its own area to the non-Christian communities like Dalits, Adivasi's and oppressed communities in the country.

[9] The term mission is expressed by the use of verbs meaning "to send," normally with God as the expressed subject. The Hebrew verb *salah* and the Greek term *apostello* emphasize an authoritative, commissioning relationship involved. The Scriptures also employ the cognates *apostolos* ('apostle,' the one sent) and *apostole* ('apostleship,' the function of being sent), referring to the one sent and his function. Horst Balz and Gerhard Schneider, ed., *Exegetical Dictionary of the New Testament*, trans. Virgil P. Howard, James W. Thompson, John W. Medendorp and Douglas W. Stott. vol. 1 (Grand Rapids: Eerdmans, 1993), 141-42.

[10] Alex Thomas, *A History of the First Cross Cultural Mission of the Mar Thoma Church 1910 - 2000.* (Delhi: ISPCK, 2007), 100-101.

traditions of the Orthodox[11] and Protestantism, the mission strategy of these ecclesial communities are also analysed to get a clear position on the concept of mission in the MTC.

1   Contesting Mission: Global Ecclesial Scenario

The mission of the Church is based on the mission of Jesus Christ. Jesus came with the mission to preach Good News to all nations (Mk.13:10). He proclaimed God's nearness to, and concern for, God's people. David Bosch points out that "mission has its origin in the heart of God. God is the fountain of sending love. This is the deepest source of mission. It is impossible to penetrate deeper still; there is mission because God loves people."[12] The Church, through its missionary activities works for the transformation of the world in Christ. The transformation of the world through the love of Christ is the meaning of Christian mission. Therefore, the very life of the Church is missionary in nature and its bearers witness as the agency of the Kingdom of God. This also cannot be proved in abstract theoretical concepts. Only missionary activities can prove that the Church is the agent through which the Kingdom of God continuously actualizes itself in history.[13]

In missiology today there are two conflicting approaches to mission work. Those who uphold the classical definition say that mission is "the spreading of Christian faith among non-believers and those who confess

---

[11] The title Orthodox refers to several Churches, which have been in conflict over doctrinal, administrative, and hierarchical matters. "The Orthodox Churches share the common roots, historical experiences, and cultural expressions. All these Churches are found in the eastern parts of the Christian world and therefore are sometimes called the Eastern Churches. The Orthodox Churches affirm a common Orthodox faith, life, practice and a conciliar nature of unity. While the Orthodox Church is separated by geographic and administrative jurisdictions rooted in the long history of Orthodox people across the globe, these Churches are united by shared doctrines and religious practices across jurisdictional, linguistic, and geographical locations." Frances Kostarelos, "Short Term Missions in the Orthodox Church in North America," *Missiology: An International Review* 41, no.2 (April 2013): 179-186.

[12] David J. Bosch, *Transforming Missions: Paradigm Shifts in Theology of Missions* (New York: Orbis, 1992), 392.

[13] Paul Tillich, "The Theology of Missions," *The Journal Christianity and Crisis* (March 1955): 27.

different faiths, and the sending of missionaries to the corresponding regions for this purpose."[14] The second approach is proclaiming brotherly communion and service (*kerygma, koinonia, diakonia*). This missiology dated back to the early chapters of Acts, which proclaimed how the apostles proclaimed the Gospel, founded communities and engaged in service. Under this definition of mission these three aspects are not means to an end but the end itself.[15]

1.1 Conceptualizing Mission: Hermeneutical Paradigms

The Christian religion is a historic religion that centres on the salvific act of Jesus Christ. The main task of the Church is to communicate the good news of Christ and to make disciples of all nations (Mt.28:18-19). Even though the term mission is not appearing explicitly in Scripture, this concept permeates the entire Bible. The concept of mission in the Old Testament lies in the understanding that the transcendent God is the God who is involved in the history, who acts in and through the history.[16] The record of His involvement in history indicates that His work is both revelatory and redemptive.[17] The act of God is manifested in and through the activities and mission of the Patriarchs, Judges, Prophets, Priests and Kings in the history of Israel. The Church's mission of inclusivity and universality has its roots in the Old Testament, particularly in the vision of the prophets (Gen.12:3, Isa.45:1-8, 49:1-6).[18] The New Testament reveals that the mission is the manifestation of the love of God (Jn. 3:16). The mission of the Church has its roots in the ministry and person of Jesus, who is both "evangelical" and

---

[14] Arthur F. Glasser and Donal A. McGavran, *Contemporary Theologies of Mission* (Baker Moor House, 1983), 26.
[15] Vladimir Federov, "Orthodox Mission Today," *Together in Mission: Orthodox Churches Consult with the Church Mission Society*, Mosco (April 2001): 13-14.
[16] Robert Hall Glover, *The Bible Basis of Missions* (Chicago: MOODY, 1976), 15-22.
[17] Geevarghese Mar Theodosius, "Mission of the Church in the 21st Century," in *Challenges and Prospects of Mission in the Emerging Context,* ed. Koshy P. Varughese, (Faridabad: Dharma Jyoti Vidya Peeth, 2010), 20.
[18] Lesslie Newbigin, *The Logic of Election in the Gospel in a Pluralistic Society* (Grand Rapids, MI: Eerdmans, 1989), 80-88. George R. Hunsberger, *Bearing the Witness of the Spirit: Lesslie Newbigin' Theology of Cultural Plurality* (Grand Rapids: MI, Eerdmans, 1998), 45-112.

"evangelizer,"[19] as he preached, served and witnessed to the reign of God and gathered around him a community[20] (Mk.1:14-45, 6:7-13, Lk.10:1-20). Jesus saw his purpose as being sent by God his Father to proclaim and accomplish spiritual deliverance for humankind (Lk.4:43, Jn.3:34, 8:42, 10:36). Before ascending into heaven, Jesus commissioned his disciples to go to the ends of the earth with a particular mission (Mt. 28:18-20). This great commissioning (Mt.28:16-20, Jn.20:19-23) is a mandate for mission. Hence the mission of the Church has its roots in the post-resurrection faith of the first disciples. They held the conviction of Jesus' universal Lordship as risen Christ, through whom humanity has direct access to God. The Holy Spirit is the guide and source of strength for mission (Jn.15.26, 14.26, Lk.24:49, 46-48, Acts.1:8). The disciples of Christ created a new community of fellowship in prayer and mutual service with the power of the Holy Spirit. For them mission begins with the self-understanding in relationship with Jesus and its manifestations.[21] For the apostles, to prove Jesus as the awaited Messiah to the Jews was the "mission." The mission outside Judaism was spontaneity, the result of a vision to Peter (Acts.10). It inaugurated new debates on the very notion of mission. It was a part of their very life and existence. They were witnessing what they experienced.[22]

The religious persecution of the early Christians during the first and second centuries has pointed up another mode of mission. For them, to

---

[19] Mortimer Arias, *Announcing the Reign of God: Evangelization and the Subversive Memory of Jesus* (Philadelphia: Fortress, 1984), 2.
[20] Hans Kung, *The Church* (New York: Sheed and Ward, 1967), 74-75.
[21] Robert Hall Glover, *The Bible Basis of Missions* (Chicago: MOODY. 1976), 22-30.
[22] The apostles, particularly Paul and John, perceive the mystery of the plan of God for the whole creation. St. Paul envisions a new cosmic community in which God seeks to gather all things (Eph.1:10), reconcile all things (Col.1:20), reunite all things so that God will be all in all (1 Cor.15:28). The evangelist John sees the Word of God enlightening everywhere (Jn.1:9) and becoming flesh to share with us his fullness (Jn. 1:16). John also sees God making all things new, so that there will be a new heaven and a new earth, where there will be no more tears and suffering (Rev.2:1-5). The missionary journeys of St. Paul were also the result of a vision and the initiation of the Holy Spirit (Acts.13:1-3, 16.6-10). His mission to the gentile community was mainly based on his interpretation of his own conversion. He emphasized the grace element in Christian faith. It was by the grace of God that he was saved, not on merit. Therefore, mission, for St. Paul is an initiation of the Holy Spirit as well as his personal understanding of God and its manifestation. Michael Amaladoss, "Challenges of Mission in the 21st century," *Theology Digest* 47, no.1 (Spring 2000): 15-20.

witness Jesus Christ was a matter of life and death, a process of persecution, dispersion and expansion that resulted in the mission (Acts.8:4). When the Romans persecuted the early Christians, they dispersed from Jerusalem. Wherever they went, they preached the good news of Jesus to everyone. apostles, and early missionaries, travelled everywhere, to the Mediterranean world, North Africa and even as far as India, with the Gospel. Paul's missionary journey in the book of the Acts of apostles narrates a descriptive report on the growth of Christianity. When the early believers scattered because of religious persecution, they preached wherever they were dispersed[23] (Acts. 8:4). Gradually Christianity "defied territorial confinement and transcended all human constraints-political, social and cultural."[24] The mission of the Christian community is to give witness to the reality of God through the Church as a sign, foretaste, and presence of the Kingdom of God. The mission of the Church must, therefore, be preoccupied with the nature of the One to whom it bears witness.

2   Mission: Ecclesiastic Traditions

The term mission has no common connotation in the history of Christianity. Throughout the centuries, diverse ecclesiastical traditions defined and practiced it differently. According to Schmemann, "a theology of mission has been always the fruit of the total being of the Church and not a mere speciality for those who receive a particular missionary calling."[25] To understand the concept of mission in the MTC, it is imperative to trace the varied understandings of mission in different Christian traditions since the Church stands in between Orthodoxy and Protestantism. The acceptance of ecclesial pluralism, practice of Eastern liturgical tradition,

---

[23] Sam George, "Diaspora: A Hidden Link to 'from Everywhere to Everywhere," *Missiology: An International Review 39, no. 1* (January 2011): 46-55.
[24] Adrian Hastings, *'150-1550': In a World History of Christianity* (Grand Rapids, MI: Eerdmans: 1999), 58.
[25] Daniel B. Clendenin, ed. *Eastern Orthodox Theology: A Contemporary Reader* (Grand Rapids, MI: Baker, 1995), 196. Alexander Schmemann, *Church, World, Mission (*New York: St. Vladimir's, 1979), 28.

and the affirmation of the Anglican theological emphasis shaped a theology of mission for the MTC. As noted above, this Church is indebted to the Antiochian Orthodox Church for its liturgical contributions, worship pattern and also it is obliged to the Protestant missionaries of Europe, especially the CMS, for its theological position. In order to understand the notion of mission in the MTC, it is imperative to analyse the mission concept of the Antiochian Orthodox Church and the Protestant traditions.

2.1 Mission: In Orthodox Tradition

The designation "Orthodox" or the Orthodox Church provides a perspective on the ecclesiological self-understanding of the Eastern Church. The term "Orthodox" is derived from a Greek word *doxazein* (to glorify) or from *dokein* (to think, to have a perspective) and means the Church that correctly praises God or the Church of the "right faith" or "right doctrine." Both interpretations form a unity of Orthodoxy and orthopraxy that pertains to the self-understanding of the Orthodox Churches.[26] In general, the missionary understanding of the Orthodox Church derives from mainly three areas: Scripture, Church Fathers and the Liturgy. These are considered as the elements of a theology of mission.[27]

(1) **Scripture**: The Eastern Church considered Scripture to be part of the apostolic tradition, which had a living continuity and was wider than the Bible alone. The richness of tradition illuminates and interprets Scripture. For them, the liturgy and writings of the Church Fathers were the basis for understanding the Bible. The Orthodox accept the Bible as the Word of God, a record of God's will. The Orthodox view of Scripture is dynamic. God's

---

[26] For Orthodox an understanding of the unity of the Church is based on shared faith and life rather than on organizational structures. It sees membership of the Church as based on participating in the life given by God rather than through membership of an organization. John Binns, *An Introduction to the Christian Orthodox Churches* (Cambridge: Cambridge University, 2002), 42.

[27] James Stamoolis, "Mission in Orthodox Theology," *The Greek Orthodox Theological Review* 33, no.1 (Spring 1988): 63-80.

revelation dealt with persons, patriarchs, prophets, priests, and ultimately with Jesus Christ. Authority was not usually accorded to the biblical books at the time they were composed, but came gradually over the course of centuries. Thus behind the books of the Bible lies a dynamic history of oral tradition.[28]

(2) **Church Fathers**: The Church Fathers bear the witness of the Orthodox to mission. In the Patristic period, the mission had not been given prominence since the Christological controversies, which consumed so much energy and time, detracted from the formulation of missionary theology. The Church Fathers had an understanding of the nature of the plan of God for the salvation of the world. According to Bosch, the monastic movement was another saving element in the Patristic and later in the Orthodox missionary tradition. Supremely, however, it has been the simple faith of thousands of ordinary believers that, to this day, gives expression to an essentially missionary dimension in Orthodoxy.[29]

(3) **The Liturgy**: In the Orthodox tradition, the liturgy is a corporate act rather than an individualistic approach. It is a means to keep their faith traditions in the midst of their challenges and persecutions. The liturgy helped them to exist in isolation from their cultural

---

[28] T. G Stylianopoulos, *The New Testament: An Orthodox Perspective*. vol. 1 (Brookline, Massachusetts: Holy Cross Orthodox, 1997), 7-13. The mission of the Church cannot be reduced only to preaching the Gospel-it implies service, i.e. witness through deeds as well as words. He further explains that the mission of the Church in its ultimate theological meaning is an expression of the apostolic faith of the Church itself. Gerald H. Anderson and Thomas F. Stransky, eds., *Mission Trends No. 1: Crucial Issues in Mission Today* (New York: Paulist, 1974), 59-70. The mission of the Church developed, as part of the Christian civilization, a social and personal ethos, which had itself been shaped by Orthodox Christianity. Anderson, eds. *Mission Trends No. 1,* 65-66. As Timothy Ware puts it, tradition has a broad, comprehensive meaning: "to an Orthodox tradition means the books of the Bible; it means the Creed, it means the decrees of the Ecumenical Councils and the writings of the Church Fathers; it means the Canons, the Service Books, the Holy icons- in fact, the whole system of doctrine, Church government, worship and art which Orthodoxy has articulated over the ages. The Orthodox Christians views themselves as heir and guardian to a great inheritance received from the past, and they believe that it is their duty to transmit this inheritance unimpaired to the future." Timothy Ware, *The Orthodox Church* (London: Penguin, 1969), 204.

[29] Bosch, *Transforming Missions*, 205-209.

roots and it has been effective in enabling the continued identity and existence of the Church. There is an interconnection between the liturgy and the mission of the Church. The supreme liturgy, the Eucharist, is the culmination of the mission of the Church that reveals the mission imperative. The Church that gathers for worship is an act of proclamation. "For as often as you eat this bread and drink the cup, you proclaim the Lord's death until he comes." (1 Cor.11:26). Therefore, the extent of the mission of the Church is confessed at every Eucharistic service.[30] The Orthodox theologians point out the centrality of the Eucharist in the mission understanding of the Orthodox Church.[31]

Schmemann rightly points out that, "the Church celebrates the Eucharist as a human response to the divine gift, its acceptance, and appropriation by humanity. This response has two aspects, i.e. the God-centered and man or world-centered. These two aspects cannot be separated for they condition each other and together constitute the dynamics of Christian life and action. The God-centered aspect is the sanctification, the growth in holiness, of both the Christian individual and the Christian community. It is the slow transformation of the old Adam in us in to the new one, the restoration of the pristine beauty, which was lost in sin. It is also the slow victory over the demonic powers of the cosmos, the joy and peace which make it partakers of the Kingdom and of life eternal. The Orthodox spiritual tradition always stressed the mystical nature of Christian life, as life hidden with Christ in God. The second aspect of the Church as response is man or world-centered. It is the understanding of the Church as being left in this world, in its time, space, and history with a specific task or mission. The Church is fullness and its home is in heaven. However, this fullness is given to the

---

[30] Ion Bria, ed., *Go Forth in Peace: Orthodox Perspectives on Mission* (Geneva, WCC, 1986), 25-30. James. J Stamoolis, *Eastern Orthodox Mission Theology Today* (Eugene: Wipf and Stock, 2001), 86-102.
[31] Timothy Ware, *The Orthodox Church* (London: Penguin, 1969), 269-314, Ion Bria, "Dynamics of Liturgy in Mission" *International Review of Mission* 82, (1993): 317-325, Ion Bria, "The Liturgy after the Liturgy," *International Review of Mission* 67, (1978): 86-90.

world, sent into the world as its salvation and redemption. In the Orthodox experience and faith, it is the Church and its sacrament that makes possible the Church-mission."[32]

Orthodoxy's liturgical-sacramental origin is the Eucharist. Currently, the Orthodox theologians widely share a Eucharistic ecclesiology.[33] The Eucharist is a single corporate action which involves the whole community.[34] In the Eucharist, "the Church becomes what it is," fulfils itself as the body of Christ, as the divine Parousia - the presence and the communication of Christ and of his Kingdom.[35] In the Orthodox tradition, the unity, holiness, catholicity, and apostolicity of the Church are centred in the sacrament of Eucharist.[36] It is through the Eucharist that the believers celebrate their union with Christ.[37] The Eucharistic community is not part of the Church, but it is the complete Church to which nothing can be added for it to function as God intends. There is equality between communities

---

[32] Alexander Schmemann, *Church, World, Mission* (New York: St. Vladimir's Seminary, 1979), 199.

[33] Christoph Bottigheimer, "Unity, Yes, But which Unity?" *Theology Digest* 52, no. 2 (Summer 2005): 119-126. The Eucharistic ecclesiology places the Eucharist at the heart and essence of the very life of the Church. The nature of the Church is seen and experienced through the Eucharist and it is the meeting point of God and humanity. They consider that the nature of the Church is *koinonia* or communion. It exists through the sharing in the life of God, given in Christ and made effective through the working of the Holy Spirit. The Orthodox faith is that through the Eucharist the divine life is given to the community of the faithful.

[34] John Binns, *An Introduction to the Christian Orthodox Churches* (Cambridge: Cambridge University, 2002), 43. The Church is created, sustained, and visible presence in the Eucharist or liturgy or communion and at the Eucharist the Church is made complete and whole.

[35] "It is in the Eucharist that the Church accomplishes the passage from this into the world to come, into the Eschaton; participates in the ascension of its Lord and in his Messianic banquet; tastes of the joy of and peace of the Kingdom. Thus, the whole life of the Church is rooted in the Eucharist and it is indeed the mission of the Church." Schmemann, *Church, World, Mission,* 198.

[36] The Eucharist, in the words of John Zizioulas, is "the locus for the prophetic presence of the Eschaton in history." Aristotle Papanikoulaou, "Divine Energies or Divine Personhood: Vladimir Lossky and John Zizioulas on Conceiving the Transcendent and Immanent God," *Modern Theology* 19, no. 3 (July, 2003): 357-385.

[37] The ministry of the Eucharist is what the Church is for, and becomes the premier, even the sole, mark of the Church: "Where the Eucharist is, there is the Church or the Church makes the Eucharist, the Eucharist makes the Church." Veli Matti Kärkkäinen, *An Introduction to Ecclesiology* (Downer's Grove: Intervarsity, 2002), 21.

and bishops too. The basic unity and identity of each local Church can be expressed by the slogan: One Bishop, one Eucharist, and one Church.[38]

According to Schmemann, the essence of Orthodox theology is its "sacramental, liturgical, mystical ethos. This is manifested primarily in the rite of the Eucharist, consisting of two complementary movements: one of ascension toward the throne of God, laying aside all earthly cares, to feast upon and offer Christ. Through participation in the Eucharist, the Christian experiences full participation in the divine life (*theosis*)[39] and then returns, yet mystically remains connected to the heavenly reality. The mission of the Church is bound up in the rite of the liturgy and the Eucharist, which is the presence of the Eschaton on earth, though an ontological abyss remains between the old and new worlds that will not be bridged in this aeon."[40]

In the Orthodox tradition, the history of salvation is the revelation of the glory of God. It is this glory, which is the manifestation of the will of God, communicated in Christ, in the Church and in the Parousia. Humanity responds to God by glorifying Him through worship. They considered the mission as participation in the glory of God. The Church is planted where God is glorified. Therefore, for the Orthodox, worship is the best means to witness the glory of God. Bosch defined "mission as an experience of worship."[41] Being a worshipping community, the Orthodox people proclaim their mission and witness as the glory of God in the world. He further states

---

[38] The Orthodox life is centred on the mystery of the Eucharist. "The closed sacramental mystery of the Eucharist in the Orthodox tradition considers the Eucharist as an eschatological event, an anticipated advent of the Kingdom to come and a fullness of divine presence. This is also why any form of inter-communion - i.e., Eucharistic communion between Christians who are divided in faith and in ultimate ecclesial commitment- necessarily reduces the Eucharist to a form of human fellowship, distinct from the union in the Kingdom of God which is the Eucharist's ultimate meaning." Binns, *An Introduction to the Christian Orthodox Churches*, 41.

[39] The Orthodox theology emphasizes the notion of *theosis* that means a process of deification in the life of the believer. Through the Sacrament of Baptism, Christians share the very life of God and they are incorporated into the body of Christ. *Final Report of CWME Consultation of Eastern Orthodox and Oriental Orthodox Churches* (Neapolis, Greece: 1988), 18. James A Scherer, and Stephen B. Bevans. eds. (*New Directions in Mission and Evangelization: Theological Foundations* (Maryknoll, New York: Orbis, 1994), 235.

[40] Schmemann, *Church, World, Mission*, 209-216.

[41] Bosch, *Transforming Mission*, 206.

that, "the major manifestation of the missionary activity of the Orthodox Church lies in its celebration of the liturgy."[42] It is clear that the Orthodox worship, mission and theological framework are constructed around the theme of "glory of God." This is the focal point of the missiology of the Orthodox Church. Stamoolis explains that, in the tradition of Orthodoxy, both its history and its theology serve as guides for the construction of an Orthodox theology of mission. He asserts that, "the primary emphasis of the Orthodox understanding of missionary work is to offer glory to God."[43] For Orthodox theology, the glory of God is a continuous manifestation and worship is the culmination of the revelation of the glory of God. The love of God and the glory of God came together in the redemption of individuals. Hence for the Orthodox, mission is participating in the glory of God.[44] Generally, for the Orthodox, mission equals being a worshipping community. The mission of the Church is to be *synergoi*, fellow-workers, with God (1 Cor.3:9; 2 Cor.6:1). The Orthodox Church understands that her task is to offer *orthodoxia*, right praise, to the living God. The entire Orthodox Church affirms that they are called out to work with God in extending that worship to the ends of the earth.[45]

The Orthodox Churches also place the doctrine of the Trinity as the centre of theological thinking about the nature of the mission.[46] The Orthodox understanding of mission is Trinitarian - Trinitarian view of

---

[42] Bosch, *Transforming Mission*, 207.

[43] Yannoulatos writes "a key to the Orthodox understanding of the process of history is, 'the glory of the most holy God' viewed in the perspective of His infinite love... the process of human history, of which the Bible speaks, begins and ends with the glory of God." James. J. Stamoolis, *Eastern Orthodox Mission Theology Today* (Eugene: Wipf and Stock, 2001), 49-51.

[44] Stamoolis, *Eastern Orthodox Mission Theology Today*, 51.

[45] Anastasios Yannoulatos "Orthodox Spirituality and External Mission," *International Review of Mission* 52, (1963): 300-302.

[46] The documents issued by the Orthodox Church in 1986, entitled "Go forth in Peace: Orthodox Perspective on Mission" begin with the assertion that while the Church's mission is based on the mission of Christ, a proper understanding of this mission requires an application of Trinitarian theology. Orthodox Advisory group to the WCC-CWME, "Go Forth in Peace: Orthodox Perspective on Mission," in *New Directions in Mission and Evangelization 1: Basic Statements 1974- 1991*, eds. James A Scherer, and Stephen B. Bevans (Maryknoll, New York: Orbis, 1992), 203.

God, a theocentric understanding of man, and ecclesiology based on communion rather than on authority.[47] A Trinitarian theology points to the radical communal nature of God as such, and this communion overflows into an involvement with history that "aims at drawing humanity and creation in general into this communion with God's very life."[48] The mission is understood fundamentally as rooted in the continual self-giving and self-revelation of God within the history of the creation; Trinitarian processions are understood not only as movements within the mystery of God, as such, but as God moving in saving love within the world. The Church is then understood as the people that God has chosen not only to participate in the saving life of the divine community, but also to be the agent and cooperators in God's outreach to the whole of creation. The Orthodox theologians like Valdimir Lossky, John Meyendorf and John Zizioulas understand the Trinity as an ecstatic communion of persons, always involved in the world, always inviting all of creation to share in the triune life of communion-in-mission.[49] Such an understanding of God as Trinity is at the basis of the Orthodox theology of mission as well.

2.2 Mission: In Protestant Traditions

Protestantism[50] is one of the three major branches of Christianity, along with Roman Catholicism and Eastern Orthodoxy. It is formed from the

---

[47] Meyndroff, "Orthodox Theology Today," *St. Vladimir's Theological Quarterly* 13, no.1/2 (1969): 77-92. Schmemann, *Church, World, Mission,* 70.

[48] God's very nature is missionary. It is not primarily about "the propagation or transmission of intellectual convictions, doctrines, moral commands, etc.," but rather about the inclusion of all creation in God's overflowing, superabundant life of communion. It is an invitation to be bearers of divine life found in the Trinity. Scherer and Bevans, eds., *New Directions in Mission and evangelization,* 204, 289.

[49] Vladimir Lossky, *The Mystical Theology of the Eastern Church* (Crestwood, New York: St. Vladimir's Theological Seminary, 1976). John Meyendorf, *Trinitarian Theology East and West* (Brookline, Mass. Holy Cross Orthodox, 1977), John Zizioulas, *Being as Communion* (Crestwood, New York: St. Vladimir's Seminary, 1985).

[50] The date often cited as the beginning of the Protestant movement is 1517, based on the date of Martin Luther's first act of dissent: the public posting of his 95 Theses, criticizing Roman Catholic practices and teachings. At the time, however, Luther had no intention of starting a new Christian tradition called "Protestantism" but hoped to reform the Catholic Church. Protestantism as a movement evolved in the decades following this act as Luther's ideas, theological arguments took root, and the Catholic Church resisted and rejected them.

split with Roman Catholicism during the Reformation in Europe in the 16th century. The main leaders of this movement were Martin Luther, John Calvin, and Huldrych Zwingli. The reformers broke from the Roman Catholic Church due to the authoritarianism of ecclesiological structures and to theological differences. The Protestant denominations formed a pattern of worship and liturgy, varying from the Roman Catholic forms of worship. The Anglican and the Lutheran Churches have maintained liturgies and rituals similar to those of the Roman Catholic Church, whereas other denominations, such as Baptists, Presbyterians, Pentecostals, and United Church of Christ, have developed less liturgical forms of worship. Most Protestants practice the Sacrament of Baptism and Communion as key rites of Christian initiation and ongoing devotion. Though originating in Europe, Protestant Christianity has spread across the globe through missionary activity and now has members from nearly every country, race, and ethnicity.[51] In the Protestant tradition, the Church is defined as a spiritual communion, a work of God, a place of gathering by the initiative of the 'Risen Christ' with the power of the Holy Spirit. Interestingly, Protestant Churches did not believe in the mission at the beginning. The early reformers like Martin Luther and John Calvin were not concerned with the mission activities. The following discourses determined their understanding of mission: (a) theologically, the concept of predestination, which they held, was not conducive to missionary outreach. (b) Their

---

Protestants share an adherence to the centrality of Scripture (both the Hebrew Scriptures and the New Testament) as well as a doctrine of salvation through faith in Jesus Christ. Martin Luther considered certain books contained in the Catholic version of the Bible (based on the Septuagint) to be of lesser value as he used the Hebrew Masoretic Text, which also excluded these books from the canon. Therefore, the Protestant Old Testament contains 39 books whereas the Roman Catholic Old Testament contains 46 books and includes sections of common books not included by Protestants. The New Testament is the same in both traditions.

[51] Mark Juergensmeyer, ed., *The Oxford Handbook of Global Religions* (Santa Barbara: University of California, 2006) 28-29. John Bowker, ed., The *Cambridge Illustrated History of Religions* (Cambridge: Cambridge University, 2002), 47-48.

biblical exegesis considered Christ's missionary mandate as directed to the twelve only. (c) Their emphasis was on reforming, not on spreading.[52]

It was in the second half of the 17th and in the 18th century that Protestants began to develop a new idea of mission. Kane points out that the modern missionary enterprise was the direct outcome of the Pietist movement which began in Germany following the thirty years' war, which ended with the peace of Westphalia in 1648. As the Protestant reformation was a revolt against the corrupted doctrines and morals of the Church of Rome, so the Pietist movement was a revolt against the barren Orthodoxy and dead formalism of the State Churches of Protestant Europe. The father of Pietism was Philip Spencer (1635-1705). The Pietists in their teaching emphasized three things: a genuine conversion experience leading to newness of life, cultivating the inner life by Bible study, prayer and Christian fellowship and missionary zeal.[53] The Enlightenment and Industrialization in Europe gave a new self-understanding of humanity- man as a rational, independent and individual-capable of rational choice. Christianity made it rational, human and dependent on God. The 18th century Protestant missionary awakening was intimately associated with the birth of Evangelicalism.[54] David Bosch claims that "the entire modern missionary enterprise is, to a very real extent, a child of the Enlightenment and similarly that the entire Western missionary movement of the past three centuries emerged from the matrix of the Enlightenment."[55]

Generally, Protestant tradition consists in keeping two decisive elements as criteria for mission: truth and faithfulness, i.e. "The Gospel

---

[52] J. Herbert Kane, *Understanding Christian Missions* (Grand Rapids, MI: Baker Book, 1983), 140.
[53] Kane, *Understanding Christian Missions*, 142.
[54] Evangelical Christianity has been interpreted as a movement whose origins and contours owe an immense debt to the philosophical and cultural patterns of the Enlightenment. Brian Stanley, ed., *Christian Missions and the Enlightenment* (Cambridge: William B. Eerdmans, 2001), 2.
[55] Bosch, *Transforming Mission*, 274, 344. According the Bosch, emphasis derived from the enlightenment which provided the defining or paradigmatic features of the Protestant missionary movement from its origins in the 18th century until the collapse of the enlightenment rationality in the postmodernist crisis of the late 20th century.

be preached purely and that the sacraments be administered in conformity with the Gospel."[56] These two criteria, defining the Church as a place and event in which the Word is proclaimed and the sacraments are celebrated, serve as reference points for all understanding of ministry in Protestantism. The ministry of the whole Church is to proclaim the gospel through preaching and the celebration of the sacraments. They affirm that each member of the Church is assigned to that task; each baptized person has a vocation, a mission, a ministry to witness, to praise, to evangelize, to obey the commands of the Lord. Each is to take his or her part in sharing the ministry of the whole Church.[57]

Following are the various features that are most frequently held to be distinctive of the conduct of Christian mission within the Protestant tradition, principally in relation to the 18th and early 19th centuries. They are (a) An almost universal belief that non-Western peoples were "heathens," lost in the degradation of sin and in need of salvation through the gospel of Christ. (b) A parallel tendency to dismiss other religious systems either as "heathen idolatry or as at best superstitions and not religions at all, and hence as devoid of any trace of the presence of God. (c) A belief in the manifest superiority and liberating potential of Western civilization in both its intellectual and its technological aspects. (d) An unshakable confidence in the regenerative capacity of rational knowledge, always provided this was linked to Christian proclamation. (e) An assumption that the Christian message was addressed principally to individuals, calling them to undergo a conscious and identifiable inner experience of personal conversion to Christ.[58] The Protestant missionaries ministered with the conviction that the non-Christian were lost in their sin and dependent on the gospel of Christ for salvation. It was grounded in the theology of the Pauline epistles and the Augustinian tradition that mediated that theology

---

[56] *Augsburg Confession* 7; Institute of Christian Religion iv, 2. http://www.ccel.org/ccel/schaff/creeds3.iii.ii.html (accessed August 12, 2015).
[57] Francois Clavairoly, "Protestantism and Theology of Ministries: Ecumenical Perspective," *Theology Digest* 49, no.1 (Spring 2002): 53-54.
[58] Brian Stanley, ed. *Christian Missions and the Enlightenment* (Cambridge: William B. Eerdmans, 2001), 8.

to Catholic Christendom. The Enlightenment movement stresses the values of rationality, progress, liberty and freedom. The enlightenment creed of humans' progress was constructed on the foundation of a Renaissance confident in the human creative capacity grounded in the philosophy of Aristotle.[59]

In the Protestant tradition, the slogan *Sola Scriptura* may be regarded as the common denominator. The role assigned to the written Word of God is more decisive in all matters. This principle expresses the reformers insistence on the sufficiency of the Word of God as the final authority in matters of faith.[60] The Bible is the supreme authority in all matters of faith and conduct, the highest court of appeal in questions of controversy in the reformed and Protestant traditions.[61] The Word of God is considered as the ultimate authority pertaining to the life and witness of the Church and all human opinions must submit to the voice of the Holy Spirit speaking in Scripture. An articulation of theology is very often embedded in songs, sermons, prayers and practices.[62] The Westminster Confession of Faith affirms that:

> "The supreme judge by which all controversies of religion are to be determined, and all decrees of councils, opinions of ancient writers, doctrines of men, and private spirits, are to be examined, and in whose sentence we are to rest, can be no other but the Holy Spirit speaking in Scripture." (I: X) this is because "All synods of councils, since the apostles' time, whether general or particular, may err; and many have erred. Therefore, they are not to be made the rule of faith, or practice; but to be used as a help in both"

---

[59] Anthony Pagden, *European Encounters with the New World: From Renaissance to Romanticism* (London: New Haven, 1993), 6.
[60] Eduardus Van der Borght, *Studies in Reformed Theology, vol.18: Unity of the Church: A Theological State of the Art and Beyond* (Boston: Brill, 2010), 113.
[61] Robert Letham, *Through Western Eyes Eastern Orthodoxy: A Reformed Perspective* (Ross-shire, Mentor, 2007), 175.
[62] Anne Richards, John Clark, Martin Lee, Philip knights, Janice Price, Paul Rolph and Nigel Rooms, *Foundations For Mission: A Study of Language, Theology and Praxis from the UK and Ireland* Perspective (London: Churches Together in Britain and Ireland, 2010), 67.

(XXXI: IV). This Assembly affirms that the primary author of Scripture is the Holy Spirit, who does not and cannot err."[63]

The European Reformation stated firmly that, all members of the Church receive a vocation and that some will be especially called and formed to exercise the ministry of preaching and of celebrating the sacraments. However, this ministry is not understood as a participation in what Catholic theology calls "the priestly ministry of Christ." While the Reformation stresses the importance of ordained ministry in the service of the visible Church, it also recalls that ministry neither represents Christ not participates in his sacrificial action. For all (the minister, the Church, and each member of the Church) are completely beneficiaries of God's salvific action. Thus, their actions can be but a response through grace, proclamation of good news and the sharing of the sacraments. For them, Christ alone is the mediator and the Church and its ministers are considered as sanctified witnesses. In the Protestant tradition, a minister is not a priest because his/her ministry does not claim to participate in the priestly work of Christ. A statement of the Reformation, therefore, deliberately locates ministries in the context of the proclamation of the gospel, of the celebration of the sacraments, and in the building up of the Church. Those statements are rooted in the reading and interpretation of the biblical texts.[64]

---

[63] Westminster Assembly, *The Confession of Faith: The Larger and Shorter Catechisms with the Scripture Proofs* (Applecross, Ross-Shire: The Publication Committee of the Free- Presbyterian Church of Scotland, 1970), I: X. The Westminster Assembly was a council of divines, called by Parliament to reform the government, worship and discipline of the Church in England, Wales and Ireland, initially to defend the Thirty-Nine Articles of Religion of the Church of England against 'false aspersions and calumnies.' This assembly considered the Trinitarian and Christological pronouncements of the first six ecumenical councils to be in harmony with the Bible. Robert Letham, *Through Western Eyes Eastern Orthodoxy: A Reformed Perspective* (Ross-shire, Mentor, 2007), 174.

[64] Clavairoly Francois, "Protestantism and Theology of Ministries: Ecumenical Perspective." *Theology Digest* 49, no. 1 (Spring 2002): 54-55.

Chapter. 2

Mission in the Malankara Mar Thoma Syrian Church: A Historical and Liturgical Overview

1 Mission Patterns of the Mar Thoma Church and its Liturgical Influence

The Christian Church is commissioned with the privilege and responsibility of participating in the mission of Jesus Christ by the power of the Holy Spirit.[65] The starting point of Christian mission is the divine commission to proclaim the Lordship of Christ over all creation. That calls for our active involvement in all aspects of human life. The proclamation of the Gospel is about using both word and deed to express the love of God to all. There are numerous missionary approaches to deal with the task of mission.[66] Hendric Kraemer has identified the ideal missionary approach of mission as the combination of "a prophetic, apostolic, heraldship of truth for Christ's sake, with a priestly, apostolic ambassadorship of love for His sake."[67] While the Church is assigned to proclaim the good news of Jesus Christ, the context is the deciding factor in shaping the paradigm for its mission.

---

[65] Vincent J Nugent, "Theological Foundation for Mission Animation: A Study of the Church's Essence." *World Mission* 24, no.1 (Spring 1943): 7-18.

[66] The Churches Together in Britain and Ireland (CTBI) identified the marks of mission as "to proclaim the Good News of the Kingdom; to teach, baptize and nurture new believers; to respond to human need by loving service; to seek to transform unjust structures of society; to strive to safeguard the integrity of creation and sustain and renew the life of earth and peace and reconciliation. Further they identified mission as "proclamation of Jesus as Universal Saviour or 'Proclamation,' mission as participation in the Triune God or *Missio Dei;* mission as liberating service of the Reign of God or Kingdom mission. Richards, *Foundations For Mission,* 15-16, 56.

[67] George K. Zachariah, "Mission of the Church," *Mar Thoma Messenger* (October 2004): 17-18.

Mission and Liturgy

The mission of the MTC is a continuation of the mission of Jesus Christ. The Constitution of the Church clearly states that

> "the ministry of the Church is the gift of the Risen Christ. The responsibility to fulfill this ministry, in history, is entrusted with the Church. The Church affirms that the people of God are sent all over the world and that they partake in the salvation work of God, to unite everything in Jesus Christ through the ministry of reconciliation begun in Jesus Christ. The Church receives the power of the Holy Spirit, which enables the Church to fulfill the redemptive work of God, who directs and controls the events in history. The Holy Spirit guides the offices of the ministry, originated (through) divine plan and ordains the people of God to build the Church which is the body of Christ, in order that they may attain maturity, akin to the fullness of Christ, through faith and knowledge in the Son of God and the Unity of the Holy Spirit. The Church believes and proclaims the above basic principles of the ministry of the Church."[68]

The Metropolitan Joseph Mar Thoma, during his presidential address of the Sabha *Prathinidhi Mandalam* (the supreme administrative body of the Church) in 2009 reiterated the mission of the Church in the following words:

> "We should never forget that we are appointed by God to share the core values of the Gospel to each and every corner of the world. The hallmark of the MTC once was lay missionary work. The emphasis of the Church was for sharing the Gospel values, rooted in the reformation principles, with others. However, we should search our conscience to find out whether we are distancing ourselves from the gospel values by conforming to the world."[69]

---

[68] *The Constitution of the Mar Thoma Syrian Church of Malabar, Division 1, Chapter 1, Declaration Part. 2, Clause 5* (Thiruvalla: Mar Thoma Press, 2000), 4-5.
[69] Minutes of the Sabha Prathinidhi Mandalam, 2009 at Thiruvalla, *Mar Thoma Messenger*, (October 2009): 14.

This is a clear indication of the priority of the Church in its mission. The Church designs its mission strategy in considering the context and the need of the time.

The MTC follows the scriptural pattern of mission. This means, the Church included the various patterns of mission expressed in the Bible, such as: the Matthean model of mission as "making disciples" (Mt.28:18-20), Lukan model of mission as "social transformation" (Lk.4:16-21), Pauline Model of mission as "ambassadors of Christ" and Johannine model of mission as "life and love" (Jn.3:16). The mission understanding of the Gospel of Mathew is disciple-centred and Luke's is boundary-centred. A general view of the mission understanding of Paul is time-centred. The Apostle Paul is supremely conscious of the fact that through Christ, God the Father has inaugurated a cosmic grace period, a suspension of his judgement for a set time[70] (Rom.1:5, 15:5, Gal.1:1-5). In the Gospel of John, the emphasis of mission is "the incarnational love." The focus of the overall scriptural mission is God's new action in the Messiah, who calls for a new response from everyone. The key text is: God sent Jesus and he sends his messengers.[71]

The identity of the Church as an "Apostolic Christian Community" gives an impetus for its mission. It is believed that the Apostle St. Thomas is the architect of the Christian community in the Malankara region. This apostolic identity and spiritual heritage provide an originality and authority to the Church in its mission. The Apostle was a missionary by himself with a vision. The post-resurrection experience of St. Thomas was unique and his missionary thrust was based on this experience (Jn.20:26-29). His experience was a result of his deep encounter with Christ. He knew Christ very personally and came to India with this Christ experience with which he communicated and shared the Gospel. The missionary thrust of St. Thomas is the mission motivation of the MTC. The Church believes that, this mystical experience of St. Thomas is entrusted with the

---

[70] Stan Nussbaum, *A Reader's Guide to Transforming Mission* (New York: Orbis, 2005), 33.
[71] Nussbaum, *A Reader's Guide to Transforming Mission,* 42.

Malankara Church.[72] In the same way that the apostle Thomas experienced Christ, the Church now experiences and encounters resurrected Christ in the Eucharist. It is in and through the Eucharist that the Church now experiences the divine. By participating in the liturgy, the faithful partake in the salvific act of Christ. The Eucharist is the culmination of human and divine fellowship which provides that solemn space where the Church encounters the resurrected Christ. It is from this mystical encounter that they are empowered and strengthen for communicating the Gospel. In short, the Christ-experience of the faithful through the Eucharist strengthens and motivates them to participate in the mission of God. The liturgy enables the people of God to internalize and enliven this Christ experience. In the final blessing in the Eucharistic liturgy, the celebrant assures the peace of Christ and exhorts them to be channels of peace and divine presence in the world. "…..depart in peace filled with gladness and rejoicing."[73] The Eucharist calls for a "liturgy after the liturgy." This Christ experience in the liturgy is the missionary thrust of the Church.

The MTC keeps tradition and Scripture in its mission journey. The mission understanding of this Church is dual in nature, which is based on the Liturgy and the Bible. It is not contradictory, but complementing each other for relevant mission. The spirit of reformation ignited the Church to take up the command of Christ seriously and that motivated them to find out new ways of engaging in mission contextually. In other words, the reformation motivated the Church to locate mission activity at the centre of the Church. The Church was open enough to receive the CMS mission's ideas and strategies for mission along with its own Oriental liturgical base. The Church combines the emphasis on Scripture and evangelism with the traditional Eastern Church forms of worship and ways of life. The Church believes that the Christian community enters into the life and love of God by celebrating the Eucharist.

---

[72] Iinterview with Joseph Mar Barnabas Episcopa on September 08, 2015.
[73] Titus II, *Qurbana Thaksa,* 44.

The missionary outreach programmes of the Church are both personal and social. It involves both evangelism and social development. In the beginning, the mission understanding of the Church was of the affirmation of the Church and activity of establishing churches. Unlike western mission societies,[74] it was a mission of the Church and through the Church. It planted churches in different part of India. Later, the concern of the Church extends to the welfare of all individuals and their salvation, which is to be realized in their social life, employment, physical growth, and social, cultural and economic development. The role played by the Metropolitans of the Church, especially Abraham Mar Thoma and Juhanon Mar Thoma, to identify the social dimension of mission is noteworthy. The Church believes that the love of God spills over from the Christian community in all directions. It is not an accident, but a deliberate intention of corporate worship and a necessary result of it. They extend to society, culture, the state, and even the world of nature.

2   Mission: A Historical Survey

The Christian community in Kerala during the 19th century accommodated itself to the caste structure of the society, and there was no possibility for the so-called outcastes to become members of the Church. The MTC remained as an exclusively "high caste Church" with members consisting of the Syrian Christian tradition. This caste identity resulted in the exclusion of the so-called low caste people. Later, from the final decade of the 19th century, interaction with the modern protestant missionaries had a drastic influence on the mission thinking and identity of the Church. In the beginning, the Church shared the purpose and goal of most of the Protestant mission of that time, which is, a soteriological focus on saving souls from eternal

---

[74] "Very often the missionary movements during the 18th and 19th centuries considered mission as sending missionaries from the west to east and making them similar to the west in religion and culture. It was associated with western imperialism. Therefore, most of the missionaries who came to India were not able to find the rich religious and cultural heritage of India. It was on the basis of their missionary consciousness; the modern missionaries have not found the same western missionary consciousness in the Mar Thoma Church." Daniel, *Ecumenism in Praxis*, 56.

condemnation.[75] The first half of the 19th century to the first decades of the 20th century was known as the "great century of missions."[76] In line with the Keswick[77] spirituality, which emphasized the individual conversion, holy living, and the immediate salvation through accepting Jesus Christ, inspired the members of the MTC and its evangelists to venture forth on missionary work along those goals of direct evangelism. Later, a paradigm shift[78] occurred in the understanding of mission and the Church searched

---

[75] Alex Thomas, "The Mar Thoma Church: Then and Now." In *In Search of Christian Identity in Global Community,* edited by M.J. Joseph (Thiruvalla: Dioceses of North America and Europe, 2008), 45.

[76] The main outcome of the evangelical awakening of the 18th and 19th centuries was the rise of modern missionary movements in Europe. They were mainly: The London Missionary Society (LMS) in 1795, the Scottish Missionary society-1796, the Netherlands Missionary Society-1797, the Church Missionary Society (CMS) -1799, the British and Foreign Missionary Society -1804, the American Board of Commissioners for Foreign Missions (ABCFM)-1810, the American Baptist Foreign Mission Society -1814, the Basel Mission -1816, the Wesleyan Methodist Missionary Society-1817-18, the Danish Missionary Society-1821, the Berlin Missionary Society -1824, the Rhenish Missionary Society -1828, the Swedish Missionary Society -1835 and the North German Missionary Society -1836. Most of these organizations were voluntary societies independent of the Church. These institutions considered themselves as separate institutions concerned with Christian missions in overseas. William Anderson, *Towards a Theology of Mission* (London: SCM, 1955), 15. Stephen B. Bevans and Roger P. Schroeder, *Constants in Context: A Theology of Mission for Today* (New York, Maryknoll: Orbis, 2004), 212. Herbert J. Kane, *Understanding Christian Missions* (Grand Rapids, MI: Baker Book, 1983), 142.

[77] The Keswick movement is an evangelical movement emerged in England in the late 19th century. The term Keswick derives its name from a small community in the Lake District of England who urged for personal holiness and high moral values. They stressed the possibility of victorious Christian life and the need for a definitive crisis experience. They conduct a spiritual convention with a view to promote personal holiness and spiritual victory. The aim of the Keswick movement is the "Promotion of Practical Holiness. "The first Keswick convention hosted over 400 individuals, who met under the banner of "All One in Christ Jesus." From Keswick the teaching quickly spread over England, Canada and the United States, with Moody himself being key to the propagation of Keswick teaching in the U.S. Keswick is not a doctrinal system, much less an organization or a denomination. Though leading churchmen and noted scholars led the movement, like Hudson Tayor, Andrew Murray, Amy Carmichael, Handley Moule, F.B. Meyer, .L. Moody, Robert McQuilley, no Keswick leader has written a treatise on its teaching. There is no official doctrinal statement and a broad variety of doctrinal positions have been held and taught by those associated with the name Keswick. Mark Steven Rathe, *The Keswick Movement its Origins and Teachings,* M.A. Thesis (San Francisco: Simpson College, 1987).

[78] A paradigm shift takes place when there is a leap from one world-view to another which allows the world to be explained and interpreted in a new way. A paradigm is defined as "an entire constellation of beliefs, values, techniques, and so on, shared by the members

for new ways to make the mission relevant to the community along with direct evangelism. Later, the Church had developed a theological vision for mission, considering the pluralistic context of India. By adopting an incarnational model of mission, the Church attempted to challenge the evils of the caste structure, serving the poor through hospitals, destitute homes and other like social institutions. The Church started day care centres for poor children, orphans and the socially deprived communities and initiated many programmes for the development of villages. The Church also attempted to provide education for all people irrespective of their caste or religious status.[79] According to Thomas, several factors contributed to the shift in the mission understanding of the MTC. A shift in the mission theory has taken place from the Willington Conference of the International Missionary Council in 1952.[80] The mission of the Church came to be understood as the work of God in the world (*Missio Dei*[81]) rather than an agenda of the Church. The concept of the Kingdom became the frame of reference of the mission of the Triune God. Jesus embodied the Kingdom of God through acts of healing, redemption and reconciliation. The Church is no longer seen as the goal of mission, but as an instrument of God's mission.[82] The mission is witness to the fullness of the promise

---

of a given community. It is an entire worldview." Spencer, *SCM Study Guide to Christian Mission,* 40-41.

[79] Thomas, "The Mar Thoma Church: Then and Now," 45.

[80] The Willington Statement was clear that "the Missionary calling of the Church is derived from the mission of God; the Church has a missionary calling rather than a mission, and that calling is to engage in God's mission. Our mission therefore has no life of its own, only in the hands of the sending God alone. The Church is both part of what God is doing, as a particular expression or embodiment of the work of God flowing from the very nature of God, and the Church has a particular vocation to engage with God in this work, in and for the world." Richards, et al., *Foundations For Mission,* 53. Bevans and Roger, *Constants in Context,* 284-285.

[81] Karl Barth was the key figure behind the coining of the phrase '*Missio Dei*', as a summary of mission's dependence on the initiative and substance of God himself. Mission was not to be seen as one of humanity's building projects, carried forward by its own strength and reason, but as a divine movement in which the Church was privileged to participate. It is his student Dietrich Bonhoeffer (1906-1945) who has been described as 'the architect' of new way of understanding the mission of the Church. Bosch, *Transforming Mission,* 375. With Barth, he saw that the foundation of faith, mission, the Church and theology is not human enquiry, reason or science but God's revelation in Jesus Christ.

[82] Thomas, "Mar Thoma Church: Then and Now," 46.

of God's Kingdom, and participation with Christ in the ongoing struggles between the Kingdom of God and the power of darkness and evil in the world. Bosch observed that all Churches, including the Roman Catholic Church, embraced the paradigm shift of the Church-centred mission to a Kingdom-centred mission. Since Vatican II, the missionary nature of the Church had been defined on the Trinitarian foundation where the focus of mission is the Kingdom of God.

The MTC has undertaken mainly two models of mission. By following the methods of Western missionary movements like London Missionary Society (LMS), Church Missionary Society (CMS), Basel mission, this Church firstly adopted a Church-centric paradigm of mission, and later shifted to a Kingdom-centric paradigm corresponding to the growth of its missiological and theological understanding. For instance, the cross-cultural mission in the North Kanara, South India, reflects these shifts in its missiology with a gradual movement towards an incarnational pattern of mission. In this pattern, the gospel becomes a way of life and its message transforms life.[83] By the middle of the 20th century, the Church had formed five mission fields altogether in Kerala and in Karnataka viz: South Travancore Mission, Central Travancore Mission, North Travancore Mission, Palakkad Mission, and Kanara Mission.[84] The paradigm shift of the Kingdom-centred mission came into the MTC considerably through the preaching of E. Stanley Jones, (1884-1973) who was a regular speaker at the Marmon convention for half a century. His theology of mission was grounded in the biblical theology of the Kingdom of God. He understood the Kingdom of God as expressed in the Nazareth manifesto of Jesus Christ (Lk.4:18) as a model for Christians to follow. He introduced the sermon of Jesus at Nazareth[85] as a missionary paradigm to the MTC. Thus, the

---

[83] Alex Thomas,. *A History of the First Cross Cultural Mission of the Mar Thoma Church 1910 - 2000.* (Delhi: ISPCK, 2007), 129.
[84] Y. T. Vinaya Raj, "When the 'Mission Field' writes the History," in *In Search of Christian Identity in the Community, of the Church,* ed. Joseph, 149-153.
[85] The reign of God has its transforming influence on the economic, the social, the political, and the moral and spiritual life of the people.

Church focused on witness to the reign of God as its goal of mission. The Metropolitan Alexander Mar Thoma rightly pointed out that,

> "Jesus Christ came to preach good news to the poor, to proclaim liberty to the captives, to give sight to the blind and to set free the oppressed. Evil is found both in individuals and in the structures of the society. The gospel has to be presented as the power of God which saves individuals and changes social structures; it is the duty of the Church to work on both levels."[86]

The MTC believes that the Church is present in the world to work for the Kingdom of God established through the person and work of Christ. The Church considers that the Christian mission is both proclamation and engaging in activities that liberate people. Evangelism, social service, struggles for social justice and truth, and uplifting of the depressed class is the inevitable responsibility of the Church. Thus, the goal of the mission of this Church is the total redemption of individuals and the society. Later, models of mission emerged in considering the need of the time such as a dialogue model, an institutional, an ecumenical model etc.

3 Models of Mission

The model of mission[87] that emerges in the Church today is a result of a theological reflection on missionary practice in current multicultural, multi-religious, globalized and religiously polarized world.[88] As the Church moves forward as a witnessing community in the 21st century,

---

[86] Alexander Mar Thoma Metropolitan, *The Mar Thoma Church: Heritage and Mission* (Thiruvalla: National Offset, 1985), 26.

[87] Mission models are the result of systematic reflection on mission strategies. Models have provided answers for understanding a reality which is not immediately accessible to the senses. Through the models theologians present the different aspects of the same reality. Mission models are employed for the purpose of explanation, and this in a more comprehensive way. These models help us to articulate and present the ideas in a systematic way. James Empereur, *Models of Liturgical Theology* (Nottingham: Grove Books, 1987), 9-12. Sallie McFague, *Metaphorical Theology: Models of God in Religious Language* (Philadelphia: Foretess, 1982), 104-105.

[88] Philip Jenkins, "The Next Christianity," *Atlantic Monthly* 290/3 (October 2002): 53-72.

Mission and Liturgy

there are various approaches communicating the Gospel, witness such as proclamation, liturgical action and contemplation, inculturation, interreligious dialogue, working for justice and peace, commitment to reconciliation. All contribute to a missionary practice that is both dialogical and prophetic, faithful to contemporary context as well as to the constants of Christian faith.[89] A new understanding of mission as expressed in the statement "mission belongs to God and not ours," motivated the Church to find new avenues for mission engagements.[90] It is about God's gracious invitation to humanity to share in the dynamic communion that is at the same time God's self-giving missionary life. It is more urgent because in a world of globalized poverty, militant religious fundamentalism and new appreciation of local culture and subaltern traditions, the vision and praxis of Jesus of Nazareth can bring new healing and new light.[91] The MTC has been employing many models to communicate the Gospel. The following are some of the more prominent mission paradigms endured by the Church.

3.1 The Church Model of Mission

This model of mission states that the Church engages in mission and mission is for the sake of planting and building the Church.[92] This mission

---

[89] Bevans and Roger, *Constants in Context*, 284-285.
[90] In his edited book, *Classic Texts in Mission and World Christianity*, Norman E Thomas enumerated the contemporary paradigms of mission in a detailed way i.e. mission as the Church-with others, as *Missio Dei*, as mediating salvation, as quest for justice, as evangelization, as contextualization, as liberation, as inculturation, as common witness, as ministry by the whole people of God, as interfaith witness, as theology, as hope in action. Studying each of these paradigms are beyond the scope of this work. Norman E. Thomas, ed., *Classic Texts in Mission and World Christianity* (New York: Orbis, 2002), 81-304. Against the earlier models of evangelization of the whole world, modern understanding of mission is most represented by the phrases of presence, humanization, dialogue, and liberation, etc. In Asia, Kim Yong-bock (1982) defines God's mission as the suffering people of Asia; Marlene Perera (1992) asserts that mission is to inaugurate the reign of God among human beings; and Prakai Nontawasee (1989), a former president of Christian Conference of Asia (CCA), sees mission in terms of mutual solidarity, meaning the work of enabling a meeting of different souls and persons, and allowing for the lives of people to be touched by one another.
[91] Bevans and Roger, *Constants in Context*, 284-285.
[92] A focusing biblical text for this model is Mt.28:19-20 "Go therefore and make disciples of all nations, baptizing them in the name of the Father and of the Son and of the Holy Spirit, and teaching them to obey everything that I have commanded you. And remember, I

model put forward the three self-understanding principles of the Church, i.e. The Church as self-governing, self-propagating, self-sustaining. The Church and mission paradigm of the ecumenical movement during 1910-1938 goes along with this line. The first meetings of the World Missionary Conference in Edinburgh, 1910, and the Tambaram meeting (1938) of International Missionary Conference (IMC) gave primary emphasis to this mission model. Missionary methods and praxis are to a great extent determined and theologically sustained by the theological foundations of mission and evangelization. The Church believes that communicating the gospel is the primary task of her mission. In this model proclamation of the gospel or Evangelism[93] is considered as the heart of all missionary endeavours. The very heart of the gospel lies in its mission and it is the mark of the Church.[94] In Evangelism, the term "missionary methods" refer to the procedure through which the reign of God is established on earth, the Church is planted in the people and the gospel is proclaimed among those who have not yet heard it.[95] In a critical view, a Church centric model of mission aimed at proselytism and church planting later proved to be inadequate for the multi-religious community of Indian society. In a cross-cultural context, this model was very often criticized as an exclusive approach towards Church planting.[96]

---

am with you always, to the end of the age." It affirms that every person converted to Christ becomes a member of the universal Church and individual churches are local expressions of that One Catholic Church. The members are added to the Church only as they are joined to Christ by faith. Kane, *Understanding Christian Missions*, 300.

[93] There are two words in the New Testament, which are pertinent to evangelism. The noun *Evangelion* means good news which occurs seventy five times in the New Testament and the verb *evangelizomai* means "to publish good news" which appears twenty four times. The word evangelism derived from the term *evangelion*. The gospel is the evangel, the good news. Evangelism is the act of proclaiming the good news. Kane, *Understanding Christian Missions*, 298, 303.

[94] Kane, *Understanding Christian Missions*, 298.

[95] Karl Muller, Theo Sundermeier, Stephen B. Bevans, and Richard H. Bliese. eds. *Dictionary of Mission: Theology, History, Perspectives* (New York: Orbis, 1999), 316-320.

[96] Thomas, *A History of the First Cross-Cultural Mission*, 130.

3.2 The Kingdom Model of Mission

The Kingdom model of mission is a highly appreciated paradigm in mission theology. The Christian Church is a community commissioned to represent the Kingdom of God in history. The Church itself is not the Kingdom of God, but it is its agent, its anticipation, and its fragmentary realization. Jesus Christ, according to Christian conviction, is the centre of history.[97] Therefore, the mission of the Church is to invite others to experience the new life in Jesus Christ (2 Cor.5:17). The model of Kingdom in the Bible describes it as the one that encompasses all of life that welcomes the most unlikely subject, exposes every pocket of evil and liberates from every injustice and oppression[98] (Lk.9:2, 14:13,21, Jn.18: 36). The life, ministry, passion, death and resurrection of Jesus enables the Church to identify with him today. This criterion leads the Church not only to discover who Christ is, but where he is to be found today; i.e. among the poor, the powerless, and the oppressed- and what he is doing; healing their wounds, breaking the chains of oppression, demanding justice and peace, giving life and imparting hope to the hurting. This model of mission affirms that the Church is commissioned to comfort the grieving, encourage the lonely, feed the hungry, minister to the handicapped, help the aged, the abused and the confused. Jesus entered into human history to redeem the whole creation and to establish the Kingdom of God. This model suggests a holistic transformation towards Christ. The involvement of the Church with the conciliar ecumenical movement provided the idea that Jesus embodied the Kingdom of God through acts of preaching, healing, reconciliation and redemption. The Church was no longer the goal of mission but an instrument of God's mission. Thus the MTC began to focus on witnessing to the Kingdom of God in its mission thought. The Church incorporated evangelism and church planting within a wider vision of a Kingdom-centered model of mission.[99]

---

[97] Paul Tillich, "The Theology of Missions." *The Journal Christianity and Crisis* (March 1955): 25.

[98] George K. Zacharia, "Mission of the Mar Thoma Church in the Context of the Diaspora Community in the West," *Mar Thoma Messenger* 26, no.4 (October 2007): 14-15.

[99] Thomas, *A History of First Cross Cultural Mission*, 130.

3.3 An Incarnational Model of Mission

Incarnation is the very heart and nature of the mission. Incarnational model of mission means that just as God became fully human in the person of Jesus Christ, the followers of Christ become fully at home in their own particular space and time. It calls for an intimate, incarnational identification with people in a particular culture where the Church communicates the Gospel. The Church is often defined as the extension of Christ's incarnation. The Church is equipped with the Holy Spirit to represent Christ to the world. The faithful embody the Gospel which means that they have Christ living in them, and therefore their lives express incarnational mission. The MTC adopted an incarnation pattern in mission, in which the goal of mission is neither proselytism nor widening the boundaries of the Church; rather, the mission is witnessing to the reign of God by identifying with the marginalized and providing opportunities for them to grow as human beings. The incarnation of God through Jesus Christ invites the Church "to become living members of Christ's earthly community and to begin a life of service to others."[100] This would bring a new social order in which the values of the Kingdom of God dominate.[101] This new social order is not limited by any earthly institution, and even by the Church. The MTC's mission, therefore, is to witness the message of "incarnation-identification" of God with the people and world realities. As a witnessing community in a multi- cultural and religious pluralistic context, the Church adopted an incarnational pattern of mission as its suitable model of mission in the religious pluralistic context of India.[102] The concept of incarnation is used as a criterion for evaluating the contextual nature of the mission.

3.4 An Institutional Model of Mission

The Church envisioned changes occurring in society. Society was becoming modern with the realization of self/individual, secular space, democracy,

---

[100] Bosch, *Transforming Missions*, 10-11.
[101] Orlando E. Costas, "Christian Missions in the America," in *New Directions in Mission and Evangelization-Theological Foundations,* eds. James A. Scherer and Stephen B. Bevans (Marknoll, New York: Orbis, 1994), 9.
[102] Thomas, A *History of the First Cross Cultural Mission,* xiii.

Mission and Liturgy

equal right of citizens, and institutionalization. In line with this modern trend, the Church itself was organized as an institution. The adoption of the constitution of the Church is a classic example of this. The MTC established many institutions to propagate the gospel. These institutions are considered as instruments of mission. The Mar Thoma Evangelistic Association itself is an institution. When we reflect on the institutional nature of the Church there are mainly three areas to which the Church gave special focus, i.e. education, health and social work.

The value of education has always been an integral part of the missionary movement. Besides preaching the gospel to the outcast, the Church gave attention to their educational and economic progress. The programme of education has been considered as an important aspect of the mission of the Church. The Western missionaries, Churches and religious organizations were in the forefront of education in India. The Anglican missionaries marked the beginning of a new deal in education. During the colonial time, education had been the traditional prerogative of the higher castes in the social context of Kerala. It was a monopoly of the high caste people. The vision that low castes also have the right to education gave an impetus for their emancipation and liberation from the social and political context. It created a space for social transformation and change. With the aim of uplifting people through education, the primary school education was given a forward thrust. The MTC took a major role in it. Rev. K. E. Oommen (1881-1984) states that the reason for starting the schools under the auspices of the MTC was "the desire of its members to read the Bible."[103] He says, "people had Bibles and they wanted to read, but there were only very few people who could read and write. Therefore, they wanted their children to learn to read the Bible at home. Hence, primary schools were started wherever possible with the grant-in-aid system. It resulted in the Church beginning several schools in various places. The Church has shown great enthusiasm to start English-medium schools also

---

[103] K. K. George, George Zacharia, Ajith Kumar, *Grants-in-Aid' Policies and Practices Towards Secondary Education in Kerala* (New Delhi: National Institute of Educational Planning and Administration, 2002), 1-3.

with a view to equip children to read the commentaries of the Bible."[104] The MTC started schools to provide learning to read and mediate the Bible with the assistance of commentaries through the medium of English and in the vernacular, and to provide elementary education to the converts from the "lower castes."[105] The educational institutions are not limited to formal learning, but to the training of the students in a variety of fields and thus enabling them to be active participants in the building up of a new society. It strives to achieve the integral development of the human personality. A Christian sense of mission impels the Church to give a preferential option for the poor and the marginalized and for the education of their children.[106] The early Mar Thoma community established more than 120 primary schools in Kerala. The Church runs many village schools to cater to the needs of the less privileged, especially in the North Indian villages.[107] It is a matter of witnessing the Christian presence and message. The schools become landmarks, symbols, and milestones of faith and witnessing.[108] Schools and colleges set up by the Church have enabled it to maintain a Christian influence in these institutions.[109] Along with the

---

[104] George, Zacharia and Kumar, *Grants-in-Aid*, 1-3. A. Sreedhara Menon, *A Cultural Heritage of Kerala*, (Madras: V. Subramanayam, 1996), 163.

[105] K.E. Oommen, M.T and E.A Schools, in *Mar Thoma Schoolukal* (Malayalam) 1-3, 89. The Mar Thoma Seminary High School was started in Kottayam in 1896 and the Syrian Christian Seminary School, Thiruvalla in 1902. Under the initiative of the MTEA, several schools were started in Puthuparambu (1904), Tiruvalla (1906), Elanthoor Vellappara (1907), Thonippara (1908), for the purpose of giving education to the newly joined members of the Church. The MTC had 65 schools including primary and higher schools by 1910. *Mar Thoma Schoolukal Charithra Samkshepam*, 1-159. This book contains the concise history of the Mar Thoma schools.

[106] Pauly Kannookadan, ed., *The Mission Theology of the Syro-Malabar Church*, (Kochi: Liturgical Research Centre, 2008), 250.

[107] The Mar Thoma Gram Jyoti Education and Development Society which was started in 1997 meant to establish village schools (Gram Jyoti Schools) in North India is a typical example of continuing the spirit of mission.

[108] Zac Varghese, ed., *Christian Witness: Revisiting the Mission Mandate of the Church*, Prathinidhimandalam 2009 Study (Thiruvalla: Mar Thoma Syrian Church, 2009), 35.

[109] Currently, The Church owns 14 colleges, 6 Higher Secondary Schools, 8 High Schools, 1 Vocational Higher Secondary School, 4 technical institutes, 1 Teachers Training Institute, 15 U.P. Schools and 114 primary schools. Besides, there are several schools and other educational institutions owned and managed by individual parishes. Joseph, *Malankara Mar Thoma Syrian Church: Sabha Directory 2015*, 23.

secular education, the Church gives priority to the theological education. The main purpose of the theological institutions is to impart biblical, theological, liturgical and pastoral training to candidates for the ministry of the Church. The principal theological institution of the Church is the Mar Thoma Theological Seminary, established in 1926, at Kottayam.

Under the institutional model of mission, a medical mission[110] is a part of the missionary outreach programme of the Church. It is an integral part of the witness of the Church. The medical mission started in 1947. Through the medical mission, the evangelistic concern for the sick and suffering is being fulfilled. The medical mission is closely connected with the Evangelistic Association of the Church. To convert people to Christianity is not the purpose of the medical mission but to render them Christian love and stewardship through their service and medical care. The medical service in itself is a part of the mission of the Church. It is an expression of the healing ministry of Christ. The Church has 49 social welfare institutions, 14 destitute homes and 9 hospitals.[111]

3.5 A Charity and Developmental Model

An act of service is an integral part of the proclamation of the Gospel. The Church has to work for the growth of society and contribute her share in nation building. The charity model of mission is significant in the Church. It is distinguished by at least three characteristics. (a) It is always self-giving. (b) It is done in the name of Jesus. (c) Its final consequence one cannot fully comprehend or calculate in the here and now. Love of God and love of neighbour is closely connected.

---

[110] The modern missionaries, taking its cue from Jesus, has actively promoted medical missions, including clinics, dispensaries, rest homes, hospitals, and in a few cases medical schools. In fact, the modern scientific medicine and surgery were introduced to the third world by Christian missionaries. Some of the outstanding pioneers of were medical men: Dr. John Scudder in India, Dr. Peter Parker in China, Dr. Paul Harrison in Arabia, Dr. Daniel Bradley in Thailand, and Dr. David Linvingstone in Africa. Kane, *Understanding Christian Missions*, 308.
[111] Joseph, *Malankara Mar Thoma Syrian Church: Sabha Directory*, 24.

The MTC gives special attention to the holistic development of the people and their life conditions. The salvific act of Christ is directly related to the world, and this is fundamental to both development and mission. In the person and works of Jesus, God proclaims sovereignty over the whole of life and not just over a religious sector of it. Likewise the Church is concerned with all spheres of life; and so it is not the Church development services which brings transformation, but, on the contrary, it is the Holy Spirit which injects transformation in the service.[112] The MTC instils new wave in its mission through its community oriented and value based programmes and projects. The socio-charitable institutions and related ministry of the church demonstrate this fact. The Navjeevan centre Mumbai[113] and Gram Jyothi school projects of the Delhi diocese[114] are examples of this type of mission. The inception of ministry among third gender (trans- gender) in honour of the Valya Metropolitan Mar Chrysostom is also prompt and relevant.[115] The Development Department of the Church

---

[112] At the World Conference for Church and Society in 1966 and at the fourth assembly of the WCC in Uppsala in 1968, the phase "responsible society" coined in Amsterdam in 1948, was taken up, and focus was on justice as such as society's constitutive element. The Uppsala assembly called on the Churches to allocate five percent of their budgets for development. The creation of a just society is possible only through a sustainable development that must be based on peace and justice. Muller, et al., *Dictionary of Missions*, 102-108.

[113] Navjeevan is a registered non-governmental organisation primarily engaged in rehabilitating the children of women working in the red-street areas in Mumbai. It was founded as part of the effort of the Mar Thoma Church to reach out to the several thousand girls who have been lured into living a life of shame in the red street areas of Mumbai. It mainly helps the exploited women and children in those areas to find new life and dignity. (http://www.navjeevan.org/home.htm)

[114] The Gram Jyothi society of schools are instituted for education, development and charity work among the under privileged people in the North Indian villages. The society is working as a light to various villages of Northern and Eastern India covering about 13 states. Currently, there are 23 schools/ balvadies under the Society. Some of the important welfare measures undertaken by these projects are: providing mid-day meals to the children in the slum/ villages, covering the education of the children, extending various helps to the parents for their livelihood, providing text books, stationaries and uniforms to the children and extending medical helps to children and their parents. (http://www.delhidiocese.com/new/web/portaltemplate.php?mainmenu=INSTITUTIONS&submenu=Gram%20Jyoti&subsubmenu=&subsubsubmenu=)

[115] Mission to transgenders is initiated by the Metropolitan of the Church in the year 2017-18. It was a historical event when Selin Thomas, representing the transgender community addressed one of the Youth's sessions in Maramon convention 2018.

Mission and Liturgy

is the most recent organization formed with a missionary concern. The work of this department is done through a registered society named Christian Agency for Rural Development (CARD). Its main objective is to act as a facilitator, an agent for change, or catalyst, to motivate and equip rural people to organize themselves for economic, educational and cultural development for social justices. There are over 40 social institutions in the Church, which are located in different geographical areas. They include counselling centres, hospital guidance centres, hospice for the terminally ill, schools for the mentally and physically challenged children. Through these institutions, the Church shows its distinctive character as a visible sign of its concern for the less privileged and the needy. It is an attempt in the area of social witness.[116]

The "Bhoo-bhavana Dana" movement (gift of land and house) initiated by Metropolitan Juhanon Mar Thoma in 1968 has now completed forty seven years. The Church, through this project, envisages building and providing houses to the people who suffer due to lack of proper housing. Around 8400 houses have been constructed and given to the needy ones irrespective of caste and religion in Kerala and other states outside Kerala.[117] Later, as part of the "home for the homeless" project in commemorating the silver jubilee of episcopal ministry of the Metropolitan Emeritus Philipose Mar Chrysostom Mar Thoma, with the cooperation of the Kerala government, the Church constructed around 5,000 houses for the homeless irrespective of caste and religion. There is also the Marriage Aid Fund started in 1972, to render financial aid to the poor for the marriage of their daughters. The relief fund designed to give immediate relief to individuals and groups who are affected by calamities such as floods, cyclone, tsunami etc. has responded well in times of need. The Church runs several orphanages and destitute homes to give asylum to the needy; all these provide many opportunities for the members in far-flung corners of the world to participate in the mission model of charity in the Church.

---

[116] Zacharias Mar Theolophilus, "The Pastoral Ministry of the Mar Thoma Church," in *In Search of Christian Identity in the Community*, 35-38.
[117] Joseph Mar Thoma Metropolitan, *Circular No.245*, dated 01st February 2016.

3.6 A Dialogue Model of Mission

Dialogue is a part of the evangelizing mission of the Church. In dialogue, there is a space for listening and speaking, learning and teaching, understanding and respecting, mutually helping and collaborating. Dialogue fosters mutual enrichment, fecundation and harmony among the followers of different religions. Besides, it challenges participants to grow deeper in their religious convictions and faith.[118] Even though the term dialogue is not in the Bible, the warm relationships and the intense personal encounters suggested by the active verb are very prominent throughout the Bible. The basis on which Christians enter into and continue their dialogue with others is their faith in Jesus Christ. Christian participation in dialogue is a part of the concrete living out of the view of life and the way of life that stem from faith in Jesus Christ.[119] Dialogue is part of the living relationship between people of different faiths and ideologies as they share in the life of the community.[120]

In the midst of the plurality of faith and multiplicity of cultural and ethnic communities, the Christian community can fulfill its prophetic role only in collaboration with others. This is a practical reason for dialogue of the Church with another religion. Dialogue is a positive attitude and profound reason to recognize the presence and action of God in other religions. A dialogue can promote mutual respect, acceptance, transformation and enrichment as well as collaboration in the fight against injustice and evil structures. Dialogue with culture and religions, then, becomes a way of mission.[121] The ministry of listening to others is important. In dialogue, there is among people a mutual listening of their experience with God and mutual learning and sharing of common experience occurs. Through dialogue, we collaborate with God's own mission of gathering all things

---

[118] Kannookadan, *The Mission Theology of the Syro-Malabar Church*, 274.
[119] S. J. Samartha, "Dialogue as a Continuing Christian Concern," in *Mission Trends No. 1: Critical issues in Mission Today,* eds. Gerals H.Anderson, Thomas F. Stansky (New York: Paulist, 1974), 259.
[120] Anderson, *Mission Trends,* 247.
[121] Michael Amalados, "Challenges of Mission in the 21st Century." *Theology Digest* 47, no.1 (Spring 2000): 16.

Mission and Liturgy

into communion.[122] Through dialogue one understands his own religion and faith in a better way.[123] Mission as dialogue requires that vulnerability, humility, and openness to other faiths encountered. A prophetic dialogue qualifies the conversation.[124] The New Delhi assembly of the World Council of Churches (WCC) in 1961 referred to "dialogue as a form of evangelism which is often effective today."[125] Uppsala 1968 pointed out that "the meeting with men of other faiths or of no faith must lead to dialogue. A Christian dialogue with another implies neither a denial of the uniqueness of Christ, nor any loss of his own commitment to Christ, but rather that a genuinely Christian approach to others must be human, personal, relevant and humble."[126] Listening and participating in dialogue can be a form of proclamation in the quest for truth.

The MTC follows a dialogue model of mission. The Church is engaged in dialogue with other religions and groups to foster unity and peace in society. The Church believes that dialogue affirms the other and at the same time helps to grow in relation, not in isolation. The Church established many dialogue centers for creative engagements with other faith communities. The Alexander Mar Thoma Centre for dialogue in Kottarakkara, Kerala is a classic example of this mission.

3.7 Sacramental Model of Mission

The Church is a sign, foretaste and instrument of God's reign in Christ entrusted with the responsibility to shape and direct the world with the power of the sacraments. Since sacraments are a visible expression of the invisible grace, (reality), the Church reveals the power of the sacraments through its very identity and mission. Sacraments point to the eternal blessings, which are meant to understand the divine grace. Sacraments are effective in two ways: culturally effective in organizing human life

---

[122] Amaladoss, "Challenges of Mission in the 21st century,"17-20.
[123] Anderson, *Mission Trends,* 247-262.
[124] Stephen B. Bevans and Roger P. Schroeder, *Prophetic Dialogue: Reflections on Christian Mission Today* (Maryknoll: Orbis, 2011), 37-38.
[125] World Council of Churches, *New Delhi Report: Section III* (London: SCM, 1961), 84.
[126] *The Uppsala Report 1968* (Geneva: WCC, 1968), 29.

and theologically effective in integrating human persons into the life of God. Cultural efficacy is not divine power, but human beings encounter the Trinity in human culture, through the incarnation and sacrament. Jesus Christ is the center of every liturgical celebration. The ecclesiological understanding of the Church as the sacrament, sign and instrument was very much dominant in the debate dealing with the missiological nature of the Church. The Church continually proclaims Christ and his Paschal Mystery through its liturgical celebrations. The worship is not just something the Church does alongside witnessing the Good news; worship itself is a witness to the world. It is a sign that all of life is holy, that hope and meaning can be found in offering ourselves to God (Rom.12:1). The celebration of Eucharist proclaims Christ's death until he comes (1 Cor.11:26). The liturgical life of the Church is a vital dimension of the mission calling.[127] The worship and liturgy proclaim the mission of the Church both internally and externally. Internally, it gives the assurance of the presence of God personally to the faithful and externally it proclaims their identity and vocation.

Stamoolis speaks of the liturgy as a method for mission. It is the source of Christian witness because at liturgy the faithful open themselves to the Spirit, through communion with the Lord's body and blood.[128] The liturgy is always the entrance into the presence of the Triune God and always ends with the community being sent forth in God's name to transform the world in God's image. Hence the mission is conceived, in other words, as "the liturgy after liturgy," the natural consequences of entering into the divine presence in worship.[129] As the document, "Go Forth in Peace put it, "the liturgy is not an escape from life, but a continuous transformation of life according to the prototype of Jesus Christ, through the power of the Spirit. The liturgy does not end when the Eucharist assembly disperses. "Let us go forth in peace"; the dismissal is a sending off of every believer

---

[127] Richards, *Foundations of Mission*, 56.
[128] Bevans and Roger, *Constants in Context*, 295.
[129] Ion Bria, *The Liturgy after the Liturgy: Mission and Witness from an Orthodox Perspective* (Geneva: WCC, 1996), 27-32.

to mission in the world where he or she lives and works, and of the whole community in the world, to witness to what they are and to the truth that the Kingdom is coming."[130]

4 Models of Mission: A Critical Assessment

Since, the MTC has extended considerably as a multi-cultural and multi-ethnic community around the world, it is imperative that, they have to design appropriate models of mission in considering its context. Otherwise the mission of the Church becomes irrelevant and the identity of the Church seems to become just a multi-ethnic minority institution. Very often the traditional pattern of mission such as Church planting, direct evangelism, emphasis on proselyticism etc., seems to be rejected by the community at large because of the arising religious intolerance, fundamentalism, inequality and injustice. At present, there is no common strategy or pattern for mission in the Church. For instance, it is important to analyse critically how far the Church could do justice to her calling of liberation of the Dalit Christians within the Church. It is unfortunate to note that there are segregation and the practice of casteism within the MTC. M. M. Thomas, an Indian Christian theologian and Chairperson of the Central Committee of World Council of Churches (1968-1975) in his analysis of the Reformation movement points out that Dalit Marthomites left the Church in large numbers because of the casteism within it. The formation of the "Prathyaksha Raksha Daiva Sabha" (PRDS) by Poikayil Yohannan is a protest against this.[131] It was only in 1981 that Dalit Marthomites were given the status of parishes in the Church. For a long time they were called Sabha, almost with a segregationist connotation, but in 1971, they came to be called chapels which later was upgraded to parishes.[132]

---

[130] Ion Bria, ed., *Go Forth in Peace: Orthodox Perspectives on Mission* (Geneva: WCC, 1986), 226.
[131] Joseph, "Abraham Malpante Naveekaranam," in Sabha Directory-2015, 353-355.
[132] Currently, the constitution of the MTC ensures representation of Dalits in decision-making bodies of the Church, such as Sabha Council, (Executive body of the Church) and Diocesan Councils. There are several development programmes being carried out for the holistic development of Dalit and Adivasi communities through the agencies

The Church has to discover new patterns of mission in considering the needs of the context. There is a fundamental distinction between the Church and the Kingdom of God in the present context. This distinction radically changes the traditional absolutists and the exclusivist understanding of the Church and its mission. The values of the Kingdom of God is radically a new reality and order, and the Church is commissioned to be a sign and servant of the Kingdom of God. Hence, the Kingdom and the historical Church are not identical. The Church has to give way to the Kingdom of God.[133] An incarnational pattern of mission is the most effective model of mission in the mission field context of the Church where the Gospel can be communicated in its best way by identifying with the people and to their cultural and social set up. The ashrams in the Church and their incarnation model of mission bear witness to this fact.[134] The extension of mission work among the so-called outcastes of the community is a classic example of this model of mission. The MTC's new mission policy to start mission work among "outcast" could be seen as a departure from its centuries old mission policy in a caste-conscious Indian society.[135] The Church attempted to incarnate the Gospel through challenging the evils of the caste structure, serving the poor through hospitals and destitute homes, and day care centres for poor children and thus focused on the development of villages though several humanitarian programs. It aims at adopting the life and engagements of Jesus Christ as the mission of the Church.[136] The goal of the Mar Thoma mission activity is to witness the redeeming power of God in Jesus Christ through its very life. Even though a conversion may have taken place because of its evangelistic work, such an event remains, strictly speaking, an individual's decision; it does not, however, constitute

---

like STARD, Christian Agency for Rural Development (CARD), and BPDP (Backward People's Development Programme) in the Church. Interview with Rev. K.Y Jacob, the director of the CARD on December 15, 2015.

[133] Kuncheria Pathil, "A Response to Religious Pluralism," in *In Search of Christian Identity in Global Community*, 89-90.

[134] A detailed study on the mission of Ashrams will be dealt in the appendix 1.

[135] Joseph Daniel, *Ecumenism in Praxis: A Historical Critique of the Malankara Mar Thoma Syrian Church* (Frankfurt: Peter Lang, 2014), 106.

[136] Thomas, "The Mar Thoma Church: Then and Now," 43-46.

the Church's agenda. As we have seen, the focus of the Eucharist liturgy is the incarnational nature of Christ and his salvific act for the redemption of whole creation. Since the Church employs the incarnational model in its mission activities, their renders Church considerably more relevant in the transformation of society. Hence an emphasis on the incarnational pattern of mission has to be reiterated in the Church.

It is worth noting the positive role played by the institutions and ancillary organizations of the Church in its mission. The auxiliary organizations of the Church through its various ministries[137] could effect a great impact in the socio-religious sphere of the community at large. These institutions employed a charity and developmental model of mission in the Church. A caution here: even though the Church could make a great impact in society through its institutions, it has nevertheless to be cautious of the danger of secular ideologies in its witnessing life. At present, institutions very often tend to become so timid and seem to keep a deliberate silence against evil practices in society such as corruption, discrimination, and injustice. There is a growing tendency that appears to move in line with the secular institutions; that is to say maintain the priority of making profit, over the communication of Christian values. Although the Church had taken education as part of ministry and mission, it worked in a hierarchical frame of paternalism (enlightened to the less enlightened - Missionaries to Syrian Christians and Syrian Christians to the new believers) challenging the spirit of mission itself.

---

[137] Mission and Ministry are not synonymous. The mission is the agenda of God and ministry is the option of the ambassadors of Christ guided by the Holy Spirit. There is an intrinsic relationship between mission and ministry. The Church has a mission but has many ministries. The mission is an inclusive term which includes every aspect of human life, but ministry is a term which refers to a particular aspect of the mission of the Church. For instance, the ministry of teaching, preaching, healing, serving. All these ministries are coming under the mission of the Church. The Church does not exist for itself, but for its mission. A ministry is the means by which mission is achieved. Mathew Mar Makkarios, "Mission of the Church: Contextual and Universal," *Mar Thoma Seminary Journal of Theology* 1, no.1 (June 2012): 59.

The religious pluralist[138] context demands new policies for Church mission. The attitude of the Church vis-à-vis another religion had been apologetic and missionary. She defended her uniqueness and invited others to join her; co-existence, collaboration and solidarity in the common struggle against atheism and evil materialism in an effort to build a better world were not within her scope.[139] In a multi- religious and plural cultural context of the world, the mission of the Church calls for it to be a truly dialogical community. It demands an attitude of openness and respect to other faiths and the role of being an agent of reconciliation and peace among the various groups. The Church has to create a common forum of dialogue and liberalize action through which mutual misunderstanding, hatred, discord and discrimination could be opposed, a forum which could together build up a nation with justice, peace and harmony. The primary task of the Church in this context is to build up a human community, which is based on freedom, fellowship, equality, justice, and peace. The mission of the Church, then, is universal reconciliation. In a multi-religious context, the Church must consciously build up a multi-religious society, in which every religious community is recognized, accepted and respected and in which this new order allows each group to contribute its riches to the good of all.[140]

In a multi-religious and pluralistic context like India, there is a need to affirm the Kingdom values of justice, peace, love, respect, and tolerance

---

[138] Plurality has existed in India for centuries but pluralism is a modern reality. Traditional India had been a land in which peoples and communal groups who followed different religions, lived according to different cultural values and social patterns, and spoke different languages, coexisted. There was a religious tolerance and mutual acceptance, and respect prevailed in the social and personal scenarios. Nevertheless, throughout the periods of history, a general dominant tendency came to birth due to colonial situations, unequal social structure, and the politicization of religion. It influenced the social fabric of Indian society. The movement from co-existence to dialogue existence is the movement from plurality to pluralism. This movement of plurality to pluralism is not only national but also local as well as worldwide. M. M Thomas, *The Church's Mission and Post Modern Humanism: Collection of Essays and Talks 1992-1996* (New Delhi: ISPCK, 1996), 129.
[139] Gregory Karotemprel and Jacob Marangattu, eds., *Evangelizing In The Third Millennium, Series No-1* (Rajkot: Deepti Publication, 2006), 55.
[140] Thomas Malipurathu and L. Stanislaus, eds., *A Vision of Mission in the New Millennium* (Mumbai: St Paul's, 2001), 77.

Mission and Liturgy

for creating a peaceful co-existence. In other words, to witness is to search for the eternal truths of the Kingdom of God and become partners in fighting for common Christian causes, celebrating festivals together and working to re-establishing and sustaining the integrity of creation. Thus acknowledging the presence of God in other religious traditions is included in the area of witnessing.[141] In the present context, the Church should make all efforts to remove every trace of triumphalism, exclusivism and any attitude of superiority in its teachings, structures, evangelizing activities and the style of the functioning of its institutions. Particularly, it has to ensure that its educational enterprises, charitable activities, health care services and social involvements are geared to the genuine promotion of people's well-being and progress and not in any way to convert from their religions. However, it should be pointed out that the Church always defends the right of individuals to profess the religion of their choice. All the same, it denounces proselytisation through the use of questionable means, such as fraud, force and allurement.

Pattern of dialogue is a crucial aspect in mission in the present context, since the Church faces various challenges in the face of nascent fundamentalism and religious intolerance. In a pluralistic context, the Church has to consider the dialogue model of mission more seriously when it encounters other faith communities. Dialogue between world-views becomes possible and indeed necessary for life. Dialogue then becomes the only possible mode of co-existence.[142] The Bible conventions and revival meetings in the Church, especially, the Maramon Convention, provides a platform for sharing the ecumenical and missional vision of the Church. These meetings are a solemn space which initiates dialogue with other faith communities and thereby fosters unity, harmony and mutual learning in the pluralistic context of Kerala. The Church's theological vision on mission affirms the mutual respect for all religious

---

[141] Zac Varghese, ed., "Christian Witness: Revisiting the Mission Mandate of the Church," Prathinidhimandalam *2009 Study* (Thiruvalla: Mar Thoma Syrian Church, 2009), 28-29.
[142] Karl Rahner, *Theological Investigations*, vol. 6, trans. David Bourke (London: Darton, Longman and Todd, 1976), 35.

faith, including the Christian faith, in relation to the universal. The Church has always been open to other religious traditions of India. The liberal and pluralistic mission outlook, which is independent of the Western theology in relation to other religions helped the Church to develop a mission pattern of inclusive paradigm in mission. According to Mundadan, before anyone, the world ever might presume demonstrate the meaning of religious tolerance and openness, the Indian Christians had already been living for centuries in a positive encounter with the high caste Hindus and had developed a theological vision of Hindu religion which was more positive and liberal.[143] The Church adapted a mission which is inclusive in nature within the Indian pluralistic context. The Malankara Church reacts to the reality of Indian religious plurality by way of two major paradigms of the modern world, viz., inclusivism and pluralism.[144] In the present context, instead of ecclesiocentrism which is exclusive in nature, Inclusivism or Karl Rahner' classic term of "Anonymous Christian"[145] is a meaningful and effective attitude for the communication of the Gospel.

---

[143] Mathias A Mundadan, *History of Christianity in India, From the Beginning up to the Middle of the Sixteenth Century.* Vol. I (Bangalore: Church History Association of India, 1989), 493-494.

[144] Daniel, *Ecumenism in Praxis,* 57.

[145] Christ's salvation and grace is given to all, even outside the boundaries of the visible Church; it is present also in other religions, though they do not know it. This expression denotes people, who live in the state of Christ's grace through faith, hope and love, yet who have no explicit knowledge of the fact that his life is orientated in grace-given salvation to Jesus Christ. Rahner, *Theological Investigations,* vol. 14, 283.

Chapter. 3

Liturgy and Community Formation: Missional Significance in the Mar Thoma Church

The Church is a community of faithful which is entrusted with the responsibility to share the good news of Christ through its very life. This community is nourished and strengthened by the table of the Word and table of the Body of Christ. Christian Faith is proclaimed in society through lifestyle. It is an expression of self. The search for this identity is manifested in the relationship between God and the human within the setting of liturgy. The faithful realize it through participating in the liturgy. A celebrated faith is proclaimed and proclamation aims at gathering people for celebration. One of the characteristics of the oriental methodology for the proclamation is the catechetical and liturgical approach. It is through the liturgy that the Church communicates its faith and theology. Here mission is an incarnational living of the liturgical, ascetical and mystical spirituality to make visible the Trinitarian-Eucharistic experience of God's saving action.[146] Therefore, the liturgical worship is a creative expression of witnessing. As mentioned in the previous chapter, the ultimate calling of the Church is to render a sacramental presence in the world. Therefore, the liturgy of the Church is specifically designed to bring God's life to His people, restoring His image in them. God's plan for the future of the cosmos is present in the Church through the liturgy. This is heaven on earth. A key phrase for all Orthodox Churches- the future is now.[147] To translate

---

[146] Kannookadan, *The Mission Theology of the Syro-Malabar Church*, 21.
[147] "The Orthodox believe that, the Church is a God-created and God-given reality, the presence of Christ's new life, the manifestation of the new eon of the Holy Spirit. The Church is an eschatological reality, a divine gift; its essential function is to manifest and

the love and life of God into the world is not an accident, but a deliberate intention of corporate worship and a necessary result of it. The worship and liturgy proclaim the mission of the Church both internally and externally. Internally, it gives the assurance of the presence of God personally to the faithful and externally it proclaims their identity and vocation.

This chapter explores how the liturgy functions as a catalyst for the formation and nurturing of communities at large. It also deals with the characteristics of the Church as a community in general and how the Sacrament of Baptism stands as an entry point to the Eucharistic community and thereby leads people to participate in the mission of the Church.

1 The Liturgy and Community Formation

Generally, the term community means, a group of people living in the same place or having a particular characteristic in common. By the word community one expects some sort of bonding, sharing, mutuality, interaction, relationship among the people, despite the diversity in religious practices and cultural traits. According to David McMillan and David Chavis, there are mainly two major meanings of the term community. When it is used more broadly: the territorial and geographical notion of community - city, town, neighbourhood; and the relational notion of community, which has to do with the quality of human relationship without reference to location.[148] They defined community as "a feeling that members have of belonging, a feeling that members matter to one another and to the group, and a shared faith that members' needs will be met through their commitment to be together."[149] Even though, it is

---

to actualize in this world the Eschaton, the ultimate reality of salvation and redemption. In and through the Church, the Kingdom of God (made already present through Christ), is communicated to people and it is this eschatological, God-given fullness of the Church that constitutes the root of the ecclesiological absolutism of the Eastern Orthodoxy." Alexander Schmemann, *Church, World, Mission* (New York: St. Vladimir's Seminary, 1979), 197.

[148] David W. McMillan and David M. Chavis, "Sense of Community: A Definition and Theory," *Journal of Community Psychology* 14 (1996): 8.

[149] McMillan and Chavis, "Sense of Community: A Definition and Theory," 9.

not a theologically based definition, it does offer important insight into what constitutes a community: belonging, membership, significance and commitment.[150] Communities exist in many forms. Mark Searle comments, "community, it appears, is above all a feeling; a sense of belonging, of being at home, of knowing and being known. Community is a place where no one feels like a stranger."[151] Similarly, George Wood and Juan Judikis define community as a group of people "who have a sense of common purpose(s) and /or interest(s) for which they assume mutual responsibility, who acknowledge their interconnectedness, who respect the individual differences among members, and who commit themselves to the well-being of each other and the integrity and well-being of the group."[152]

God designed humanity to live in community. For the early Christians, evangelisation was a way of life in the community, by the community, and for the community. Continuing from the apostolic tradition, where the household had often been the venue and focus of the mission, formal and informal discussions as well as worship took place in private homes during this house-church period of Christianity.[153] The Disciples of Christ, were empowered by the Holy Spirit to preach the resurrection of Jesus Christ. Then they lived as an Easter community and celebrated their plurality. For them, the Eucharist was a sacred space which was inclusive in nature. Their ministry was to form the community of believers wherever they

---

[150] C. Randall Bradley, *From Memory to Imagination: Reforming the Church's Music* (Cambridge: Grand Rapids, 2012), 112.

[151] Mark Searle, *Called to Participate: Theological, Ritual and Social Perspectives* (Collegeville, MN: Liturgical, 2006), 72.

[152] This definition contains six essential elements that determine whether community is present: A sense of common purpose(s) or interest(s) among members, an assuming of mutual responsibility, an acknowledgment (at least among members) of interconnectedness, mutual respect for individual differences, mutual commitment to the well-being of each other and Commitment by the members to the integrity and well-being of the group. The other traits that are important for community involve inclusion, safety, geographical location, beliefs, values, particular practices, decision making, and community spirit. In addition, they divided communities into five categories such as Nuclear community, Tribal community, Collaborative community, Geopolitical community, and Life community, George S. Wood Jr and Juan C. Judikis, *Conversations on Community Theory* (West Lafayette, Ind.: Purdue University, 2002), 12, 46-51.

[153] Bevans and Roger, *Constants in Context*, 86-87.

went and preached the Gospel. They emphasized community living and shared spiritual nourishment and it helped the growth and the nurturing of the community.

In the Christian theological circle, the term community is meant to highlight personal communion with the Trinitarian God and among believers in the Church. Trinity is the model for a perfect community.[154] The Trinity is a community where there is intimate, loving and sharing, full participation of the three members, absolute equality of persons and outreach to others. The Church is a community of believers.[155] As the key to ecclesiology, *communio* (according to biblical teaching and Patristic tradition) always encompasses a double dimension, i.e. a vertical (communion with God) and the horizontal (communion with one another). The *communio* of the Church is prefigured, enabled, and sustained by the intra-Trinitarian *communio:* Hence the Church is seen to be "a people brought into unity from the unity of the Father, the Son and the Holy Spirit."[156] Thus the Church is now often represented as the icon of the Trinitarian community. A theology of community is fundamentally a concretization of the dogmatic teaching about the Church, which is a pilgrim people of God, the all-encompassing sacrament of salvation, the body of Christ and the temple of the Holy Spirit. The Christian community basically grounded in the sacraments of initiation- Baptism, Confirmation and the Eucharist is the primitive source of ecclesial communion, and hence Christian community.[157]

---

[154] Richards, et al., *Foundations For Mission*, 22.

[155] The ecclesiological foundations of the new theology of community lie in the Second Vatican Council's Dogmatic constitution on the Church *Lumen Gentium*, its Constitution on the Sacred Liturgy *Sacrosanctum Concilium*, as well as in its decrees *Christus Dominus, Presbyterorum Ordinis, Apostolicam Actuositatem*, and *Ad Gentes*. At issue is, above all, the meaning and scope of the following terms found in the conciliar texts: *Ecclesia particularis* (individual church), *Ecclesia localis* (local/regional church), *congregatio fidelium localis, communitas paroecialis, communitas altaris* (local congregation of the faithful, local community, parish community, community of the altar) Michael Figura, The Works of Communion: Christian Community in Act," *Communio-International Catholic Review* XXIX, No.2 (2002): 220-238.

[156] This citation is found in Cyprian, *De dominica oration* 23 (CCL 3A, 105, Z.448f).

[157] David S. Crawford, "Christian Community and the States of Life," *Communio-International Catholic Review* XXIX, no.2 (2002): 340-341.

The liturgy is a component for community formation. The identity of a Christian community is based on the way it worships. Worshipping is what gives communing people their identity. A fundamental role of liturgy is to be a channel of communication between God and the faithful. The liturgy helps the faithful to be in touch with the creator God through their corporate fellowship. Hence liturgy has to express the need, context, aspirations and even the life of the people. In general, the Church is a liturgical community. The liturgy is a fundamental form of Church community life. Through liturgy a sense of community within the parish is encouraged. The highpoint of the Christian community is the Eucharist. By participating in the body and blood of Christ, the Church is taken up into communion with God and with one another. Through the Eucharist, the community becomes a sign of God's salvific work on behalf of all humanity and the world. It is in the liturgical celebration that the Church transcends her societal context and manifests her special character.[158] The Church is a praying community. Prayer is the fundamental action of the Church. Through prayer and liturgy, the Church expresses herself and also constitutes herself and makes herself known therein. In other words, where Christians gather together in prayer, the Church becomes visible.[159] The gospel writer Luke depicts the original Christian community in Jerusalem as a praying community. Prayer is the foundation of the life of a Christian community. The *lex orandi* follows upon the *lex credenda*.

1.1 The Characteristics of the Church as a Community

While considering the term "Christian community," the Greek term *koinonia* is most often used to describe it. Craig Nissan says, "*koinonia* comes from the initiative of God in establishing communion with human beings by the power of the Spirit."[160] The incarnated Word - Jesus - came

---

[158] Figura, "The Works of Communion: Christian Community in Act," 226. St. Paul calls his collection for the community in Jerusalem *diakonia tes leiturgias* (2 Cor.9:12).
[159] Figura, "The Works of Communion: Christian Community in Act," 235.
[160] Craig L. Nessan, *Beyond Maintenance to Mission: A Theology of the Congregation*, 2nd ed. (Minneapolis: Fortress, 2010), 4-5. According to him, the essence of Christian *koinonia* can be determined by asking the following questions: Does a community reflect

into the world to initiate fellowship with God and with human beings. He gathered a community around him, as exemplified in the group of twelve disciples.[161] Nessan continues, "Jesus was renowned and even notorious for the fellowship he initiated, and practiced open table fellowship with the so called "sinners" in society such as tax collectors, lepers, and women."[162] The early Church continued to practice the *koinonia* of Christ by gathering together for worship and by the breaking of bread. They shared everything and fellowship in Christ was their strength (Acts.2:44-45). There are different dimensions of *koinonia*, such as *martyria* (witness), *diakonia* (service) and *leiturgia* (worship), fulfilment in the communication of the gospel, and in the celebration of the sacramentality of life. The theological concept of *communio* is complex. This term refers fundamentally to communion with God through Jesus Christ in the Holy Spirit. This communion occurs in the Word of God and in the sacraments.[163] A Christian community is not a company of strangers, rather it is a body of believers (1 Cor.12:12-31) which is diverse in nature - male and female, rich and poor, black and white - yet one in Christ.[164]

1.1.1 A Community of Word and Sacraments

An engagement with Scripture is always central to the identity of a Christian community. The Christian community is built up through the proclamation of the Word of God. It is the Word of God that unites the people of God. Scripture is normative, not because it possess a privileged theoretical status independent of the community of believers, but because the early Christian community and generations of Christians have recognised in

---

the spirit of mutual love and concern shown by Jesus to those who followed him? Are all made welcome in the name of Jesus? Is the ultimate source of power that of the crucified Christ, and is that power shared in common? Is special effort made to express concern for 'the least' of sisters and brothers? When there is failure to live up to the ideal, is there readiness to ask for and grant forgiveness for Christ's sake? These questions are important for measuring the quality and genuineness of Christian community.

[161] Bradley, *From Memory to Imagination*, 113.
[162] Nessan, *Beyond Maintenance to Mission*, 4.
[163] Figura, "The Works of Communion: Christian Community in Act," 231.
[164] Bradley, *From Memory to Imagination*, 115.

Mission and Liturgy

the reading of the text, a definitive expression of their communal faith. In Scripture, the Church recognises its shared faith. This experience of shared recognition helps the Church to bind together as a faith community. Thus the Scriptures are normative for the faith of Christians. The Bible is the earliest written testimony to the Christian faith and countless other generations over two millennia have also recognised their own faith in these writings. The Christian communities are not just hearers of the Word, but also the proclaimers of the Word. Just as every individual Christian is obligated to pass on the faith given to him/her through Sacrament of Baptism, so the whole community is called to witness their faith and to proclaim it as missionaries.[165]

The Bible is the Word of God, in the sense that it helps the faithful to realize the presence of God in their life experiences. As a sacramental word, Scripture presents Christ to the believing community. "As a sacramental word, Scripture is not only a witness to the revelation that has taken place in Christ; rather, it draws the faithful into the presence of Christ and invites them to be transformed into his image. It opens the possibility of relationship between the divine and the human."[166] On this view, the Bible forms the community into the body of Christ through the liturgical gathering. Scripture becomes a means by which Christians are gathered into the body of the living Lord. Lathrop remarks that, "a community gathers in prayer around the scriptures read and proclaimed. This community of the word then tastes the meaning of that word by keeping the meal of Christ, giving thanks over bread and cup and eating and drinking. It is this word-table community, the body of Christ, which gathers other people to its number, continually teaching both itself and these new comers the mercy and mystery of God and washing them in the name of that God."[167] Scripture is a means of grace used by the Holy

---

[165] Figura, "The Works of Communion: Christian Community in Act," 220-238.
[166] Witvliet, John D. "The Opening of Worship-Trinity." In *A More Profound Alleluia: Theology and Worship in Harmony*, edited by Leanne Van Dyk. Grand Rapids, MI: William B. Eerdmans, 2005. 65-66
[167] Gordon Lathrop, *What are the Essentials of Christian Worship?* (Minneapolis, MN: Augsburg Fortress, 1994), 22.

Spirit to nourish and build up the community of faith. The Holy Spirit uses Scripture as a sacramental element, as it were, to unite the believers to Christ. Scripture unites believers to Jesus Christ, himself the Word of God. The Bible is the Word of God in a sacramental sense, uniting us to Christ, the one true Word of God. It brings Christ to believers.[168]

1.1.2 A Eucharistic Community

The worship and sacraments keep the members together as a community. Through participation in the Eucharist, the members of the Church experience a mystical union with Christ. It connects the individual with the wider fellowship of the community of believers. The Eucharist celebrates and creates the communion of believers with the Trinity while at the same time strengthening the bonds of communion between believers as fellow members of the one body. Hence the Eucharist is both "the sign and sublime cause of that communion in the divine life and that unity of the people of God."[169] Eucharist is a celebration when the bonds of communion are formed and deepened. In the Eucharist, the mutual indwelling of Christ in the believer and the believer in Christ is given full expression and leads to a deeper assimilation of the believer to Christ and a fuller immersion into Trinitarian life. Eucharist not only conforms us to Christ individually, but transforms us collectively into his body by the power of the Holy Spirit. In him all become one. For Christ is the centre where all lines converge.[170]

The Church is a Eucharistic community and its identity and mission derives from the Eucharist. The Eucharist is a symbolic act of the abundance of divine love. It expresses Christians' identity as a Eucharistic community based on their relationship to God and to their fellow human beings. When the Disciples of Christ translate the love of God - which they experience in Christ in the Eucharist - into their everyday lives, into their relationship with each other and with other human beings, then they are building a new

---

[168] Dyk, "Proclamation: Revelation, Christology," 66-67.
[169] Billy Swan, *The Eucharist, Communion and Formation-Proceedings of the International Symposium of Theology* (Dublin: Veritas, 2013), 995.
[170] Swan, *The Eucharist, Communion and Formation*, 997.

society and part of a new creation. Basically, the Eucharist brings together two basic aspects of the entire mystery, i.e. the Eucharist strengthens and deepens the bonds of community, and also Eucharistic sharing means that one must divide, separate and give to another what is shared and this denotes the self-giving of Christian life.[171] In this sense, the Church is a Eucharistic community and its mission and identity derives from the Eucharist. An example of this basic formula would be the theological rationale for the shape of the Eucharistic action. For instance, in the preparation service of the Eucharist (pre-anaphora), the faithful gather to be formed into a community, ready to attend to God. This recognition of who and where we are prepares us to incorporate our story into the story of what God has done for us. The key moment of this incorporation and engagement in the celebration is the proclamation of the gospel at the climax of the Liturgy of the Word. Then in the anaphora, in the Eucharistic action, the God who has come to share our life in the Word made flesh, catches us up into his transforming action of grace, as we, the broken fragments of his body, are made one as we receive his body, broken for us. Renewed by this mystery, the faithful are charged to share this life of engagement and transformation. The final blessing in the Eucharistic liturgy is key to the mission of the Church.[172] Through the Eucharist, the Church reminds us that sharing is possible only through breaking and the Church prepares herself for the mission of sharing by breaking. It is the mission of self-emptying. "Caring by sharing" is an integral part of the mission.[173] Relationship with other communities is inevitable for an effective ministry. This community must

---

[171] Kurt Koch, "Principles for a Christian Theology of Baptism," *Theology Digest* 52, no.3 (2005): 235-236.

[172] David Stancliffe, "The Making of the Church of England's Common Worship," *Studia Liturgica* 31, no.1 (2001): 16. "A tradition common to both the East and the West is that all ordinations must be related to a concrete community and must take place within the context of a Eucharistic assembly. Both of these point to the close relation between ministry and community. The Eucharistic assembly is the natural milieu for the birth of ministry understood in this broader soteriological perspective." Zizioulas, *Being as Communion*, 211-212.

[173] Geevarghese Mar Theodosius, "Mission of the Church in the 21st Century," in *Challenges and Prospects of Mission in the Emerging Context,* ed. Koshy P Varughese (Faridabad: Dharma Jyoti Vidya Peeth, 2010), 26.

be in relation with other communities in spite of the divisions caused by space and time. Thus the Eucharist has been offered not just on earth but before the very throne of God and in the company of all the saints, living and departed, as well as in the name of the "Catholic Church in the world."[174]

1.1.3 A Missional Community

Before ascending into heaven, Jesus commissioned his disciples to go to the ends of the earth with a particular mission (Mt.28:18-20). This great commissioning (Mt.28:16-20, Jn.20:19- 23) is a mandate for mission. The Church is entrusted with this mission of salvation through Christ by the power of the Holy Spirit. The work of evangelisation belongs to this missionary commission as a fundamental task of the people of God. This community is called together for worship and sent forth to minister not only to each other, but to the larger community within their context. The missional Church is not foremost a gathering place, but a place from which to be sent.[175] There is a new way of understanding the Church as the body of people sent on mission. The Church is being conceived as a community, a gathered people, brought together by a common calling and vocation to be a sent people.[176] The Christian community is missionary in its proclamation, liturgy and service to the neighbour; it testifies to its missionary calling particularly by entering into the various needs of people, whom out of faith and love it seeks to ameliorate. This community ceaselessly proclaims the salvation of God to the world.[177] The Eucharistic liturgy affirms that the community gathered for worship must be dispersed for mission. It orients the believing community towards new responsibilities such as witness to Jesus Christ, preservation of creation, and service to society. These new responsibilities are carried out in various spheres of life, such as family,

---

[174] John Zizioulas, *Being as Communion* (Crestwood, New York: St. Vladimir's Seminary, 1985), 236-237.
[175] Bradley, *From Memory to Imagination*, 138.
[176] Guder, *Missional Church*, 81.
[177] Figura, "The Works of communion: Christian Community in Act," 234.

Church, society, environment and the entire creation. The praxis of the Church in the community symbolizes the Christian identity. The liturgy, traditions, institutions, and other outreach programs like development and charity proclaim the nature and identity of a community. A ministry in the Church is a response and a commitment to the call and commission of the Lord of the Church. It is within the community, and by the community the ministry of the Church is nurtured and proclaimed.

1.1.4 An Eschatological Community

The Church is a community of people who are called out to live with values of the Kingdom of God and look forward for the fullness of time. The Kingdom of God is active and present in the world, powerfully thrusting towards eschatological fullness. As a community of faith, the Church survives in the reality of the "already, but not yet." The Church is already in fellowship with Christ, but not fully in the presence of Christ. The Church is a community of hope and vision, which always anticipates the glorious return of Christ in awe and wonder. This community anticipates the second coming of Christ and prepares herself for eternal glory. Here, the worship connects the faithful to the future reality of our being fully present with Christ. The Church believes that the earthly liturgy is a mirror image of the heavenly liturgy.[178] According to Newbigin "the Church lives in the midst of history as a sign, instrument and foretaste of the reign of God."[179] She finds her identity and mission in what it points to as a sign, in what it savours as a foretaste, and in what it pursues and bring about as an instrument. All three of these terms, sign, foretaste and instrument, are closely linked to the mission and unity of the Church. As a sign, the Church admits that it is not itself the eschatological end of redemption, but rather its means (or instrument) and foretaste, and it also serves to usher it in primarily through its mission. The Christian mission is not only a sign

---

[178] Giles Dimock, *The Eucharist* (New York: Paulist, 2006), 135-137.
[179] Lesslie Newbigin, *The Open Secret: An Introduction to the Theology of Mission* (Grand Rapids, MI: Eerdmans, 1975), 110.

of the Kingdom, but the "instrument of a universal and eschatological salvation."[180]

Eschatologically speaking, the Church is a manifestation of the choice of God to redeem humanity through chosen individuals and people. An eschatological view considers where history is moving to, and also where it is moving from. Newbigin articulates that the "Church is not to be defined by what it is, but by that End to which it moves."[181] The eschatological nature of this faith community is not the negation of the world, but on the contrary, its affirmation and acceptance as the object of divine love. In other words, the whole other worldliness of the Church is nothing but the sign and the reality of the love of God for this world, the very condition of the Church's mission to the world.[182] The mission of the Church is, according to Newbigin, "itself the sign of the coming consummation."[183] The Church is not the Kingdom to which it points, but it is a foretaste of that Kingdom. The liturgy of the Church is designed to experience a communion with God and believers. It unites people, breaks down barriers, and enables them to experience fellowship in Christ. The worship (liturgy) and community are interdependent. Genuine community will deepen and strengthen the spirit of worship in the same way meaningful worship enhances the community spirit.[184] A Eucharistic community which deliberately lives in isolation from the rest of the community is not an ecclesial community. This is what renders the Church "Catholic" not only on the level of "here and now" but also on that of "everywhere and always." The ministry of the Church must reflect this catholicity by being a unifying ministry both in time and in space.

---

[180] Newbigin, *The Household of God* (New York: Friendship, 1954), 145.
[181] Newbigin, *The Household of God*, 19.
[182] Schmemann, *Church, World, Mission*, 199.
[183] Newbigin, *The Household of God*, 142.
[184] Bradley, *From Memory to Imagination*, 110-111.

2   The Sacrament of Baptism: An Invitation to the Eucharistic Community

The Sacrament of Baptism is a Christian symbolic action[185] that involves pouring or immersion in water. As one of the dominical sacraments,[186] Holy Baptism stands as a pillar of Christian life, its identity and mission. Christian baptism is rooted in the ministry of Jesus of Nazareth, in his death and resurrection. According to Gregory of Nyssa, baptism is a sacramental initiation into the mystery of Christ's death and resurrection, which at the same time accomplishes in us the effect of Christ's action.[187] The decisive distinction of early Christian baptism from its roots in John's baptism was that it was carried out in the name of Jesus Christ (Acts.2:38, 8:16, 10:48, 19:5). It was understood as the participation of the baptized person to Christ, so that from that point the baptised person belongs to Christ.[188] It is the sacrament of the Church, i.e. the act in which and for which the Church manifests and fulfils herself as the body of Christ and the temple of the Holy Spirit.

St. Paul, the Apostle taught baptism as a process of being crucified with Christ by dying to sin and death in the waters of baptism and sharing in Christ's resurrection (Rom. 6:1-10). In the Gospel of John, baptism is seen as rebirth (Jn.3:1-7). This image is reinforced by the other Johannine writings of the New Testament as well as by the image of baptism as the

---

[185] The symbolic aspects in baptism are of special importance. It is the Aramaic word *mamodisa*, which means immersion or washing that best describes the Sacrament of Baptism. The closest Greek equivalent is *baptisma*. John the Baptist used water as a sign of repentance and conversion to God, as a sign which was used throughout the ancient world for cleansing and purification. The Old Testament also recognizes the life-giving power of water (Isa.41:17-20, Ezek.47:1-2). The New Testament symbolism of water signifies purification, sanctification, and paradoxically life-giving and death-dealing. The Greek word *baptizo* originally signifies "to sink" or "art drawn."

[186] The holy baptism and holy Qurbana are called Dominical Sacraments. These are called so because they are directly commanded by the Lord. (Dominical - having to do with Jesus Christ as Lord).

[187] Everett Ferguson, "The Doctrine of Baptism in Gregory of Nyssa's *Oratio Catechetica*," in *Dimensions of Baptism: Biblical and Theological Studies,* eds. Stanley E. Porter and Anthony R. Cross (New York: Sheffield Academic, 2002), 226-227.

[188] Koch, "Principles for a Christian Theology of Baptism," 232.

water of rebirth.[189] In line with this, the baptismal liturgy of the MTC affirms that, through Holy Baptism, a person identifies with the death and resurrection of Jesus Christ. It is a sign of a renewed life in Christ and participation in his life-giving mission.[190] Syriac writers like Severus of Antioch[191] (465-538 CE) and Bar Habreas[192] (1226-1286 CE) held that by baptism the divine life (Trinitarian life) is communicated to the baptized, that baptism cleanses from sin, brings renewal, effects rebirth, incorporates into the Church, makes the baptized person a child of God, causes the dwelling of the Holy Spirit in the baptized and so on.[193] These realities of faith are not explained speculatively or rationally, but as indicated above, by making use of the Old Testament typology, images, figures and similes. It is a response in faith to the call of God in and through Christ. This call is freely made by God and is experienced as a gift of God.

The Sacrament of Baptism is a gateway into Christian life, directed towards the fullness of faith and discipleship of Christ. It is the first means of ritual incorporation into the life, death and resurrection of Christ.[194] Incorporation into Christ means it is also incorporated into his mystical body- the Church. Baptism intimately connects the baptized with Christ's whole Church and its manifestation within a particular, visible denomination and the local congregation. Believers are baptized into one body and

---

[189] Muller, et al., *Dictionary of Mission*, 40. Philippe Bordeyne and Bruce T. Morrill, "Baptism and Identity Formation: Convergence in Ritual and Ethical Perspectives: A Dialogue," *Studia Liturgica* 42, no.1-2 (2012): 154-175.

[190] *Baptismal Liturgy of the Mar Thoma Church* (Thiruvalla: Mar Thoma, 1995), 8-11.

[191] Severus the Great of Antioch (465-538 CE) was a Greek monk-theologian, who was the last non-Chalcedonian Patriarch to reside in Antioch and is considered one of the founders of the Syriac Orthodox Church. Severus is also considered a Church Father and a saint in Oriental Orthodoxy.

[192] Bar Habreas was a Catholicos (bishop) of the Syriac Orthodox Church in the 13th century. He is noted for his works addressing philosophy, poetry, language, history, and theology. He has been called one of the most learned and versatile men from the Syriac Orthodox Church.

[193] CBCI Inter-Ritual Committee, *Baptism and Confirmation* (Bangalore: Theological Publications in India, 2010), 58-59. Mullar, et al., *Dictionary of Mission*, 39.

[194] Karen B. Westerfield, "Baptism and Ecumenism: Agreements and Problems on the Journey Towards Mutual Recognition." *Studia Liturgica* 42, no.1-2 (2012): 8-9.

become members of one another.[195] This sacrament brings re-generation and renewal of the individual. It stands as a unique experience in the life of a believer. The baptized experience the construction of a subjective identity which centres on the life of Jesus Christ.[196] This subjective identity is the result of a personal conversion from the sinfulness of the world with the help of the Holy Spirit (Rom.6:8-10). It is considered as the medium for the remission of sin, and a sign and seal of Christian discipleship.[197] In baptism, the heavenly Lord took possession of the baptized person, bestowed salvation upon him/her, and invited him/her to a personal relationship. This relationship proves fundamentally meaningful that the baptized person obtains entrance into the Kingdom of God. Through baptism Christians are brought into union with Christ, and with each other.[198] It is through this spiritual act that one enters into a new content of life and he/she receives newness of life. It is an experience of entering and growing in new life in Christ. The fruit of baptism is new life, more moral or even more pious life, and a life ontologically different from the old one.[199] The very content of this newness is that it is life with Christ.

The Sacraments of Baptism and Eucharist are essentially connected. The Eucharist is the foundational sacrament of the Church and the Church is born in and through the Eucharist.[200] The Eucharistic table is an

---

[195] *One Baptism: Towards Mutual Recognition. A Study Text*, Faith and Order Paper No.210. (Geneva: World Council of Churches, 2011), 57.

[196] Bordeyne and Morrill, *Baptism and Identity Formation*, 168.

[197] Faith and Order Paper No.111, *Baptism, Eucharist and Ministry* (Geneva: WCC, 1982), 1-2.

[198] Koch, *Principles for a Christian Theology of Baptism*, 239.

[199] Alexander Schmemann, *Of Water and the Spirit: A Liturgical Study on Baptism*. (Crestwood, New York: St. Vladimir's Seminary, 1974), 120.

[200] "In the early Christian tradition, Baptism, Chrismation and the Eucharist "belong together" and form one liturgical sequence and "ordo" because each sacrament within it is fulfilled in the other in such a way that it is impossible fully to understand the meaning of one in separation and isolation from the other two. If chrismation, fulfils baptism, the Eucharist is the fulfilment of chrismation. In baptism we are born again of Water and the spirit, and it is this birth which makes us open to the gift of the Holy Spirit, to our personal Pentecost. It is the gift of the Holy Spirit that opens to us to the Church, to Christ's table in his Kingdom. We are baptized so that we may receive the Holy Spirit; we receive the Holy Spirit so that we may become living members of the body of Christ, growing within the Church into the fullness of Christ's stature. There is a sacramental interdependence

indispensable part of the identity and nature of Christian Church. As cited above, the Church is a Eucharistic community and without the Eucharist, it has no existence at all. This sacrament brings the baptised into the Church as the body of Christ (1 Cor.12:13). In this process, it is the same spirit who fills all the baptized and makes them members of the one body of Christ. Indeed, it is the spirit who joins everyone together in baptism (Eph.4: 4-6). Thus baptism is the "entrance gate" to the Church. It is not only an entry point to the Church, rather it has its goal, the achievement of the fullness of life in Christ. It is ordered toward a complete profession of faith, a complete incorporation into the event of salvation, and finally towards a complete integration into Eucharistic communion.[201] Reception into the Church proves to be an essential dimension to the understanding of baptism in the early Church (Acts. 2:41). This sacrament not only marks one's adoption of the Christian faith but also implies entrance into the Church.

In the West Syrian liturgical tradition, the sacrament of regeneration is celebrated in and with the Eucharistic community. It is believed that, baptism is completed and perfected with the Eucharistic communion which is the fulfilment of baptism.[202] The newly baptised member enter into the Church in a procession. This procession is a symbol of spiritual rejoicing. This procession is always important and an integral part of the liturgy of initiation. According to Schmemann, the "Trisagion" is a processional hymn in the earlier tradition of the Church.[203] Baptism was organically connected with the Eucharistic gathering. It finds its fulfilment in the entrance to the Church, which symbolises[204] the celebration of the resurrection of Christ. The post-baptism procession connects the baptism

---

between the Eucharist and baptism. The Eucharist, as the sacrament of the sacraments, is a means of grace, which aims for the personal sanctification of the faithful." Schmemann, *Of Water and the Spirit*, 116.

[201] Koch, *Principles for a Christian Theology of Baptism*, 238.

[202] CBCI Inter-Ritual Committee, *Baptism and Confirmation*, 65.

[203] Schmemann, *Of Water and the Spirit*, 111.

[204] The main door of church building is called royal door, the whole Church is a symbol and of the expression of the Kingdom of God. It is the baptismal regeneration and the anointment with the Holy Spirit that open the door to that Kingdom, the door shut by sin and man's alienation from God.

Mission and Liturgy

and the Eucharist. The procession connects the sacrament of regeneration, with the Eucharist.[205] Baptism is the foundation of Christian equality and unity; it creates and realizes a unique relationship with Christ and his Church, thus making possible a distinctive bond of unity among those who are baptized.[206]

The Sacraments of Baptism and the Eucharist are known as dominical sacraments since Jesus Christ Himself initiated it. By practicing it, the Church affirms the apostolic nature and commissioning of the Church. The Church is an apostolic community, called out to share the Gospel by its teaching, preaching and its very life. "Apostolicity indicates coherence and continuity with the faith, life, witness and ministry of the apostolic community, chosen and sent by Christ."[207] An individual joins with Christ through the Sacrament of Baptism and continues by participating in the Eucharist. Participation in the holy mysteries with the fellowship of the community strengthens in virtue of the power of the Holy Spirit and

---

[205] "In the Orthodox tradition, the Holy Qurbana is viewed as the fulfilment, the crowning point and the climax, of the whole Eucharistic liturgy. Its meaning is precisely that it actualizes the Church as new creation, redeemed by Christ, reconciled with God-given access to heaven, filled with divine glory, sanctified by the Holy Spirit. Therefore, one is capable of and called to participation in divine life, in the communion of the body and blood of Christ. Schmemann says only such understanding and experience of the Eucharist reveals it as the self-evident and necessary fulfilment of baptism." Baptism integrates the faithful into the Church. The Church's ultimate being and essence are revealed in and through the Eucharist. The Eucharist is indeed the fulfilment of baptism. The newly baptized enter into the Church in procession, join the body of the believers and together with them begin their participation in the Eucharistic celebration. The entrance of the baptised is first of all the act of joining the gathered community, the *Ekklesia,* which means the assembly or gathering. They are united with the people of God, constitute one family, one body, one fellowship in Christ. This gathering is a sacramental gathering because it reveals and makes visible the invisible unity in Christ." Schmemann, *Of Water and the Spirit,* 17-119.

[206] Together the baptized are joined in sharing Christ's suffering (Phil.3:10-11), called to be of the same mind as Christ (Phil.2:5), clothed with Christ (Gal.3:27), grafted onto a common vine/tree (Jn.15:1-5, Rom.11:17-24), adopted as siblings and coheirs of the Father (Rom.8:14-17, Gal.4:6-7) and filled with the Holy Spirit (1 Cor.3: 16-17). As Christ's new creation, they are liberated from old ways of divisions (Gal.3:28) and are entrusted with the ministry of reconciliation (2 Cor.5:18-19). Westerfield, *Baptism and Ecumenism,* 9-10.

[207] *One Baptism: Towards Mutual Recognition,* 14. "Ecclesiological and Ecumenical Implications of Common Baptism: A JWG Study," in Eighth Report: Joint Working Group between the Roma Catholic Church and the World Council of Churches, Geneva-Rome, 2005 (Geneva: World Council of Churches, 2005), 91.

moves out for mission to proclaim the gospel. In this sense one can say that baptism is a *doorway* to the community of witnesses and the Eucharist is the *fuel* for its mission journey. Hence the Sacrament of Baptism qualifies a person to be part of the Eucharistic community and its ministries. Baptism commissions the baptized to the Church's mission and also defines that mission. The baptized are commissioned to minister to the world, to proclaim the good news of God's saving love and to practice the ethics of the Kingdom of God.[208] The Christian life is thus a baptismal life, lived out in the royal, priestly, and prophetic community that is the Church wherein the spiritual gifts bestowed for service in the Church and the world are exercised.[209] Just as the baptized have heard and responded to Christ's invitation to conversion, the baptized in the name of Christ are to issue the call for repentance, new life, and service to the neighbour so that others may hear and believe.[210]

2.1 Baptism: Call to Mission

The baptismal text used in the MTC is of West Syrian origin. However, due to the reformation in the Malankara Church, certain adaptations and revisions were made to the original text.[211] At present the Church uses a revised baptismal liturgy which has been translated from Syriac by Maplan Maliakkal Zacharia, with the first official English translation published in 1988.[212] The West Syrian liturgy has been attributed to Severus of Antioch (512-518 CE). In the 13th century, Gregorios Bar Hebraeus (1284 CE) revised and shortened this text; later this was published in Pampakuda,

---

[208] *One Baptism: Towards Mutual Recognition*, 74-75.
[209] *One Baptism: Towards Mutual Recognition*, 48.
[210] Westerfield, *Baptism and Ecumenism*, 11.
[211] An analysis of the baptism liturgy of the MTC is beyond the scope of this research.
[212] Mar Thoma Syrian Church, *Order of Services: Baptism, Matrimony, Prayer for Sick, House Dedication and Funeral* (Thiruvalla: The Mar Thoma Sabha Book Depot, 1988), 9-23. A detailed textual analysis of the Mar Thoma Baptismal Liturgy, see George Mathew, "The Baptismal Liturgy of the Mar Thoma Syrian Church of Malabar," in *Baptism Today*, ed. Thomas F. Best (Geneva: World Council of Churches, 2008), 118, 115-132.

Kerala. This text is in use in the Orthodox and the Malankara Catholic Churches in India.[213]

In the Syriac tradition,[214] the mystery (sacrament) of regeneration from water and Spirit holds a significant place in the life of a Christian. According to the Oriental tradition, the Sacrament of Baptism is one unit of the celebration of the mystery of regeneration from water and Spirit.[215] The Church believes that the baptism is a process that incorporates an individual into the body of Christ (1 Cor.12:13). A new world comes into being in the life of an individual. A believer enters into a new covenant inaugurated through the atoning death of Christ and his resurrection.[216] Baptism is administered within the context of the community of believers, which confesses faith in Jesus Christ. Faith is not an intellectual affair; rather it suggests trust, obedience, and commitment to God in Christ. When one trusts and commits to God, it is God who responds. The MTC affirms that there is only one baptism, which is in the name of the Trinity, i.e. the Father, the Son and the Holy Spirit. The Church recognizes both infant baptism and adult baptism. Adults are baptized and admitted to the fellowship of the Church if they were not baptised before, but now accepting the Lordship of Jesus Christ. However, if an adult was already baptized in another tradition of the Church universal, he/she does not have to go through this sacrament again to become a member of the MTC. The

---

[213] Baby Varghese, *Baptism and Confirmation in the Syriac Tradition* (Kottayam: SEERI, 1989), 26.

[214] The text of the baptismal liturgy of the West Syrian Antiochian liturgical tradition has been attributed to Severus of Antioch (512-578 CE). The different baptismal text indicates that 5th-13th centuries was a period of great creativity of the West Syrian baptismal tradition. The Severus text contains the most elaborate structural details. Bar Hebreya' text, which is adopted and still followed in its entirety in Malankara rite, is a revised and abridged edition of the Severus text. Currently the West Syrian baptismal tradition (rituals and theology) is followed in its entirety in two text forms, namely the Mosul form and Tikrit form. The Mosul form is the Severus text followed in the Antiochian Syrian Orthodox Church and the Antiochian Syrian Catholic Church. The Tikrit form is followed in the Malankara Catholic Church, the Malankara Jacobite Church, the Indian Orthodox Church, and the Mar Thoma Church. CBCI Inter-Ritual Committee, *Baptism and Confirmation*, 61.

[215] CBCI Inter-Ritual Committee, *Baptism and Confirmation*, 58.

[216] Mathew, "The Baptismal Liturgy of the Mar Thoma Syrian Church of Malabar," 118-119.

emphasis of the Church is that baptism occurs only once: those born of Christian parents are baptized at infancy; believers coming to faith are baptized as adults.[217] The Church affirms that baptism involves growing; it is not a static and momentary experience. It is unrepeatable and is, in fact, the ordination by which every believer is incorporated into the corporate, priestly ministry of the Church.[218] In the MTC, as in other Oriental Eastern Churches, the Sacrament of Confirmation is administered immediately after baptism.[219] This being the second sacrament, there is a separate order of service. In the confirmation service[220] the celebrant anoints the candidate with *mooron*[221] (consecrated oil), which symbolizes the Holy Spirit. In this sacramental moment, the Church specifically prays for the gift of the Holy Spirit. Baptismal anointing with *mooron* is also to signify the candidate's ordination to the priesthood of believers.[222] In the tradition of the Western Churches, confirmation occurs only when one becomes in an age of maturity. Being an Oriental Eastern Church, the MTC follows the prayers (rubrics) and practices of the West Syrian liturgical traditions. Even though the Church follows the West Syrian traditions, it is not completely adopting it. For instance, in the Orthodox tradition children are allowed to

---

[217] Mathew, "The Baptismal Liturgy of the Mar Thoma Syrian Church of Malabar," 128.
[218] Max Thurian, ed., *Churches Respond to BEM: Official Response to the "Baptism, Eucharist and Ministry" Text,* vol. IV, Faith and Order Paper No. 137 (Geneva: World Council of Churches, 1987), 7-13. Sebastian P. Brock, *The Holy Spirit in the Syrian Baptismal Tradition, The Syrian Church Series,* vol.9 (Poona: Anita Press, 1979), 58-62.
[219] The common Syriac tradition and the West Syrian tradition originally did not have a separate sacrament of confirmation. The Antiochian post-baptismal anointing with *mooron* (Chrismation) later came to be distinguished as the Sacrament of Confirmation. There is no baptism without confirmation by the same minister. West Syrian tradition renders four main meanings of the post-baptismal Chrismation: Chrismation is a sweet fragrance of Christ, it the sign and mark of the true faith, it is perfection of the gift of the Holy Spirit, and it is the royal-priestly and prophetic anointing of the New Israel. CBCI Inter-Ritual Committee, *Baptism and Confirmation,* 63.
[220] In the MTC, it is not mandatory to have bishop to be the celebrant in the baptism and confirmation service. An ordained person can officiate the service.
[221] The MTC keeps the practice of using the *mooron* that is blessed by the Patriarch of Antioch in the time of Palakkunnathu Mathews Mar Athanasius Metropolitan while he was in Antioch. This practice connects the MTC with the Antiochian Church. Interview with the Metropolitan Joseph Mar Thoma on April 15, 2015.
[222] Mathew, "The Baptismal Liturgy of the Mar Thoma Syrian Church of Malabar," 124-125.

receive the holy mysteries after the confirmation. This practice is not in the MTC since the Church is in line of thought with the Anglican tradition.[223] In the MTC, only a baptised member can partake in the Lord's Table. Even though children are incorporated into the life of the community, participation in the Lord's table is allowed only after the service of the First Holy Communion, in which the participant publicly pronounces his/her faith in the Lordship of Jesus Christ. By proclaiming faith in the Lordship of Christ, the Church believes that, faith is not just a personal affair, rather a communitarian reality. A child is nurtured in faith in and through the community of the believers. Along with the parents, the Church has the responsibility to nurture children in Christian ethos and values. The role of godparents in the baptismal service symbolises this truth. The Church keeps a balance between the personal and corporate dimension of salvation and faith through this act. The Church practices a primitive Christian practice and the expectation is that baptism should be conducted before admitting a person to the Table.[224] As a Reformed Church, the MTC follows this practice of not giving communion to children preferring to postpone communion to an 'age of understanding,' as in other Protestant churches. This practice needs to be addressed further and considered ecumenically.[225]

The historic order of reception of baptism before the reception of the Eucharist should be observed for the sake of the unity of the Churches.[226] The Eucharist expresses, enhances, and focuses the *koinonia* established and the faith professed in baptism.[227] The MTC appreciates the "open

---

[223] When one reaches the period of teenage, classes about the faith and practices of the Church are given and the candidate understands the implications of leading a Christin life. The Church conducts similar classes to young people who are ready to receive their first Holy Communion.

[224] Maxwell E. Johnson, *The Rites of the Christian Initiation: Their Evolution and Interpretation* (Collegeville, MN: Liturgical, 1999), 3-6.

[225] Mathew, "The Baptismal Liturgy of the Mar Thoma Syrian Church of Malabar," 129.

[226] *One Baptism: Towards Mutual Recognition*, 14. "Ecclesiological and Ecumenical Implications of Common Baptism: A JWG Study," in Eighth Report: Joint Working Group between the Roma Catholic Church and the World Council of Churches, Geneva-Rome, 2005 (Geneva: WCC, 2005), 91-92.

[227] *One Baptism: Towards Mutual Recognition*, 59. *Ecclesiological and Ecumenical Implications of Common Baptism: A JWG Study*, 93.

table" or "open communion"- a general unconditional invitation - which has been justified from the perspective of Jesus' radical hospitality at table fellowship along with his preferential option for the poor and marginalized (Lk.19:1-10). Any baptized person with a heart of repentance can partake in the Lord's Table.[228] The Eucharist is for the baptized as a spiritual food which allows them to live a life of/in Christ and to be incorporated more profoundly in him and share more intensely in the mystery of Christ.[229] The Eucharistic community is thus appropriately the baptismal community, united by faith in the risen Lord, incorporated into him by the spirit, and sustained by him with the bread of life.[230]

---

[228] Interview with Joseph Mar Barnabas Episcopa on 10th July 2013. The advocates have focused on the gospel narratives of Jesus' unconditional meal ministries with culturally-labelled "sinners" and especially the account of the visit to Zacchaeus (Lk.19:1-10) in which Jesus dines with the rich tax collector.
[229] *Ecclesiological and Ecumenical Implications of Common Baptism*, 94. *One Baptism: Towards Mutual Recognition*, 59.
[230] Westerfield, *Baptism and Ecumenism*, 10.

Chapter. 4

Cultural Landscape of the Mar Thoma Community: Liturgical Significance and Challenges

The industrial revolution and rapid development of science, technology, transport and communication of the previous century made tremendous impact in the thought pattern and the living conditions of people in general. This draws new employment opportunities and better living conditions for people all over the world. Many of the educated people from Kerala migrated to foreign countries. Because of this rapid migration, the small Travancore -centred Syrian reformed Malankara community was transformed into a global Church by crossing the boundaries of the broad cultural, geographical, ethnic and social fabric of the world. Currently, the MTC is an inclusive faith community which gives fellowship to a wider section of people around the globe. For this Church, the last quarter of the 20th century was a period of transition. Within this short span of time, this community has extended beyond the traditional boundaries of Kerala into North America and Europe, South Africa, Malaysia, Singapore, Australia and other places of the Middle-East such as Dubai, Bahrain, Abu-Dhabi, Doha, Kuwait. Wherever the Mar Thoma Christians emigrated to, they carried with them their spiritual heritage, traditions of Christian life and Oriental worship pattern. In their countries of adoption, they organized themselves in small congregations and sought pastoral help from their mother Church in Kerala. Then they sought official recognition in establishing themselves as members of the Mar Thoma parishes in these countries.[231] Since the time of reformation in 1836, an extensive involvement of laity in the mission and ministry of the Church is evident and that stands as a backbone to the existence of the Church. The mutual respect and co-operation of the laity, clergy and bishops of the Church became the reason for the development of the new ministries and mission field in the Church locally and globally. This Church, though reformed, retains its inherited liturgy of St. James, and is the only Church of Eastern rite with which the worldwide Anglican Church is in communion.[232] Since the revised Eucharistic liturgy is a liturgical foundation for mission in the Church, the sacramental and incarnational aspect of mission reflected in the liturgy has to be much emphasized in the Church at large, especially in its developing diverse cultural context. A major challenge of the MTC in the 21st century is to assume its global nature by transcending the boundaries set by the familiar religion and culture. Can the Church incarnate in a cross-cultural, inter-racial, inter-generational context? The Church has to cross all barriers to reach out to all ethnic groups, class, tribes, social classes and cultures

Since the MTC has *de facto* emerged as a global Church, this chapter primarily explores the basic concept of culture and Christianity. Further, it deals with diverse cultural and geographical background of the MTC at large, especially the settings of diaspora and mission fields and the role of liturgy in shaping its identity and mission. Along with this, the historical growth of the Mar Thoma communities in diaspora and their liturgical life is analysed in detail. In the progression of mission fields, the question of how the Church integrated the liturgy and evangelism in its mission is a matter of study.

---

[231] Zac Varghese, "Mission of the Mar Thoma Church in the Global Context," in *The Mar Thoma Church: Tradition and Modernity*, 190-196.
[232] Collin Buchanon, ed., *Anglican Eucharistic Liturgies 1985-2010* (London: Canterbury, 2011), 195.

1 Culture: What is it?

Human beings are naturally cultural beings and culture is a unique characteristic of human existence. Generally, culture means a total way of life of a society or community.[233] The human culture distinguishes them from other living creatures and it exists everywhere and differs from one place to another. Culture is referred to as more material, technological and socially organized sphere of human life. It has helped to shape the identities of nations, groups, and peoples. Etymologically the word culture (from the Latin *colere* - cultivate, to modify nature correctly) refers to the activity through which people influence the environment in which they live with their physical and spiritual powers. All cultures are subject to continuous change, which could be rapid or slow.[234] Consequently cultures can be understood only from a dynamic and diachronic perspective.

The Latin word *cultura* describes what a person does and what a person cannot do. The modern concept of culture came from cultural contact. Modernity maps culture as a comparative concept.[235] It has been defined in various ways. There is no universally accepted definition of culture. Kroeber and Kluckhohn, in their book *Culture: A Critical Review of Concepts and Definitions*[236] listed about two hundred and fifty definitions of culture. Culture means much more than art, architecture, sculpture, literature, music, morals, law, customs and other activities and habits acquired by humans as members of society.[237] A cultural anthropologist, Geertz describes culture as "a system of inherited concepts expressed in symbolic forms which enables us to communicate, perpetuate

---

[233] Xavier Koodapuzha, ed., *Eastern Theological Reflection in India* (Kottayam: Oriental Institute of Religious Studies, 1999), 9.
[234] Muller, et al., *Dictionary of Mission*, 94-95.
[235] Regina Ammicht Quinn, "Ethics of Integration," in *Concilium*, 28-29.
[236] A.L. Kroeber and C. Kluckhohn, *Culture: A Critical Review of Concepts and Definitions*, vol. XLVII, no.1 (Cambridge: Museum of American Archaeology and Ethnology, 1952).
[237] E.B. Tylor, "Culture at the Service of Evangelization in India" in *The St. Thomas Christian Encyclopedia of India*, vol.1, ed. G. Menachery (Thrissur: St. Thomas Christian Encyclopedia, 1982), 198.

and develop our understanding of life, and traditional customs."[238] He emphasises the importance of inherited traditions, the modes and methods of communication, the habits and customs that guide and help people to find space within their society and access to the wider world.

Raymond Williams, an eminent sociologist provides a definition that "culture is the signifying system through which a social order is communicated, reproduced, experienced and explored."[239] Culture incorporates individual and society, nature and art, religion, morality and history within an ordered, complex configuration of reality.[240] Cultural anthropologists sometimes define culture according to its components such as values, patterns and institutions. Values are principles which influence and give direction to the life and activities of a community and its members. They are formative of the community's attitude or behaviour towards social, religious, political and ethical realities. The cultural patterns[241] are a typical way for members of a society to think or form concepts, to express their thoughts through languages, ritualise aspects of their life and create art forms. The area covered by cultural patterns are thus: thoughts, languages, rituals and symbols, literature, music, architecture and all other expressions of fine arts. We call them cultural patterns because they are predictable, in the sense that they follow an established course. Every cultural group has its typical way of thinking, verbalizing concepts, expressing values and so on. Cultural patterns are society's norms of life into which a person is born and reared. Through the process of "enculturation," as anthropologists calls

---

[238] Clifford Greets, *The Interpretations of Cultures* (New York: Basic Books, 1973), 89.
[239] Raymond Williams, *The Sociology of Culture* (New York: Schocken Books, 1982), 13.
[240] M. Francis Mannion, *Masterworks of God: Essays in Liturgical Theory and Practice* (Chicago: Hillenbrand, 2004), 88.
[241] According to Stauffer, "Cultural patterns do not eliminate individuality, they shape members of society within the established bonds of social acceptability. Cultural patterns have the power to shape the life of an individual, as they conform him or her to the image society has for itself and for its members. Cultural patterns are at the root of social and racial identities. The typical way in which members of a group think, speak, and ritualize allows us to distinguish one cultural group from another. Thus, each cultural group has its own thought process, style of language, and rituals with which to express the values of hospitality, community spirit and leadership. Thought pattern, language pattern and ritual pattern are important in all cultural contexts." Anita Stauffer, ed., *Worship and Culture in Dialogue* (Geneva: Lutheran World federation, 1997), 158-159.

it, a person is initiated and trained to behave according to such patterns that these become second nature to each member of the community.[242] Thus, each cultural group has its own thought process, style of language, and rituals with which to express the values of hospitality, community spirit and leadership. Thought pattern, language pattern and ritual pattern are important in all cultural contexts.

1.1 Culture and Christianity

It is important to set the topic of Christian worship and culture within a large framework, which is the relationship between Christ and culture. One helpful model for considering this larger theological context is a typology developed by H. Richard Niebuhr (1894-1962). Niebuhr has laid out five possible relationships between Christ and culture - Christ against culture, Christ of culture, Christ above culture, Christ and culture in paradox, and Christ the transformer of culture.[243] In these five typologies the final one - Christ the transformer of culture- is more hopeful about culture, when it describes culture as not inherently evil, although it is the locus of disorder and sin. What is needed is a conversion or transformation of the culture. The Christian Church often assimilated various components of culture into the liturgy. We can say that it became one of the methods of the Church for incarnating the Gospel in the life and history of people. By assimilating new cultural components into the liturgy, the Church allows the liturgy to be shaped and influenced by the culture.[244]

The Church ultimately traces its liturgical origin to the Jewish tradition and culture. Christianity adopted a lot of cultural aspects of its diaspora regions such as Greek and Roman soil in addition to the Jewish tradition and culture. It is difficult to understand the original core of Christianity since it has assimilated a lot of cultural genres from Hellenistic, Roman,

---

[242] Louis J. Luzbetak, *The Church and Cultures - New Perspectives in Missiological Anthropology* (Maryknoll, New York: Orbis, 1988), 64-65.
[243] H. Richard Niebuhr, *Christ and Culture* (New York: Harper and Row, 1951), 190-198.
[244] Stauffer, *Worship and Culture in Dialogue*, 153.

Franco-Germanic backgrounds.[245] Christianity always opens itself to other cultures and it adopted and transformed whatever they found good and noble in paganism from the days of its origin.[246] A statement of the Commission of Faith and Order of the WCC on culture observes the following as important. They are "God can be encountered in all culture; that Christ awaits to be discovered in every culture; that sinfulness also exist in all cultures; and that the Church is called to evangelize culture in order to bring out fully the presence of Christ."[247]

To consider the connection between Christian worship and culture we should examine two other interlocking areas of content. Worship itself is multifaceted. It includes not only texts, but also actions, music and space. The topic is interdisciplinary: it contains not only liturgy, but also its texts, actions, church music, art and architecture. Christian worship is deeply shaped by space in which it occurs. The design and iconography and symbol-systems of the church building are expressions of theology.[248] Christian worship is always celebrated in a given local cultural setting. It draws our attention to the dynamics between worship and many local cultures in the world. All liturgical rites are vested in culture and no liturgy is celebrated in a cultural vacuum. The worship relates dynamically to culture in at least four ways.[249] First, it is *transcultural*, the same substance for everyone, everywhere, beyond culture. The salvific act of Christ transcends and indeed is beyond all cultures. The mystery of the resurrection of Christ is the source of the transcultural nature of Christian worship. Reading from the Bible, the ecumenical creeds and the Lord's Prayer, baptism in water in the name of Trinity, sharing of the table and so on are examples of this transcultural element. Second, it is *contextual*, varying according

---

[245] Stauffer, *Worship and Culture in Dialogue,* 154. Luzbetak, *The Church and Cultures,* 85-86.
[246] Anscar J. Chupungco, *Cultural Adaptation of the Liturgy* (New York: Paulist, 1992), 9.
[247] Commission of Faith and Order, WCC, "Towards Koinonia in Worship: Consultation on the Role of Worship within the Search of Unity," *Studia Liturgica* 25, no.1 (1995): 16.
[248] Stauffer, *Worship and Culture in Dialogue,* 10-11.
[249] Lutheran World Federation, "Nairobi Statement on Worship and Culture: Contemporary Challenges and Opportunities," *Studia Liturgica* 27, no.1 (1997): 89.

to the local situation (both nature and culture). Even though Christ was born in a specific culture of the world, the mystery of his incarnation is the model and the mandate for the contextualization of Christian worship. Contextualization is a necessary task for the mission of the Church in the world, so that the Gospel can be ever more deeply rooted in diverse local cultures. Thirdly, it is *counter-culture* that challenges what is contrary to the Gospel in a given culture. The mission of Christ was to transform all human beings and all cultures. In the mystery of Christ's passage from death to eternal life is the model for transformation, and thus for the counter-cultural nature of Christian worship. From the perspective of the gospel, all sinful, dehumanizing, exploitative aspects of all cultures need critique and transformation. The contextualization of worship necessarily involves challenging all types of oppression and social injustice wherever they exist in earthly cultures. Fourthly, it is *cross-cultural*, that is, it makes possible sharing between different local cultures. The breaking of the cultural barriers helps to enrich the whole Church and strengthens the sense of the *communio* of the Church. The sharing of the common values and patterns, witnessing and the fellowship of worshippers, foster the unity of the Church and the oneness of baptism. Cross-cultural sharing is possible for every Church, but is especially needed in multicultural congregations and member churches. It accepts the uniqueness in every culture and respects the elements for fostering the unity and fellowship.[250] In all four dynamics, there are helpful principles which can be identified.

India is a country or sub-continent of many cultures. Cultural pluralism is a significant feature of India. With different tribal religions and world religions like Hinduism, Jainism and Buddhism, religious pluralism is another prevailing reality of India. When we consider the cultural life of the St. Thomas Christians in Kerala, it is clear that it has emerged throughout the centuries by adopting various cultural elements from different communities and ecclesial traditions of the world such as the Persian, the Roman Catholic, the Syrian, and the Anglican. Both native and

---

[250] Lutheran World Federation, "Nairobi Statement on Worship and Culture," 91.

foreign elements influenced its cultural growth and entity. The St. Thomas Christians in India generally see themselves as Hindus in their culture, Christians in their faith and their liturgical life is rooted in the Syrian rite.[251] Indian historian A. Sreedhra Menon writes: "Nevertheless, the Christians have completely assimilated themselves in a community in which they live by adopting the language, dress, and habits of the Hindu brother. Though Christian in faith, they are Keralites in all other aspects."[252] They have imbibed the social and cultural practices and traditions of Hinduism, which represents the crux of Indian culture.[253] Many ritual activities, such as, tying of *minnu*[254] in the marriage ceremony, *Arinjanamkettu* (tying of golden chain to the new born baby), *Vidhyarambham* (ceremony related to the beginning of formal education), lighting of lamp before prayer, processing around the church with wind instruments, drums, using ornamental umbrellas, elephants and occasionally fire crackers in the celebrations and processions, floral garlands, or fruit etc., may be observed both in churches and Hindu temples.[255]

---

[251] Vellian, *The Malabar Church,* 12. Christoph Baumer, *The Church of the East-An illustrated History of Assyrian Christianity* (London: I.B. Tauris and Co. 2006), 244.

[252] Menon, *A Survey of Kerala History,* 86.

[253] Daniel, *Ecumenism in Praxis,* 52-53.

[254] In the Syrian Christian marriage, the bridegroom presents a gold pendant known as the *minnu* to his bride. The celebrant blesses the *minnu* and then holds the thread with the *minnu*, for the groom to tie it around the neck of the bride. By this they declare that they are tied together for life. A *minnu* is in the shape of a banyan tree leaf. The banyan tree spreads out to cover a wide area and provides shelter and comfort to others. It represents eternal life and symbolizes unity. Thus the *minnu* represents a long and happy married life. On one side of the *minnu* is a cross made with twelve small beads (*muthu*) signifying the Holy Trinity: Father, Son and Holy Spirit (3) and the Fruits of the Holy Spirit, the nine visible attributes of a true Christian love, joy, peace, forbearance, kindness, goodness, faithfulness, gentleness and self-control (9) A married Christian woman should always wear her *minnu*. Keep in mind the *minnu* is not an ornament it is part of her life.

[255] Several customs associated with the whole life of a person are practiced by both the Hindus and the Christians in India. Some such practices are: First rice feeding custom, marriage customs, puberty customs, and so on. Both the Hindus and Christians practice arranged marriages, and respect and honour their parents, priests, teachers and elders. Vellian, *The Malabar Church,* 12-13, Menacherry, "Indian Church History Classics," 485-507, Chaillot, "The Ancient Oriental Churches," 160.

2 Cultural and Geographical Diversity

The MTC is a global Church, which has been moved from the central Travancore region of Kerala to other regions of India and all continents of the world as a result of evangelization process and constant migration. As mentioned in the previous chapter, reformation process in the Malankara Church influenced the early Marthomites to extend its boundaries to a wider spectrum through their mission activities. Through diverse missionary activities, the Church extensively accepted members of other faith communities[256] into its wider fellowship irrespective of caste, class, tribe or region. Currently, this Church can be defined as a multi-cultural Church which comprises members from various cultural, ethnic, and linguistic backgrounds. The multicultural identity of the Church stands as a paradigm for its inclusive mission. Multiculturalism encourages cross-cultural understanding and racial and ethnic harmony. This term ensures that all members in a society could be proud of their ancestors and maintain their identity and a sense of belonging. Accordingly, an acceptance of traditions should foster the confidence, cooperation and tranquillity of the believers who are living in different regions.[257]

Migration from central Travancore caused a great impact in the life and mission of the MTC. It gave a new identity to the Church as a "migrant Church" in outside regions. Migrants travel with their religion. It is a general fact that, when a group of people move, they take their own religious ideas, beliefs and practices with them. Thomas Sowell, in his study of migrations, asserts that "each group has its own cultural pattern... these patterns do not disappear upon crossing a broader or an ocean."[258] Historian Peter Stearns

---

[256] Dalits and Tribal people in the Indian sub-continent. The evangelistic work among Dalits (Tamil Nadu, Karnataka, Andhra Pradesh) and Tribal people (Orissa, Madhya Pradesh, Chhattisgarh) show that mission is the core and foundation of the Church's identity and witness. Dalits are the most vulnerable group of people in Indian society who are marginalized and alienated from the main stream of Indian society because of their colour, occupation and social situations.

[257] Solange Lefebvre, Denise Couture and K. Gandhar Chakravarty, eds., Living with Diversity, *Concilium* (London: SCM, 2014), 7.

[258] Thomas Sowell, *Migrations and Cultures: A World View* (New York: Basic Books, 1996), 18-21.

aptly describes peoples' movements as culture in motion.[259] Religious beliefs and spirituality are vital to the survival of migrants in a new land that gives them a sense of belonging (community). Immigrants are very often religious, because religion is one of the most important identity makers that helps them to preserve individual awareness and cohesion in a group.[260] The migrated Marthomites sprouted with the ignited spirit of reformed doctrines based on Scripture. Biblical interpretation played a major role in establishing the foundation of the Church and nurturing faith in the people. This global Church has encountered multi-cultural and multi-ethnic atmosphere and assimilated various cultural practices and faced faith confrontation in its own geographical regions. This confrontation caused a renewed view of the nature, identity and mission of the Church in a positive manner.

The MTC continues to seek opportunities for enlarging its horizon and to expand its mission of witness globally. However, one should not forget the fact that a great diversity of theological thought forms, liturgical life, and Church governance are the result of an encounter of the Christian faith with cultural traditions - a fact, which is not always recognized or admitted.[261] In order to understand the current Mar Thoma ecclesial landscape, it is important to analyse the various cultural contexts of the Church.

In order to analyse the cultural patterns of the MTC in general, the members of the Church can be categorized into three. They are central Travancore Syrian Christians, Diaspora Mar Thoma Communities, (especially in urban India and outside of India), and members in the Mission Fields who became part of the Church through conversion from other cultural and linguistic regions by mission work. The cultural settings and values of these three groups are diverse and each has its own specialities.

---

[259] Peter Stearns, *Cultures in Motion: Mapping Key Contacts their Imprints in World History* (New Haven: Yale University, 2001), 28-31.
[260] Raymond Williams, *Religion of Immigrants from India and Pakistan: New Thread in American Tapestry* (Cambridge: Cambridge University, 1988), 11.
[261] Alexander, *The Mar Thoma Church: Tradition and Modernity*, 106.

Mission and Liturgy

The basic culture of the Kerala Christians is intermingled with the Hindu religious and cultural ethos. Generally one can say that the Mar Thoma Christians in Kerala are basically Indian in culture, Christian in religion, and Oriental in worship.[262] A kind of "hybrid identity" is the hallmark of the Mar Thoma community now. It is interesting to note that diaspora communities find their identity "in-between" the Indian and external[263] cultures. The newly joined members stand in between the St. Thomas spiritual heritage and their own varied cultural traits of traditions, values and practices of their regions. Now, the MTC has missionary works and outreach programmes in more than twenty states, including two union territories of India and many other parts of the world such as USA, UK, Middle-east, Australia, Africa, Mexico, Nepal, etc.[264]

2.1 The Mar Thoma Diaspora: An Analysis

The term diaspora is a widely used concept in academic discourse. It has always been a reality in the world history because there were many diasporas in the pre-colonial, colonial and post-colonial times, but its expression and understanding appeared to be different. Generally, this term refers to an increasing flow of people who are migrating to different parts of the world because of multiple reasons. A central theme in this discourse is that it is an "experience of away from home."[265] According to William Safran, this label has been stretched to cover almost any ethnic or religious minority that is dispersed physically from its original homeland, regardless of the conditions leading to dispersion, and regardless of whether, and to what extent, physical, cultural or emotional links exist

---

[262] Podipara, *The Thomas Christians,* 76-77.
[263] External or foreign culture means, an influence because of their associations with the East Syrians, the Catholics, the Syrian Orthodox, the Anglican etc.
[264] *Report of the Mar Thoma Evangelistic Association* (Thiruvalla: Mar Thoma, 2011), 13.
[265] Previously it has been used for different minority groups who had been dispersed and uprooted from their homeland and spread to other parts of the world. Terms like migration, diaspora, multicultural and transnational have frequently being used without theoretical grounding and conceptual clarity.

between the community and the home country.[266] The reasons for diaspora are found to be many which vary for each community. Robin Cohen, in his work, *Global Diasporas: An Introduction,* categorized the diasporas in five different classes like: (1) Victim diasporas (Jews, Africans and Armenians) (2) Labour diasporas (Indian) (3) Trade and business diasporas (Chinese and Lebanese (4) Imperial diaspora (British) (5) Cultural diaspora (Caribbean).[267]

The term diaspora is used by the people living outside their country of origin to describe themselves. In the Greek root as it is used in the Bible, it refers to the scattered Christian communities.[268] Etymologically the word "diaspora" derives from the Greek, *dia,* "through" and "spread in" or "to scatter." According to Webster's dictionary, this term refers to "dispersion from." Hence, the word embodies a notion of a centre, a locus, a home from where the dispersion occurs. Cohen defines diaspora as "the communities

---

[266] Willaim Safran, "Deconstructing and Comparing Diasporas," in *Diaspora, Identity and Religion: New Directions in Theory and Research,* eds. Waltraud Kokot, Kachig Tololyan and Carolin Alfonso (London: Routledge, 2004), 9.

[267] Robin Cohen, *Global Diasporas: An Introduction,* 2nd ed. (London: Routledge, 2008), 1-19.

[268] Y.T. Vinayaraj. "Border Lives and Border God: Diaspora Reconfigures Heritage, Mission and Theology," *Mar Thoma Messenger* XXX, no.2 (2011): 10-11. The diaspora became a permanent feature in the life of the Jewish community, who scattered all over the world from their traditional lands, the Kingdom of Judah and Roman Judaea, and later emigration from wider Israel, who always longed to return to Israel. This term is used to designate the dispersal of the Jews at the time of the destruction of the first temple in 586 BC, and their forced exile to Babylon by 70 CE. The Jewish communities existed in Babylon, Syria, Egypt, Asia Minor, Greece, and Rome. It invokes images of multiple journeys. Stuart Hall, "Cultural Identity and Diaspora," in *Identity, Community, Culture Difference, ed.* Jonathan Rotherford (London: Awrence and Ishart, 1990), 443. Jews were a diaspora community; similarly, Christians in diaspora, who received the name as Christians in Antioch, dispersed through the apostles around the world. This term occurs three times in Scripture (Jn.7:35, Jas.1:1, 1 Pet.1:1) and is translated as "scattered" (NIV). The verb form, *"diaspeiro"* also appears three times (Acts. 8:1, 4, 11: 19). For more on migration and Diaspora references in the Bible see Scott Moreau, ed., *Evangelical Dictionary of World Missions* (Grand Rapids: Baker Academics, 2000), 18-20. "Diaspora Missiology: Mission among Chinese's Diaspora," http://missiology.org/missionchina. ChineseDiaspora-Missiology.pdf (accessed August 07, 2010). The translation of the Bible, liturgy and songs in local languages was carried out by bilingual and bicultural migrants so frequently that "translatability became the characteristic mode of Christian expansion through history." Lamen Sannneh, *Translating the Message: The missionary Impact on Culture* (New York: Maryknoll, Orbis, 1989), 214.

of people living together in one country who acknowledge that 'the old country'- a notion often buried deep in religion, language, custom or folklore- always has some claim on their loyalty, emotions, identity, and subjectivity."[269] In this sense each member of that diaspora community shares a common story of their past migration history and a sense of co-ethnicity with others of a similar background. Many of the migrants have found "home" in the new land and for them "home country" may not be at all nostalgic because of the possibilities of the new spaces. However the diaspora identities are not homogeneous but varied and contested in accordance with generational/ gender differences. The diaspora identities are contested identities which must be attended to differently.

The term diaspora means the scattering of people from one geographical location to another location. The diasporic subject is seen to look in two directions - towards an historical, cultural identity on one hand, and the society of re-location on the other.[270] The dispersal of large groups of people throughout the world generates hybrid and heterogeneous societies that problematize the very notions of unity, racial dominance and civilization on which empires were built. Diaspora highlights the global trend of creating, constructing and reconstructing identity, not by identifying with some ancestral place, but through travelling. While the diasporic subject travels, so does their culture. A travelling culture means a culture that changes, develops, and transforms itself according to the various influences it encounters in different places. Thus, while diasporas change their countries of arrival, so are their cultures changed in turn.[271] Diasporic identity demonstrates the extent to which identity itself must be constructed and reconstructed by individuals in their everyday life. Diaspora is not simply of an ethnic affiliation and cultural movement, but also of social position. Diasporas have come to mean cultural minorities in social power if not always in number and as such are always seen

---

[269] Cohen, *Global Diasporas: An Introduction*, ix.
[270] Bill Shcroft, Gareth Riffiths and Elen Iffin, *The Post-Colonial Studies Reader*. 2nd ed. (London: Routledge, 2006), 425.
[271] Shcroft, *The Post-Colonial Studies Reader*, 427.

to be establishing their sense of identity and cultural affiliation, their sense of home, their sense of subject position, against the background of a majoritarian' rule.[272]

2.1.1 The Mar Thoma Diaspora: A Historical Glance

Broadly considering the Indian diaspora, it began as part of the British imperial movement of labour to the colonies. The end of slavery produced a massive demand for labour on the sugar plantations and Indian labours were brought to Guyana, Mauritius, Fiji and South Africa.[273] But when we speak of the Mar Thoma diaspora situated in different parts of the world, its formation over the years has happened neither as the consequence of any forced expulsion nor as the end result of mass immigration of refugees. It has occurred and continues to happen as part of a different kind of migration, mostly voluntarily of the Mar Thoma communities in search of better living conditions, quality education and better job opportunities.[274] It is a fact that the present migrant generation of the Church as diasporas has already been settled in the countries were the faithful have migrated and are accepted as respected citizens of respective countries.

The MTC emerged as a global Church from its roots in central Travancore within a short span of time. With the advancement of English education, and in search of better job opportunities, a large number of educated populace from Travancore and Cochin migrated to big cities like Kolkata, Chennai, Mumbai and Delhi in India. Also, a large number of women joined the work force, and many of them are working in nursing and in other professional fields. Along with internal migration, there were three streams of migration to foreign lands. The first was to British colonies like Malaya, Ceylon, and East Africa, which took place in the 1920's and early 1930's, where an Indian work force and professionals were needed for plantations and industrial related works. After the end of

---

[272] Shcroft, *The Post-Colonial Studies Reader,* 426.
[273] Hall, "Cultural Identity and Diaspora," 447.
[274] M.C. Thomas, "Diaspora, Mar Thoma Church Identity and Mission: Theoretical Considerations" in *Beyond the Diaspora,* 51-73.

Mission and Liturgy

World War 1 (1918), more Malayalees including some Marthomites went to Malaya for work. In the 1920's approximately seventy Syrian Christians were in Malaya and Singapore. This is the oldest Mar Thoma diaspora community established outside India. The second exodus began in the 1940's to the Gulf region, as opportunities to work in the oil industries opened. The third opportunity for mass movement of the Indians was to the Western hemisphere, which began as a trickle in the 1960's and 1980's with the liberalization of visa restrictions and opportunities for employment of Indian professionals, particularly in USA, UK and other European countries.[275]

In the early phases of migration, the Church was not interested in establishing parishes in the newly found spaces for her members or to form dioceses. The Church administration encouraged the members to attend local mainline churches for worship and fellowship. The leaders of the Church discouraged any attempt to form a local parish of the Mar Thoma parish or to send clergy to attend to the pastoral needs of the people in the diaspora because of the long distance from the mother land, less membership and financial constraints. But later, due to the increase of members, the laity of the Church took the initiative to organize gatherings for their community fellowship and divine worship. These prayer fellowships were mostly conducted in houses which catered not only to their spiritual and religious needs, but also to their cultural aspirations. Initially they lacked their liturgical worship but later this liturgical oriented community made arrangements to have ordained clergy to administer sacraments and to lead them spiritually.[276]

According to Zac Varghese, there are three sorts of diaspora of the Mar Thoma Christians:

---

[275] Karinjappally, *Roots and Wings*, 102-103.
[276] Geevarghese Mar Theodosius. "Shifting meaning in Public, Religion and Domestic Spaces: Theological, Ministerial and Missional Challenges," *Mar Thoma Messenger* 34, no. 3 (July 2015): 15-16.

(a) Those people who voluntarily left Travancore and Cochin and moved to other parts of India. The very first Mar Thoma diaspora worshipping community was established in Madras in 1915. Those who moved to Malabar region for agricultural opportunities should be included in this category.

(b) Those who voluntarily accepted citizenship of other countries such as Malaysia, Singapore, UK, USA and Australia.

(c) Expatriates, particularly in the Middle East, Africa, and other regions who may eventually return to India.[277]

Currently MTC is a global Church and there are parishes in almost all continents. Five dioceses of the Church are in the diaspora regions and five bishops minister exclusively to the needs of the communities in the diaspora sections. For administrative purpose parishes in the Gulf regions are attached to different dioceses of the Church in India. A brief history of the Mar Thoma diaspora community is highlighted below

2.1.1.1 The Malaysian and Singapore

The Mar Thoma presence in the Malaysian region went back more than a century ago. The first Marthomite in Malaya landed at Port Swettenham (now Port Klang) in 1911. The first Marthomite in Singapore arrived in 1920. Starting as a trickle, the 1920s saw the first steady stream of Syrian Christians reaching the Klang Valley, a hinterland centered around Klang town and Singapore for employment. True to their faith, the members organized prayer meetings and participated in regular Divine services from as early as 1926. Very Rev. V. P. Mammen arrived in Malaya in 1928 on a survey mission and conducted the first Holy Qurbana service at the Methodist church in Klang. The subsequent arrival of Rev. T.N. Koshy on Friday, 21st August 1936, signalled the formal establishment of the Mar Thoma Church in Malaya and Singapore. As the first overseas resident

---

[277] Zac Varghese, "Mission and Message of the Mar Thoma Diaspora," in *In Search of Christian Identity in Global Community,* 49.

priest, he celebrated the Holy Qurbana service on 23rd August 1936 at Jubilee School, Klang. Regular divine services were held in Kuala Lumpur at the Penuel High School since 1929.

In the early years (from September 1936), divine services in Singapore were held at the Teo Hoo Lye Institute and the subsequent regular church services were conducted by Rev. T. N. Koshy at the Armenian Church and at St Andrews School. Rev. V.E. Thomas joined the ministry in Malaya in 1947. The posting of Rev. P. C. John as the third resident priest in 1955 further consolidated the church ministry in the country. In 1953, the churches that were built in Kuala Lumpur, Klang and Singapore were consecrated by Rt. Rev. Dr. Mathews Mar Athanasius Episcopa. Subsequently, members residing in other towns built their own churches, viz. Malacca (1958), Kluang (1961), Johore Bahru (1962), Labis (1951), Banting (19681967) and Sungei Petani in 1985/1998. Two new congregations were established at Damansara (2008) and USJ (2012).[278]

Currently MTC in Malaysia has sixteen parishes of varying sizes, consisting of 2000 members, dispersed within peninsular Malaysia with a concentration of members in the main parishes of Kuala Lumpur, Klang, Johore Bahru, Kluang, Banting and Seremban. The Pandamaram mission is an outreach programme of the Church in Malaysia. The Mar Thoma evangelistic Association of Malaysia was also inaugurated in 1955 and the first Mission field of the Church outside of India with a full-time evangelist was operational at Pandamaran near Klang in 1960.[279]

The early settlers in Singapore started their regular worship services in 1936 under the leadership of the very Rev. T. N. Koshy. They constructed a church building in 1953 and later purchased a piece of land with a bungalow in 1954 to start an English secondary school for over-aged and under-privileged students in Singapore. The School started functioning in January 1955. The School hall was used for worship services in the interim period. The School

---

[278] E-mail correspondence with the Vicar of the Singapore MTC, Rev. John G. Mathews on 11th November 2015.
[279] Abraham Mattackal, "The Mar Thoma Church and its Diaspora Communities around the world", *Mar Thoma Messenger* 10 (2009): 12-13.

was closed because of falling attendance and the parish had to move out in January 2001. The congregation worshipped at a rented hall at the Catholic Archdiocese till end of 2003. By 2004, the Mar Thoma Church in Singapore constructed a church building and currently the parish has a membership of 231 families, a majority of whom include second and third generation Marthomites as in the case of parishes in Malaysia.[280] The establishment of the St. Thomas school in Singapore in 1955 as a mission project is commendable. The first overseas mission field work at Panadamaran Klang was a blessing to the local community. The pioneer 27 parishes, many of them with small memberships, were formally established as Malaysia - Singapore Diocese on February 1962. It is commendable that the Singapore Mar Thoma church has taken the initiative to translate the Malayalam liturgy into English for the use of the community. A circular from the Mar Thoma Metropolitan following a Synod decision in 1982, formally divided the two countries, Malaysia and Singapore, into two separate zones in the diocese, with Australia first and New Zealand some years later.[281]

2.1.1.2 The Australian and New Zealand

As a result of the discussion between Dr. Zacharias Mar Theophilious and Bishop John Reid of the Anglican Church in Sydney, Australia after the 7th General Assembly of the World Council of Churches held in Canberra in 1991, it was agreed by both leaders that a Mar Thoma priest would be appointed by the Anglican Church in Sydney. This was proposed as a joint mission to serve both the Anglican parish as well as Mar Thoma congregations in Sydney and Melbourne. The synod of the Church approved the Mar Thoma congregation in Sydney and Melbourne in 1991 and appointed Rev. Dr. Abraham Kuruvilla as the first Mar Thoma priest in Australia. In November 1998, the Mar Thoma congregations were recognized as a full-fledged parish in Australia. Currently MTC has six parishes/congregations in Australia-Sydney, Melbourne, Brisbane,

---

[280] Mattackal, "The Mar Thoma Church and its Diaspora Communities," 12-13.
[281] Joseph, *Mar Thoma Sabha Directory-2015* (Thiruvalla: Mar Thoma Syrian Church, 2015), 145.

Canberra, Adelaide, and Perth. Melbourne parish has about 180 families and the one in Sydney has 170 families. [282]

There were migrations to New Zealand from early 70s, but no formal church groups were started until November 2002. The first communion service was conducted in New Zealand on 14 November 2002 by Rt. Rev. Zacharias Mar Theophilus Episcopa. Mar Theophilus helped to form a congregation in Auckland. Rt. Rev. Isaac Mar Philoxenos Episcopa conducted the first Holy Communion service in Wellington on 25 December 2003 and a congregation was started. The first priest in New Zealand was Rev. Raji Eapen who started his services on 4th November 2006. [283] At present there are two parishes in the Island such as in Auckland and in Wellington.

2.1.1.3 Middle-East

The migration of the Marthomites to the Gulf countries started as far back as the early fifties of the last century. In fact the flow started with the professionals like doctors, engineers and nurses, followed by skilled workers in the sixties and unskilled workers in the seventies as there was a construction boom. The first base for the MTC in the Gulf started in the Emirate of Kuwait under Rev. Philip Oommen (Metropolitan Emeritus Dr. Philipose Mar Chrysostom). Our priests moved from Kuwait to Bahrain where also the presence of American and British people and their missions helped to form our parishes. It started with prayer groups which gradually developed in to small parishes; such forerunners of full-fledged parishes came up in Oman and Qatar also. From a small group to larger groups, the Mar Thoma community was increasing in number and later developed into churches.[284] The Mar Thoma diaspora communities in Middle East area formed as churches in different countries such as Bahrain, Abu Dhabi, Doha, Qatar, Dubai, Kuwait, Sharjah, Muscat etc.

---

[282] Mattackal, "The Mar Thoma Church and its Diaspora Communities," 12-13.
[283] Joseph, *Mar Thoma Sabha Directory*, 146.
[284] George John, "Mar Thoma Syrian Church in the Arabia Gulf Context," in *In Search of Christian Identity in Global Community*, ed. M.J. Joseph (Thiruvalla: The Dioceses of North America and Europe, 2008), 63-67.

2.1.1.4 African Continent

The Mar Thoma population in South Africa is scattered in various provinces like Botswana, Swaziland and the mountain Kingdom of Lesotho. Roughly there are only two hundred Marthomite families in South Africa. With the establishment of a Mar Thoma centre in Pretoria and the appointment of the first vicar of the region Rev. Varghese Jacob on March 2000, the MTC also began to take root on African soil.

2.1.1.5 North America and Canada

There are mainly three stages in the development of the Mar Thoma diaspora in the North America and Canada region. In the first stage, the Marthomites who came to North America were students and gradually the number of students increased.[285] The second stage began with the arrival of professionals and other highly educated Marthomites who secured jobs or those who were seeking for jobs in North America. The change of immigration laws in 1965 resulted in many Marthomites finding jobs and reaching US in late 1960s. A sizeable number came only by the early 1970's and then Mar Thoma congregations were formed in various cities of North America.[286] Those who remained for a few years brought their family members and the third stage began by 1980s. Marthomites who came at different stages organized themselves as parishes[287] and worked

---

[285] Available sources reveal that the first student was deacon N M Abraham who studied at Wycliffe College, Toronto, Canada in 1912-14 and received his MA degree in 1914, and who later became a Bishop of the Church with the name Abraham Mar Thoma Metropolitan. After him, K. K. Kuruvila came to Hatfor Seminary Foundation in Connecticut, USA in the early 1920 and then served the Mar Thoma Church as a lay person. He became the first principal of the Mar Thoma Seminary, Kottayam in 1926. T.M. Thomas, "Mar Thoma Identity in the North American Context" *In search of Christian identity in the Global Community,* 58-59. Abraham Mar Thoma, *Focus-A Publication of Diaspora* 2, no.1 (2014): 20.

[286] There were several student priests who conducted Holy Communion services and other sacraments for the Marthomites in various cities of the United States like New York, Boston, Los Angeles, Dallas, Houston, Chicago, Philadelphia etc. During the early 1970's three of our Bishops visited United States a few times and they were Most Rev. Dr Alexander Mar Thoma and Rt. Rev. Dr. Thomas Mar Athanasius and Rt. Rev. Easow Mar Timotheos.

[287] The first Mar Thoma worship was conducted in Boston in January 1969 by Rev. Cherian Thomas (Sr.) and in New York in February 1971 by Rev. Thomas Varghese. The

together under the episcopal guidance of the Church, and accomplished many goals one after another. The role and initiative taken by the laity in forming prayer groups and congregations in major cities throughout the Diocese should be commended.

The history of the MTC in the North American started with an ecumenical worshipping fellowship of Mar Thoma and CSI members in the early Sixties. After this, commencing as a small prayer group in Queens, New York, in 1972, the first approved parish was recognized in New York in 1976. In terms of functionality, the churches in this part of the world were grouped as a Zone of the MTC in 1982. The leadership of the Suffragan Metropolitan Thomas Mar Athanasius and then Alexander Mar Thoma, presided over the Zone and guided the Church in its new socio-cultural and geographical habitus. As per the decision of the Episcopal Synod, the churches in North America and United Kingdom became constituents of the newly formed "Diocese of North America and United Kingdom." Philipose Mar Chrysostom took charge as Diocesan Bishop. Due to the expansion of the Church, the nomenclature of the Diocese has changed slightly to its current name, "Diocese of North America and Europe" with its headquarters at South Merrick Avenue, Merrick, New York. The Episcopal Synod appointed the first resident Bishop, Zacharias Mar Theophilus with effect from October 1993. Later, Dr. Euyakim Mar Coorilos and Dr. Geevarghese Mar Theodosius became bishops of this diocese. Currently Dr. Isaac Mar Philaxinos is in-charge of this diocese.

When more and more Marthomites migrated to the United States, the need for regular worship became a necessity. But the leaders of the MTC during that period were not in favour of establishing parishes, and directed Marthomites to take membership in local Episcopal Churches in the United States and Anglican Churches in Canada. But because of an increase in number, this policy of the Church had changed, when it

---

first congregation was formed in Queens, New York in April 1972 and a Mar Thoma - C. S. I Congregation in New York City in September 1973. T.M. Thomas and Abraham Mattackal, *In the Beginnings' 2008.*

approved the first Mar Thoma congregation in New York in 1976.[288] A large number of Marthomites are settled in New York and therefore New York is the centre of the Mar Thoma community in the region. Now the Diocese of North America and Europe has seventy two parishes, seven congregations, seventy four priests and 8,478 families spread out in two continents.[289] To honour the sacrifices and commitment of the early settlers of the Mar Thoma community, since 2000, the Diocese of North America and Europe observes one Sunday of November as Diaspora Sunday.[290] On this day special order of worship is conducted before the Holy Qurbana which is published with the approval of the Metropolitan.[291]

2.1.1.6 Europe

In August 1948 Metropolitan Juhanon Mar Thoma passed through London to attend the meeting of WCC in Amsterdam. Though only very few Marthomites lived in London at that time, a Holy Communion service was conducted which was the first Mar Thoma Holy Communion service held in Europe. In early 1950's, a few more Marthomites came to the United Kingdom as students for higher studies and others for employment. Once a month they met in the chapel of the Indian YMCA Students' Hostel in London. At that time there were no other Malayali Christian services in the UK. This encouraged other Malayali Christians also to participate in our service, and it became a very effective ecumenical gathering and worshipping community. In 1957 the first Mar Thoma congregation in London was approved and Rev. V. V. Alexander was appointed as the first vicar. He started a regular service, according to Mar Thoma rites at the

---

[288] The first full time Vicar appointed was Rev. M. V. Benjamin in 1979 for the Mar Thoma Congregation of Greater New York for two Sundays, one week for the Mar Thoma Congregation in Philadelphia and one week for the Mar Thoma - C. S. I. Congregation in New York.

[289] *Annual Report of the Sabha Pradhinidhi Mandalam 2014-15*, II-33.

[290] Circular No. 125, Thomas Mar Timotheos, dated 18th September 2013.

[291] Joseph, *Mar Thoma Sabha Directory*, 150.

chapel of the Indian YMCA at Fitzroy Square, London, and it continued there for 21 years.[292]

During the 1970s more Marthomites and other Christians came to England from Malaysia, Singapore, Uganda, Zambia, India and many other countries. In 1979 they moved to St. Mary's Parish Church in Newington in Kensington. Although they had services once or twice a month, most of the members took membership in the local parishes of the Church of England, with which the MTC have full communion.[293] In 1978 these gatherings became an official congregation of the MTC. In October 1978 the Diocesan Bishop Mar Chrysostom, approved the congregation as a parish. Rev. Philip Varghese and then Rev. Abraham Philip arrived during this period and ministered. In 1982, they conducted their Silver Jubilee, in the presence of the Suffragan Metropolitan Thomas Mar Athanasius, the Archbishop of Canterbury, Robert Runcie, and host of Bishops and dignitaries. Later this group, with a congregational status was recognized as a parish. In 1989 the parish moved to the St. Katharin Church in Central London. On 1st April 1996 the original parish was divided into two parishes, namely St. Johns parish at Hounslow, and St. James Parish in the City to provide pastoral care for the growing population of Marthomites in London.[294]

The history of the MTC in Ireland starts in early 2005. On 1st of October 2005, the first Holy Qurbana of the Mar Thoma community in Ireland was conducted under the leadership of Rev. Thomas Koshy Patteril (London) at St. Maelruains Church, Tallaght. Gradually the gathering became a congregation and in March 2009, the Hon. Episcopal Synod of the MTC elevated the congregation to the status of a parish under the North America and Europe Diocese. Rev. Mathew Philip served as the

---

[292] E-mail correspondence with Dr. Zac Varghese on October 15, 2015. Varghese is one of the senior most members of the MTC in UK and he is the first secretary of the Council of Mar Thoma Parishes in Europe (COMPE).

[293] Joseph, *Mar Thoma Sabha Directory*, 148.

[294] 6th Annual Report of the Council of Mar Thoma Parishes in Europe (COMPE). Currently there are eleven parishes and six congregations in the Europe region. The parishes are in Belfast, Birmingham, Bristol, Cardiff, East London, Edinburgh, Harrow, Hounslow, Kent, Liverpool, London, Manchester, Newcastle, Peterborough, Dublin, Heidelberg (Germany) and Zurich (Switzerland).

first resident vicar of the Dublin Nazareth Mar Thoma Church and later, at the time of Rev. K Jameson, the Church got charity registration form the government of Ireland. Now there are worship services in Galway, Cork and Belfast which altogether comprises of 150 families.

2.1.2 Liturgical Life in the Diaspora: A Critical Observation

The Church is not only summoned to minister to the people of the diaspora, but, theologically speaking, the Church itself is a Diaspora community- a pilgrim community that is involved in a journey to fulfil God's ultimate purpose for humanity and for all God's creation. The growth of the MTC outside Kerala, was facilitated largely by the hospitality extended to them by the sister churches. In the beginning, the mission model of the Church in diaspora region was to be an "approach of presence." It was mainly a worshipping community which gave spiritual guidance and fellowship to its own members. But later, the immigrants from India continued to follow the incarnational model of assimilating themselves within their new society, establishing theological faculties, launching neighbourhood mission projects in their own particular areas and eventually using English language in their worship especially in USA. At the same time, the focus of the diaspora communities was on serving the immigrants and preserving their religious/cultural identity and faith. However, a transition happened after 1985 due to the large scale migration to other countries seeking better living conditions.

As already seen, the MTC is a bridging Church that integrates the St. Thomas heritage, Oriental liturgical traditions and the Anglican reformed theological positions as well as a Church giving rise to generations of ecumenical commitment. The Church upholds a commitment to work ecumenically in those places where they have an extensive mission activity. The Church lays emphasis on leadership development which couples with the conviction that "every Marthomite is a missionary." The neighbourhood ministries, as well as the wider mission projects in Mexico and among Native Americans, prove the inclusive nature of the mission pattern of the Church.

Mission is not an activity; it is the heart of the Church. It is an empowerment of every generation towards the total care of the society. The Church has to respond appropriately to contemporary needs of the people. The Church must be part of a constant process of evaluation and evaluation in becoming a true body of Christ. Participation of youth in the ministry of the Church is important. Connecting them with liturgy is the need of the time since liturgy is an expression of the faith and theology of the Church, and liturgical celebrations reveal the identity of the community. An active participation of youth and their leadership in the liturgical celebration enhances the quality of their fellowship and witness and makes worship more creative and contextual. The Church has to conscientise it members liturgically and there should be a renewed awareness of liturgical practices of the Church through systematic study, exhortation and experiments in the liturgical celebrations. The younger generation needs to foster the Christian community through ministration and spiritual nurture. The Church has to find new avenues to assure the participation of youth in the worship and ministry of the Church. The participation of the "altar boys and girls" introduced by the North American dioceses in the liturgical celebration of the Church is a novel step in this process. A new development in the dioceses of North America and Europe is the inauguration of the Cross Way Mar Thoma Congregation, Dallas on 20th September 2015, which was launched by the initiative of the second-generation Marthomites in the United States.[295]

In case of the Mar Thoma diaspora community, the liturgical life is a matter of serious concern. The Church accepts that it is the liturgy that unites the community of the faithful. When it unites the faithful, there should be space to include everyone irrespective of their differences. Liturgical celebration should be taken seriously in the various cultural settings of diaspora community. One of the emphases of reformation was

---

[295] Circular No. DC/568/15 by Dr. Geevarghese Mar Theodosius Episcopa, Dioceses of North America and Europe on 20th September, 2015. This is a new Mar Thoma Congregation which is mainly for the second and third generation Marthomites in the region.

to make the liturgy accessible and understandable to all people. Here language of worship should be the language of the people. In the diaspora context, it is an urgent need to translate the prayers into the vernacular of people, especially to youth. The Church has to teach their identity, liturgical traditions and theological emphasis to younger generations which would help them to analyse the nature and identity of other independent churches in their regions. Very often, younger generations tend to become influenced by the teachings of independent Churches.[296]

Currently, the Mar Thoma diaspora community- all over the world- appears to be a full grown community with great diversity and multiple socio-cultural mixture. For instance, the new generation Marthomites born and brought up in North America have reached the fourth and fifth generation with different inter-marriage ethnic combination. Consequently it created theological, liturgical, ministerial and missional challenges.[297] This community negotiates and engages with different types of diasporic spaces like domestic social, economic, cultural, religious and the like. An analysis of the identity of the diaspora community reveals its basic characterises as multiplicity of spaces, languages and belongings. At present, the traditional identity of the early settlers tend to be marginalized and not fully identified with. When into the diaspora communities are born new members, who are distanced from the homeland and from the ethos of the original migrants, one then sees a hybrid generation which has different attitudes and a different definition of one's own identity and traditions. This differs from the defining parameters of their parents. Hence a new meaning system in their personal relationships, liturgical gathering etc., are to be studied afresh. Can we conceive of and engender a hybrid liturgy for a hybrid generation? Hybrid liturgy is to evolve though dialogue, openness, in-depth study of Bible and meditation. The Church has to come up with alternate forms of liturgy by recognizing the multi-dimensionality of the

---

[296] Independent Churches are basically non-denominational, not in association with any mainline Churches. They are run by the charisma of their independent leaders who propagate the "gospel of prosperity."
[297] Theodosius, "Shifting meaning in Public, Religion and Domestic Spaces," 17.

diasporic identity of members.[298] The Church has the obligation to give new answers to the new questions of the diasporic community pertinent to their context.

The Church and diaspora community have to face many cultural situations and inter-cultural, inter-religious issues which have to be addressed relevantly. In the diaspora settings, very often the youth do not feel welcome within the larger parish life and administration of the Church. The Church should be open every day and provide a service in which all may grow. The new generation in the diaspora finds difficulty in imbibing the meaning and means of expression of faith and liturgy. The traditional liturgical pattern of worship is not addressing their experience and expressions in faith practices. The modern media and technologies have given multi-dimensionality to their identity. In the diaspora region, the local culture, religious belief, and practices have an influence on the new generation. Young people are influenced and fashioned by the popular culture of the transnational social fields. Traditional liturgical pattern hymns, and traditional pattern of authority/structures and organized patterns are reshaped or discarded by the new experiences and understanding of the people. Very often the diaspora youth seem to live in a virtual world which becomes a kind of real world for the new generation. The individualistic and technologically oriented mind of young believes more readily in the images on the technology screen than in the letters of written texts. This is specially so for liturgical text; its world and word are not familiar to the diaspora community.[299] In this juncture, a strong scriptural and liturgical texturing has to happen in the diaspora region. The Church has to rewrite the liturgy and provide relevant hermeneutics in the changing scenes of the diaspora community. Diasporic culture gives new perception to the understanding of human body, values, ethos appertaining to their generation. In such a setting, the diasporic context demands a re-reading, re-writing, re-articulation and re-interpretation of all sources of spirituality.

---

[298] Theodosius, "Shifting meaning in Public, Religion and Domestic Spaces," 20.
[299] Theodosius, "Shifting meaning in Public, Religion and Domestic Spaces," 20-21.

2.2 Mission Centers: An Overview

As has been demonstrated, the reformation in the Malankara Church resulted in a renewed understanding of mission on the basis of Scripture. The reformed group responded positively to the summons to evangelize within the Church and outside with Christian love to care and serve.[300] It inaugurated missionary movements within the Church, aiming to cross the caste boundaries, with the Gospel, into different parts of India diverse in language, culture, manners and religious background.

The Church, especially the Mar Thoma Evangelistic Association (MTEA) places primary focus on propagation of the Gospel through its missionary activities. Initially mission work in the villages mainly concentrated on evangelization through family visits and prayer units. In the course of development it organized various programmes like retreats, conventions and spiritual gatherings. Later, in order to take care of the spiritual and social needs of the people, the Church initiated many programmes for the development of social and educational needs of the community.[301] Programmes for empowering women and other weaker sections of the society are taken serious consideration. As mentioned in the previous chapter, for more than 126 years, MTEA takes missionary initiatives with a vision - "evangelization of India." Thus far, the Gospel have been preached in difference parts of India such as a Karwar, Ankola, Hoskote, (Karnataka) Sihora, Satna (Madhya Pradesh) Tibetan Border and Nepal. Initially the Evangelistic Association came up to support these

---

[300] Theodosius, "Maramon Convention: Mission and Ministry," 28-31. The MTEA is a missionary organization which mainly focuses its work among non-Christians and mission fields.

[301] The main missionary outreach programmes of the Church especially MTEA includes distribution of the Bible and leaflets, conducting prayer meetings and house visits, organizing spiritual meetings for believers and seekers, establishing village school (*Baalavadi*), Gram Jyothi schools, conducting classes for HIV/AIDS, Alcoholic anamnesis, rendering tuition for village children, offering training of stitching, type-writing to the poor people, organizing medical camps, Scripture camps, vacation Bible schools, Sunday schools, distribution of medical aids, hostels for financially backward children, crèches, educational help for economically backward children, and employment of training programmes for women. There are more than 15000 children who participates in the Sunday school ministry of the Church in India. *Annual Report 2012-13*, Malabar Mar Thoma Syrian Christian Evangelistic Association (Thiruvalla: MMTSCEA, 2013), 14.

mission centres. Now there are 62 mission fields, reaching out to 2600 Indian villages that are supported by the various auxiliary organizations of the Church, and different dioceses. They established many schools, medical clinics, and caring centres for Mother and Child, etc. Altogether the MTEA could be responsible for the formation of 350 parishes and faith communities for the MTC and they could have reached out to more than 2,700 villages in 19 states and 2 union territories of India.[302] There are more than 750 evangelists who take responsibility of various mission work in Indian villages. Those who have accepted the faith of the Church are incorporated into the fellowship through baptism and thereby enter into the communion of the Eucharist. The Church conducts bible classes, prayer meetings, community development programmes and liturgical worship for the faith formation, spiritual upbringing and social development of the villagers.[303]

2.2.1 Liturgy in the Mission Field Milieu: An Analysis

Liturgical life and liturgical developments among newly converted people in mission fields are a matter of study since reformation ideals influenced the Church to open its gates widely to accommodate new believers from other ethnic and cultural backgrounds of India through its evangelization process. In a traditional Christian circle, a Christian is born into a community: i.e., a parish. In mission centres, these Christian communities have yet to be formed or the phase of formation is very slow. In the formation of such a Christian community, the liturgy plays an important role. As already seen, the liturgy is a tool that provides an identity to the worshipping community. The identity of a Christian community can be understood by the way the faithful worship and by their socio-religious engagements. There are three main elements needed to build up a Christian

---

[302] *Annual Report of the Malankara Mar Thoma Syrian Church 2014-2015* (Thiruvalla: Mar Thoma Sabha Council, 2015), II-60, 61. Malabar Mar Thoma Syrian Christian Evangelistic Association, *Annual Report 2012-13*, (Thiruvalla: MMTSCEA, 2013), 14.

[303] Since an analysis of the history of mission, nature and various models of mission employed in the Church is mentioned in the previous chapter, the present focus is on how the Church integrated the liturgy and evangelism in mission centres.

community, i.e. faith related aspects such as doctrines, rituals, and rubrics, the Christianization of morals (discipline and actions) and the liturgical life (celebration of faith).[304] As a community of faith, the liturgy provides a new space and identity to the converted Christians. It motivates them to gather around the Table and enables them to experience a mystical union with Christ and to have a fellowship with human beings as well. As in the traditional Christian community, the liturgy helps the newly converted faithful to form a new community around the Table and Word of God. The liturgy creates a solemn space to experience a community fellowship and spiritual nurturing. The liturgical life and worship is a binding force for a traditional Christian community. Very often in the mission centres, the newly converted believers remain somewhat isolated individuals. Because they have not yet formed as a Christian community in which to live as members caring for each other. Hence the primary task of evangelization then is the building up of a truly local church. The local church is a church incarnate in a people, indigenous and inculturated.[305] One of the main tasks, therefore, of present day missionary work is the formation of these Christian communities by intensification of an active communal liturgical life. There are mainly three things important in this regard, i.e. the necessity of active participation in the liturgy, the liturgical living of the *kerygma*- the message of the gospel and the reciprocal interworking of catechetic and liturgy. The value of liturgy as a means of instruction could be exploited much more.[306]

Since liturgy is a component of community formation and community living, the Church has to give adequate attention to develop a liturgy for the newly formed faith communities. Along with the traditional mode of worship and liturgy, the Church has to be open enough for new adaptations and liturgical experiments for making liturgy relevant and meaningful to

---

[304] Johannes Hofinger, ed., *Liturgy and the Missions: The Nijmegen Papers* (New York: P J. Kennedy and Sons, 1960), 43-44.
[305] G.B. Rosales and C.G. Arevalo, eds., *For All Peoples of Asia: Federation of Asian Bishops' Conferences; Documents form 1970-1991* (Quezon City: Claretian Publications, 1992), 14.
[306] Hofinger and Johannes, *Liturgy and the Missions,* 45.

Mission and Liturgy

the local community. In this regard, the Church has to include not only the liturgical texts, calendars, actions and gestures, but also such externals as ecclesiastical music, architecture, art, vestments which are all in some way conditioned by the physiognomy of a liturgy. The language, however, in which a liturgy is developed does not contribute greatly to its physiognomy and could be changed with no great harm done to the latter. The other externals such as music, architecture, art, vestments, and to some extend actions and gestures, insofar as they do not condition, but are conditioned by the physiognomy of a liturgy, could be adapted to new circumstances, in accordance with the spirit of the liturgy.[307] Adaptation should not destroy the individuality or characteristics that embody the spirit of the liturgy, since the individuality of a liturgy is one of the different providential means in which faith is expressed and tradition is safeguarded.

A dialogical existence in harmony with the Indian culture, traditions and spiritual heritage is a unique way of life followed by the Church to bear effective witness to the Gospel. This includes an incarnational quality of self-emptying for identification with everyone, especially the poor, downtrodden and the marginalized. It calls for inculturation, which enables the Church to take roots and flourish in new places.[308] Inculturation of the gospel and of Christian way of life is a task that the Church faces today, especially in societies where evangelisation is taking place among new peoples and cultures. It is a very delicate and difficult task. Inculturation does not mean a new gospel or a new composite religion. Inculturation requires a long process. In considering the areas of Inculturation, as a ritual action the liturgy is a confluence of texts, gestures, material objects, music, time, and space. Texts are either proclaimed or sung, and they can be classified as prayers, admonitions, and homilies, greetings and responses, and song lyrics. Gestures, on the other hand, are bodily actions with ritual with a meaning and purpose. For example, the gestures of hand–laying, standing, kneeling, sitting, and the exchange of peace.

---

[307] Placid J. Podipara, *Reflections on Liturgy* (Kottayam: Oriental Institute of Religious Studies, 1983), 20.
[308] Kannookadan, *The Mission Theology of the Syro-Malabar Church,* 8.

Bread, wine, water and oil are material objects that are commonly used in sacramental celebrations. To these we can add vestments, furnishings like the altar, lectern, chairs, vessels, lighted candles, wedding rings, and other such objects. Music is the preferred language of the liturgy. All of the above ritual elements originated and developed in cultural traditions, in conjunction with the teachings of the Bible.[309] They are culturally bound and hence are the subject of inculturation. The task of framing the liturgy should not be left alone to some experts who may often be outsiders to the particular community and culture; rather, along with their contribution, it should be the outcome of the faith experience of the community. Any change by way of inculturation must be compatible with Scripture and teaching of the Church. The local parish cannot live in isolation, it must think and act in union with the universal Church.

2.2.2 Major Challenges in the Mission Field Context

Socio-religious and political background of the mission field context is a matter of discussion since India is a country with diverse cultures, religions, manners, customs and traditions. As mentioned in the first chapter, the social landscape of Indian society is intermingled with Hindu religious traditions and ethos. Very often Christianity is considered a foreign religion and a by-product of Western Imperialism because of its historical connections with outside India. Unfortunately, there is an unhealthy tension in the relationship between evangelization process of Christians and the Hindu fundamental groups in India. Aloysius Pieris observes that "the whole of Christian mission history of the colonialists was the period of conquest of other religions and cultures for Christ."[310] The majority of the Hindu religious groups consider Christianity as a foreign religion which stands for proselytism.

---

[309] Koodapuzha, *Eastern Theological Reflection in India,* 23-24.
[310] Aloysius Pieris, "The Church, the Kingdom of God and the other Religions," *Dialogue* 22 (1970): 3-7.

In this context, evangelization in mission field setting is numerous and wide, yet full of challenges. The major challenges of mission work are analysed in the following order: social, economic, religious, and political.

(a) **Social Challenge: Caste System** - Even though there are considerable changes in the socio political scenario of Indian society because of the development of education, communication and transport, Hindu religious ideologies still continue to play a major role in constructing the socio-political consciousness and identity of the common populace. The social system of India is structured on intense caste system which discriminates people and communities in the name of caste and religion.[311] From time immemorial Indian society is based on "chathurvarnya" (colour code) in which the societal strata is divided into four groups based on the status of the birth and occupation of the people.[312] By this rule, a person from the high caste would be polluted if touched by a Dalit or low caste person.[313] The caste Hindus branded the low castes as untouchables and outcastes. The high caste always kept a distance with the law caste to avoid ritual pollution. An account of the manners and customs of the people of Travancore written in 1860 stated that ritual pollution infected a person in three ways: by approaching, touching or eating with an inferior.[314] Even though Kerala society is an exception[315] due to English education and

---

[311] Paul de la Gueriviere, "Caste and Christian," *Jeevadhara* 11 (May-June, 1981): 156.
[312] The "Brahmin" enjoyed the upper class position who were taking care of the activities related to religion and study. "Kshythria" mainly warriors and rulers, "Vaishyas" who were engaged in trade and commerce. "Sudras" who indulged in other menial works.
[313] The word "Dalit" means oppressed, broken, and crushed, which most realistically describes the lives of almost all of those who are part of this cluster of communities. The term has been self-chosen and self-applied by people belonging to this group. Sathianathan Clarke, *Dalits and Christianity: Subaltern Religions and Liberation Theology in India* (Calcutta: Oxford University, 1998), 18.
[314] Day, *Dawn in Travancore*, 9.
[315] Many scholars have studied the society of Kerala and observed that during the 19th century an awakening emerged within Kerala for a radical social and religious change in its caste structure. This awakening prepared the people to question the validity of the

influence of missionaries, and so many other political and social factors, many of the Indian societies are continued to be dominated by Hindu caste ideologies,[316] which is based on inequality, social discrimination, untouchability and inapproachability.

It is apparent that very often people converted to Christianity from the rest of the community still retain nevertheless their caste identity. Thus caste has persisted to be a part of Christian's identity in India. Even the legal reservation policies of the Indian Government is based on caste identity. It is unfortunate to note that a Christian convert is not entitled for any social welfare concessions and other reservations in job/study from the government since Christians are considered as a higher caste. This social reality has been studied very well in reference to the south Indian states of Adhra Pradesh, Tamil Nadu and Kerala.[317]

(b) **Economic Challenge: Poverty** - Poverty in India is not just an economic challenge. It is intermingled with the socio-political factors. In India the main cause of poverty is injustice of the systematic exploitation of the poor by the rich through manipulation of the system of economic, political and cultural relationships.[318] Joseph Vadakkan analyses the term poverty into four categories: ignorance, hunger, disease and homelessness.[319] The poverty leads

---

caste structure and to fight against its oppressive manifestations. Jeffrey, *The Decline of Nayar Dominance,* 72-73. Mathew and Thomas, *The Indian Churches of St. Thomas,* 48-52. Kawashima, *Missionaries and a Hindu State,* 83.

[316] The high caste Brahmanical domination of its society is based on a legend in the Brahmanical tradition about its creation. It is believed that the Brahmins introduced the caste system into the community structure of the indigenous people. This process is known as "Aryanisation" or "Sanskritization," a cultural domination of pre-Aryan people by a Brahmanical culture by which non-Aryan people gradually adopted Vedic practices and Brahmanical authority. It is considered that the caste rules and barriers were deliberately created the Brahmins. Kusuman, *Slavery in Travancore,* 25.

[317] Parkas G. Reddy, "Caste and Christianity: A study of Shudra Caste in Rural Andhra Pradesh," in *Religion in South India,* eds. V. Sudarsen G. Prakash Reddy and M. Suryanarayana (Delhi: B. R. Publishing, 1987), 113-124.

[318] D.S. Amalorpavadass, ed., *The Conclusions of the Interdisciplinary Research Seminar on the Indian Church in the Struggle for the New Society* (Bangalore: TNBCLC, 1982), 46.

[319] Joseph Vadakkan, *A Priest's Encounter with Revolution* (Bangalore: ATC, 1974), 37, 118.

to other evil social practices like prostitution, child labour, forced migration, cheap labour, abortion etc. The relevance of the Church depends upon the response of the Church towards these issues. The Church has to address positively the issues of poverty, economic disparity, corruption, violation of human rights and all other forms of injustice in society by developing its own theological reflection and action.

(c) **Religious Challenges: Pluralistic Context of India** - Generally Indian society is pluralistic in nature. Unity in diversity is the hall mark of the country. There are many religious streams in the country. According to the 2011 census, the religious compositions of India's population is as follows: Hindus- 80.51%, Muslims, 13.4%, Christians 2.3%, Sikhs 1.90%, Buddhist's 0.8%, Jains 0.4%, and others 0.60%.[320] Indian religious reality is complex. When considering the term religious pluralism, it generally refers to a belief in multiple religious worldviews as being equally valid or acceptable. More than mere tolerance, it accepts multiple paths to God as a possibility. Pluralism or multiculturalism is not merely the existence of different religions, cultures and ideologies.[321] It is the mutuality, justice and love among the cultures and religions which is absent in both the Indian[322] and world scenario. S.J

---

[320] censusindia.gov.in/census_and_you/Religion.aspx (accessed August 25, 2013).

[321] Plurality has existed in India for centuries but pluralism is a modern reality. "Traditional India had been a land in which peoples and communal groups who followed different religions, lived according to different cultural values and social patterns, and spoke different languages, coexisted. There was a religious tolerance, and mutual acceptance and respect prevailed in the social and personal scenarios. Nevertheless, throughout the periods of history, a general dominant tendency originated due to colonial situations, unequal social structure, and the politicization of religion. It influenced the social fabric of Indian society. The movement from co-existence to dialogue existence is the movement from plurality to pluralism. This movement of plurality to pluralism is not only national but also local as well as worldwide." M. M Thomas, *The Church's Mission and Post Modern Humanism: Collection of Essays and Talks 1992-1996* (New Delhi: ISPCK, 1996), 129.

[322] In the Indian context, even Hinduism that prides itself on its tolerance had actively opposed Buddhism and Jainism in the past and opposes Islam and Christianity as 'foreign' in the present. Exclusivist attitude in religion causes ignorance and prejudice concerning the others. It creates a negative attitudes that consider others as untrue and immoral in one's own point of view. The binding force of religious identity, because of its strength and

Samarth, an Indian theologian explains that a pluralist society is "one where people of different religions, cultures and ideological commitments, of languages, regions and ethnic groups, live and work together in the larger community, sharing the burdens and joys of human existence."[323] In a multi- religious and plural-cultural context, the mission of the Church calls for it to be a truly dialogical community. It demands an attitude of openness and respect for other faiths and the role of being an agent of reconciliation and peace among the various groups.

(d) **Political Challenges:** The rise of radical fundamentalist groups in India is an emerging problem for Christian mission and threatens the spirit of inter religious harmony in general and Christian evangelization in particular. Hindu fanatic groups like Hindu Maha Sabha, Rashtriya Swoyam Sevak (RSS), Bajrangdal, Shiva Sena, Vishwa Hindu Parishad (VHP) etc., oppose religious and cultural pluralism and create difficulties for members of other religions, including Christians. Religious fundamentalism and communalism are very inhuman and destroy the harmony of society. Communalism is closely related to fundamentalism, which can be defined as an "exaggerated adherence to one's religious identity that draws the members of a religious community into a tightly knit defensive group and maintain a hostile aggressive stance against members of other religious groups."[324] The root causes of communalism are political, economic and social interests.[325] The militant religious fundamentalism is often exploited by persons and groups whose motive is purely political, which is to gain

---

integrative power, is often used as the basis of group power in situations of social conflict. Amaladoss, "Our Mission in India Today," *Vaigarai* 6, no. 2 (September 2001): 12-15.

[323] S. J Samartha, "Exegetical Preaching in a Pluralist society," *Masihi Sevak* XVI (January 1994): 30.

[324] George M. Soares Prabhu, "Religion and Communalism: the Christian Dilemma," in *In Responding to Communalism: The Task of Religions and Theology*, ed. S. Arokiasamy (Anand: Gujrat Sahitya Prakash, 1991), 138-142.

[325] Asghar Ali Engineer, *On Developing Theory of Communal Riots* (Bombay: Institute of Islamic Studies, 1984), 3-8.

social control or economic advantages. Very often, politicians instrumentalize religion and manipulate religious symbols for their own self-interest and advantage.[326] As a result, contemporary India has witnessed a number of clashes between different religious communities in recent times all over the country.[327]

2.2.3 Relevant Approaches to Mission in the Indian Mission Field Settings

In order to address the above mentioned challenges the Church has to design new modes of mission appropriate to the context. Currently, above mentioned challenges in India could be encountered mainly by three kinds of trends such as: a trend of inculturation, a trend of interreligious dialogue, and a trend of liberation.

An approach of inculturation is the affirmation of God's presence in the Indian cultural terrain. The Church has to integrate the principal elements into its proclamation, celebration and ecclesial life. The process of inculturation is both an element of religio-cultural integration and social incorporation of the Christian faith with realities of the society. The Church has to engage herself in dialogue with the poor and marginalized with a view to alleviate their massive poverty and oppression. A detailed description on the process of inculturation follows at the end of this chapter.

An approach of interreligious dialogue demands oneness and a vision of inclusive approach towards other religions and culture. It is based on the realization that Christ is present and active among all peoples and all religions and that the saving grace of Christ is present and operative in them; hence we need to enter into dialogue with them. The Church,

---

[326] Errol D'Lima, "The Church Mission of Love and Service in the context of Asia's Socio-Economic and Political Realities," *Jeevadhara* XXVIII (July 1997): 160.

[327] In specific, cities like Ahmedabad, Allahabad, Ayodhya, Hyderabad, Meerut, and Mumbai there have been clashes between Muslim and Hindus that have caused the destruction of temples, mosques, houses, shops, despoliation of properties, even killing of innocent people. John Britto Michael, *The Church's Marian Profile And Evangelization in India: In the Light of the Federation of Asian Bishop's Conferences' Documentation on Evangelization.* (Unpublished PhD Thesis, St. Patrick's College, 2014), 38.

while accepting Christ as God's final and full revelation, is at the same time aware of the fact that our realization of the fullness of the mystery of Christ will be possible only at the end of time, and that it is her task to grow in the realization of this mystery through sharing with others.[328] In a diverse cultural context of India, the Church has to create a common platform to have healthy dialogue and liberalized action through which mutual misunderstanding, hatred, discord and discrimination could be identified and opposed. The primary task of the Church in this context is to build up a human community, which is based on freedom, fellowship, equality, justice, and peace. The mission of the Church then is universal reconciliation.[329] Building a genuine human community that brings together people of all religions and cultures with the dialogical framework of pluralism is the common historical responsibility of the time. The uniqueness of each human person and diversity in the community invite us to the possibility of accepting the "other" as "other."[330] In a multi-religious context, the Church must consciously build up a multi-religious society, in which every religious community is recognized, accepted and respected and in this new order allowing each group to contribute its riches to the good of all. The witness of the Church is to follow the lifestyle of the cross in the context of respecting differences and accepting pluralities. For effective Christian witness, it is necessary to have increased trust and unity between faith communities. There is a need to re-engage and continue conversations with other religions and churches. There is an urgent need to affirm the Kingdom values of justice, peace, love, respect, and tolerance for creating a peaceful co-existence. In other words, to witness is to search for the eternal truths of the Kingdom of God and become partners in fighting for common Christian causes, celebrating festivals together and

---

[328] D.S. Amalorpavadass, "Approaches, Meaning and Horizon of Evangelization," in *Light and Life We Seek to Share* (Patna: All India Consultation on Evangelization, 1973), 54-55.
[329] Thomas Malipurathu and L. Stanislaus, eds., *A Vision of Mission in the New Millennium* (Mumbai: St Paul's, 2001), 77.
[330] Joseph, *In Search of Christian Identity in the Community,* 89-92.

working to re-establishing and sustaining the integrity of creation.[331] Thus acknowledging the presence of God in other religious traditions is included in the area of witnessing.

In the present context, the Church should make all efforts to remove every trace of triumphalism, exclusivism and any attitude of superiority in its teachings, structures, evangelizing activities and the style of the functioning of its institutions. Particularly, it has to ensure that its educational enterprises, charitable activities, health care services and social involvements are geared to the genuine promotion of people's well-being and progress and not in any way to convert from their religions.[332] The Christian task to witness and not to convert is important in the pluralistic context of India. M.M. Thomas argues that "a Christian is called not to convert but to witness. The burden of responding to the messages of Christ is that of the hearers and not of those who proclaim."[333] However, there is nothing wrong in inviting those who respond positively to the person of Christ to experience fellowships around the Table of the Lord and the Table of the word as 'part of the Church' within their religious and cultural community-settings.

A liberational approach of mission urges the Church to consider socio-economic injustice as unacceptable to the justice of God. Our faith in a liberator God compels us to involve ourselves to affirm solidarity with the poor and liberating them from the unjust structures. The mission strategy of the Church in the mission field context is not that of extending its boundaries; rather it has to share the true spirit of unity, cordiality, solidarity of the people in their struggle for justice and peace and equality and to focus on God's Kingdom revealed in Christ. A major mission mandate in the village of India is to work for social and economic justice,

---

[331] Zac Varghese, ed., "Christian Witness: Revisiting the Mission Mandate of the Church," *Prathinidhimandalam 2009 Study* (Thiruvalla: Mar Thoma Syrian Church, 2009), 28-29.
[332] Rienze Perera, "Religion, Cultures and Peace: The Challenge of Religious Pluralism and the Common Life of Asia," in *Faith and Life in Contemporary Asian Realities,* eds. Feliciano V Carino and Marina True (Hong Kong: Christian Conference of Asia, 2000), 112-113.
[333] Thomas, *The Church's Mission and Post Modern Humanism,* 122-123.

peace and development with a strong emphasis on liberating the poor, from oppressive structures.[334] It is an invitation to share the joy of Christ in His Kingdom. Participation in issues such as human rights, minority problems, social and economic injustice which we commonly face, gives a basis for dialogue.[335] In this juncture, the mission of the Church must be holistic and it should address all aspects, threats and challenges of the whole of humanity.[336]

2.2.4 Liturgical Orientation and Training

Liturgical orientation and training are essential elements for relevant liturgical life, not only in the mission centres but also in the entire Church. Since liturgy expresses the faith of the Church, there should be a detailed and systematic way of liturgical training and orientation in the mission centres of the Church. At present, there is no such systematic liturgical orientation or training happening in the Church or in any mission centres. The liturgical orientation for the new believers depends on the initiative of the clergy who are in charge of the mission centres. There should be a system for an ongoing systematic liturgical orientation and training in the Church. In addition, the Church should focus more on serious research and studies in the field of liturgy to enrich members to lead a Eucharistic centred lifestyle. It is high time to think about the possibility of giving liturgical freedom to the mission centres and to the diaspora community, so that they could express their own cultural elements in their corporate worship. This will help to constrain the influx of people to independent charismatic groups. A liturgical reformation is the need of the time to have a renewal in the Church. The liturgy has to be the centre of the Church along with Scripture.

---

[334] Rosales and Arevalo, *For All Peoples of Asia,* 15-16, 94.
[335] K.C. Abraham, "Mission and Ministry of the Church: A Liberative Perspective," *Bangalore Theological Forum* XXI, no.3 (September, 1989): 42.
[336] Amaladoss, "Challenges of Mission in the 21st Century," 18-20.

2.2.5 An Integration of Liturgy and Evangelism in the Church

The primary task before the MTC after the formation of the mission organization -MTEA-was to integrate the eastern liturgical base of the Church to the new evangelical fervour. In the initial stage of evangelization, the missionary approach was mainly through conducting prayer meetings, visiting houses, and conducting community development programmes.[337] Along with these, later, the Church took initiative to translate the Malayalam Eucharistic liturgy and introduced liturgical worship in their own vernacular.[338] Currently, in the majority of the worship centres, the celebration of the liturgy and divine services are conducted in native languages.[339] According to Daniel, the MTC's integration task was dual in nature. Primarily it was an assimilation of the eastern liturgical and evangelical faith of the CMS as well as the integration of the Church and mission to create a Church with a missionary zeal.[340] The vision of the Church combined the "evangelical faith and experience within the framework of corporate life" with the "liturgical devotion of the Oriental Eastern Church."[341] Therefore, the MTEA had to assert its independence of western missionary societies and churches in thought and action. According to Daniel, the eastern liturgical basis of the MTC led the Church to devote time for integrating, first, the Church's sacramental life and missionary consciousness in its teachings and, subsequently, the integration of the Church and the MTEA.[342] As to the leaders of the MTC, the Church's integration with the MTEA was a main concern as it faced the autonomous

---

[337] Malabar Mar Thoma Syrian Christian Evangelistic Association, *Annual Report 2012-13*, 14.
[338] A detailed description on translation of liturgy is highlighted in the second chapter.
[339] Interview with Rev. Philip Baby on August 08, 2015, who was the first missionary priest of the MTC in Orissa, Andhra region among the tribal community. According to him believers and faith seekers very actively participate in the celebration of the liturgy and wholeheartedly welcome it.
[340] Daniel, *Ecumenism in Praxis*, 101.
[341] The Malabar Mar Thoma Syrian Evangelistic Association was a registered organization under the Indian companies act VI, under the Travancore Regulation I, of 1882, in 1904. Mathew and Thomas, *Indian Christians of St. Thomas*, 89.
[342] Daniel, *Ecumenism in Praxis*, 102.

existence of Western missions and organizations.[343] The leaders of the Church were very much open and particular in this integration process. For instance, Thomas Mar Athanasius, the then Metropolitan, wholeheartedly supported the integration process.[344] Besides, MTEA leaders like Thomas Kottarathil,[345] Mathai Edavanmelil, and Yohannan Kottoorethu were loyal churchmen and had been known for their efforts to amalgamate the missionary spirit and eastern liturgical ideals in their thoughts and actions.[346]

According to Daniel, "the Church employed two methods for integrating the missionary spirit and eastern liturgical ideas; it started an "educational phase to edify the Church whereby it prepared teachings on "mission" and "eastern liturgical practices" for Sunday worship, Bible convention meetings, and conferences, etc. Convention meetings and conferences were to conclude with the Holy Qurbana, explaining the Church's paramount importance of the eastern liturgy. Constitutional efforts were made to safeguard the Church's integration with the MTEA by providing checks and balances. For instance, the third annual meeting of the MTEA made a decision that the reports of all meetings of the MTEA shall be submitted to the Metropolitan.[347] The purpose of this decision was to bring all proceedings of the MTEA before the Metropolitan for his perusal and approval. This was later included as a clause in the MTEA constitution. Similarly, the Church's sacramental life made its oriental liturgical faith lively and the Church's constitution made its liturgical

---

[343] Most of the missionary organizations including the CMS were voluntary societies independent of the Church. These institutions considered themselves as separate institutions concerned with Christian missions in overseas.

[344] George Alexander, "Malankara Mar Thoma Suvishesha Prasanga sangham," in *Maramon Convention Sathabdhi Valyam*, 160-302. Rev. George Alexander is a clergy of the MTC. He was the General Secretary of the MTEA during 1981-1987 and he wrote a concise history of the MTEA since its inception in 1995.

[345] Thomas Abraham Kottarathil was a clergy of the MTC, who was one among the twelve instrumental in the formation of the MTEA.

[346] Daniel, *Ecumenism in Praxis*, 102.

[347] *Report of the Third Meeting of the MTEA*, M.E. Dhanu 27, 1064. (February 7, 1889). Daniel, *Ecumenism in Praxis*, 102-103.

observance mandatory.[348] C. P. Philipose (1868-1948), the first general secretary of the MTEA, helped the Church to keep the balance of these two elements by integrating missionary spirit and oriental liturgical piety in the MTEA's mission praxis.[349] Instead of keeping the independent nature of the organizations who initiated the evangelisation process, the MTC bases all mission work at the center of her very life from its inception, which is in contrast to the administrative pattern of the Church Missionary Society.[350] The leaders of the Church were very cautious to avoid the possible division of the Church-mission dichotomy as it appeared in western missionary societies.[351] The "evangelical-oriental liturgical" and "church-mission" integration stood in contrast to the organizational pattern of the ministry enterprises in the West. This was an expression of the Indian Church's assertion of autonomy and independence in the new missionary context.[352] As cited above, the conviction of the early leaders of the Church to renew the Church through revival meetings and Bible conventions made a great impact in the life and mission of the Church. Revivalism in the Church was effected through two phases. In the first phase, which could be termed evangelisation phrase, "the lower caste" communities were sought to be drawn to the Church. Revival preachers, including converts from other religions, were encouraged to speak at the annual convention in different parishes. This practice still continues. M. M. Thomas says, it is "where the spiritually revived received stability

---

[348] "the ministry of deacon, priest and episcope, rites of the Church viz., Church dedication, Church consecration, holy baptism, holy communion(Qurbana), holy matrimony, unction of the sick, funeral services and observance of Lents, Sundays and dominical feasts shall not be abolished at any time" *Constitution, Mar Thoma Syrian Church,* Declaration, Part. I, (Thiruvalla: Mar Thoma Church, 2002), 1.
[349] Daniel, *Ecumenism in Praxis,* 103.
[350] The Travancore mission of the CMS was an independent mission agency and therefore it was not under the Anglican Dioceses of Cochin. Stephen Neill, *Creative Tension* (Duff Lectures) (Edinburgh: Edinburgh Press, 1959), 86.
[351] *Report of the Third Meeting of the MTEA,* M.E. Dhanu 27, 1064 (February 7, 1889); the Malabar Mar Thoma Syrian Christians Evangelistic Association: Memorandum and Articles of Association, as amended in 1106 M.E. (1931), reprinted, 1-12; cited in *Mar Thoma Sabha Directory,* ed. Thomas, 150.
[352] Daniel, *Ecumenism in Praxis,* 104-106.

and nurture through preaching and teaching of Scripture."[353] The revival meetings and conventions brought converts from so called "lower caste" communities and other Church members together under one roof, which was not common in the early period of the 20th century in the social context of Kerala.[354] The emerging new social context within the Church enabled both the Church members and newly converted to reap religious and social returns of mutual acceptance from interactions with each other.[355] In the second phase, the revival meetings inspired the Church to turn to the gospel with a burning conviction, which led them to intensify its mission to spread the message of the Gospel. A former Vicar General of the Church, Rev. K. E. Oommen described the influence of the revival meetings at the Church as: "they had come to set a very high value of the daily readings and study of the Bible and also to accept the Bible as the primary authority in the doctrinal matters. In public worship, on Sundays and other holidays, a sermon came to be an inevitable part of the service."[356] The revivalism in the Church helped the members to maintain a serious personal piety with a new emphasis on spontaneity and to interpret the Bible in the light of the contemporary context.

A critical analysis of the influence of revivalism in the MTC shows that there was a certain lack of ecclesiological and liturgical emphasis in the annual conventions at the parishes as well as in the conventions in the regional and diocesan levels, and the Marmon convention. This lack of emphasis is one major reason for the outflow from MTC to the Brethren and Baptist Churches, in the early decades of the 20th century, and later to the Pentecostal and other independent groups. It was clear that the Church found it difficult to connect effectively its traditional oriental liturgical piety with the major changes in its evangelical revival context.[357] This

---

[353] Mathew and Thomas, *The Indian Churches of St. Thomas*, 104-105.
[354] K. T. Jacob, "Maramon Convention Uthbhavavum Valarchayum," In *Maramon Convention Sathabdhi Valyam,* 61.
[355] Daniel, *Ecumenism in Praxis*, 108.
[356] Jacob, "Maramon Convention Uthbhavavum Valarchayum," 61-62.
[357] Daniel, *Ecumenism in Praxis*, 109-110.

resulted in some less-informed preachers criticising the Church's unique nature of blending evangelical faith with its oriental liturgical mooring.

Instead, they wanted to emphasize spirituality based on individualistic poeticism, over and above the oriental liturgical positioning. This provided a space for some of the Church members to try to lessen its liturgical corporate worship base. This eventually developed into tension within the Church between its liturgical heritage and the newfound revivalism, which emphasised adult baptism, speaking in tongues and the second-coming of Christ.[358] This tension prepared the ground for churches such as Baptist and Brethren to work among the members of the MTC since the last decade of the 19th century. Added to this were other reasons which were to result a fresh schism within the Church in 1961.[359] The MTC continues to struggle with all those sectarian tendencies in the name of a Church-centered evangelicalism.

---

[358] Mathew and Thomas, *Indian Christians of St. Thomas*, 102-103, Mathew, *Malankara Mar Thoma Sabha Charithram* vol. II, 174-175.

[359] Having influenced by evangelicalism, some member of the Church showed reluctance to integrate evangelical and liturgical base in the Church. They gave more emphasis on evangelicalism. This lead to an internal struggle within the Church and later the friction resulted in a schism in the Church and subsequent formation of the St. Thomas Evangelical Church in 1961. Its headquarters is at Manjadi, Thiruvalla, Kerala.

Chapter. 5

Challenges in Mission: A Liturgical Review

The growth of the MTC as a global Church through migration and the evangelistic outreach is of great significance. Even though the membership of the Church has increased numerically, it has still to equip herself to face up to ever emerging challenges. The personal, corporate and structural dimensions of the Church should be reviewed comprehensively to ensure relevance, missiological effectiveness and meaningful mission. Earlier, during the first period of reformation, this Church was entirely rural and geographically limited to the Central Travancore regions. Now this Church is spread all around the globe. Prevalent contemporary values springing from market economy and the electronic media have become influential in shaping to a considerable degree the thought patterns, values and behaviour of the faithful, especially among the youth, in the migrated urban context.[360] The very relevance of the Church rests indeed on its commitment to Christ who sends forth his faithful into the world, but also on how successfully it adapts its life and ministerial forms to major changes against the background of global scattering and the emergence of widespread plurality. Though admittedly numerically small, the Church is nevertheless highly pluralistic and is no longer an exclusively Malayalam-speaking Church of "Syrian Christians." The following can be listed as

---

[360] The world view of the urban Indians are now dominated by radical individualism and the values of the market economy. There has been an idealisation of affluent living and a diminution in the concern for the poor. Poverty and plenty are both leaving many people unsupported and isolated. The migrant urban youth are deeply influenced by the changes in the world. Alongside, corruption has made deep inroads into national life, including the democratic processes. Corruption has spread to public life, religious movements and to the churches. The above changes in Church and society have raised several issues which demand urgent attention.

the pertinent challenges facing the Church in the course of its growth both in the diaspora and in the mission fields of differing rural areas in India.

1 Challenges of the Mar Thoma Diaspora Community

The challenges facing the MTC, especially in the diaspora, vary according to the geographical region. Although local situations may differ, nevertheless problems facing the diaspora in general remain the same. This general challenge posed by the diaspora is the need to discover and assess new forms of expressing identity and activating meaningful mission. Being an immigrant Church in the overseas locations, it has to encounter in due course various challenges to the very old traditions, heritage and values. At the same time the Church is open enough to adapt to changes required to meet its changed locations. Wherever it finds itself, the MTC would, of course, retain deep roots in India and would uphold its Oriental liturgical traditions along with the spiritual heritage that blossomed in the Malankara reformation. However, other issues arise with which the Church must wrestle, for the diaspora community faces some immense spiritual as well as liturgical challenges, such as the following:

(a) There is an inter-generational difference which necessarily engenders internal conflicts. The generation gap between the first generation immigrants and those born in various parts of the world with different cultures creates a sort of misperception regarding identity, values and world view. While the first generation tries to cling on to the faith, practices and rich heritage of the mother Church, succeeding generations might very well feel more a part of the local community and do not show any deep loyalty to the mother Church. Accordingly, these latter in most cases neither speak Malayalam at home nor resonate to a liturgy steeped in poetic language and rich in symbolism. The younger generations tend to seek new identities in a different cultural context and they are being detached from an ancestral tradition and culture.[361] Consequently, in such a conflicting situation it is little wonder that the Church itself encounters difficulty in maintaining and manifesting a meaningful existence.

(b) The new generation found itself ill at ease with the hierarchical and "charismatic, person centred" leadership nature of the Church. Tensions are possible between leaders, including bishops, who are born and educated in India and those who are born in other countries. Very often, the appointed leadership[362] in the Church is inadequately equipped to take care of the spiritual needs of the diaspora community, especially the needs of the youngsters because of barriers in language, culture and ethos. In a word, the new generation finds it difficult to identify and to associate with ecclesiastical leadership.

(c) The liturgy is not addressing various issues existentially pertinent to people in their daily life, issues such as single parents, children born out of wedlock, widows and widowers, children with special needs, divorcees, people afflicted by guilt and shame, etc. The aim of any Church must be to assist her members to address their problems, which means clearly to assist them in an atmosphere of openness and an attitude of mercy and compassion, such as Jesus taught. At present, there is no forum established to address the social, ethical and moral issues which may arise such as

---

[361] In many of the major cities in US, there are independent congregations largely attracting second and third generation Marthomites. For instance, Chicago, New York, Philadelphia, Washington, Dallas, Houston, the pews of many of these congregations are filled with second and third generation Marthomites and similar younger generation from other Christian denominations from Kerala. Lal Varghese, "Commitment to Mar Thoma Church and Ardor for Giving it a Global Identity- Mar Theodosius," in *Beyond the Diaspora,* 248.

[362] The Mar Thoma priests' are ordained for the Church in general and each of them will get a chance to serve at least three years in a diaspora region outside of India either in North America, Canada, Europe, Middle East, Australia, Malaysia and Singapore. The Episcopal Synod of the Church in India takes the decision of appointment for the clergy and bishops.

homosexuality, abortion, euthanasia, etc. The Church remains silent about these kinds of concern.[363]

(d) As alluded to above, there is for the younger generation a decline in the appeal of the traditional liturgical style of worship and historic Eucharistic liturgies. Tension arises between retention of the riches of inherited liturgical patterns and the embrace of forms of worship that speak to the new generation. The second generation Marthomites, and especially the young, struggle to make sense of the historic forms of worship. There is in many of the diaspora Churches a trend to adopt the style of worship that finds among independent evangelical Protestant groups.[364] So far, the response of the Churches to explain to the young the existential meaningfulness of the liturgy is admittedly limited. The fundamental issue is that the prayers appear distant to the modern mind set and no really serious effort is being made to bridge this gap. The "praise and worship style" (with the help of modern musical instruments) has a considerable following among the younger generation. What is required is a proper programme of biblical, theological and liturgical instruction to bring the young to

---

[363] Geevarghese and Mathew, *Beyond Diaspora*, 231-233.

[364] Traditional Churches like Mar Thoma Churches tended to adopt some of the music, worship practices and style of the nondenominational evangelicalism. "Nondenominational churches de-emphasize theology, sacraments, and the sacred liturgical calendar of the Church. Their services are informal, anti-liturgical and anti-ceremonial. They are held in buildings that avoid religious symbolism, by clergy who do not wear the traditional robes, who may not have a theological degree from established seminaries and are sometimes not ordained. Such churches tend to have minimalist but clear doctrines, which include the certainty that Christianity is the only true religion, the assurance of salvation to those who are born-again in Christin and the belief in the inerrancy and authority of the Bible. They use the spirited contemporary music with a rock band and multimedia presentations, sometimes including skits and plays. Very often they do not have a consecrated worship space. The non-denominational churches also tend to decentralize and flat the authority structures and provide considerable autonomy to the local church and the lay leadership. These groups articulate an individualistic concept of spirituality and religion that stresses individual salvation. The goal, attending worship is to obtain 'spiritual food' or sermon applicable to life which will help the individual to grow spiritually." Prema Kurian, "Denominationalism to Post-Denominationalism: Changes in American Christianity," *Mar Thoma Messenger* 30, no. 2 (April 2011): 24-25.

understand the need for worshipping God. This is a very important matter that merits to be discussed and resolved in conjunction with the youth members themselves.[365]

(e) The need to give priority to the mission imperatives of diaspora settings and the need to show mission solidarity with the Church in India. The priority of the Church in its mission journey is to reach out with its reformed identity. Very often more emphasis is given to the collection of finance for the mission work in India rather than the outreach mission in its own diaspora context.

(f) It seems that there is an upsurge of hybrid forms of non-denominational congregations founded by second-generation leaders, targeting the Kerala Christians in the US. The Church should launch new English-speaking congregations to accommodate the spiritual liturgical needs of those youngsters whose primary language is English. It is a fact that second and third generation Marthomites are leaving their mother Church and moving elsewhere. From a study conducted in the North American Mar Thoma diaspora community, it is found that only 20% of the second generation and third generation Marthomites attend their mother Church on a regular basis.[366]

(g) Lack of in-depth study of the riches inherent in the tradition, heritage, liturgy and spirituality of the MTC.

(h) Translations of the liturgy and an incorporation into worship of cultural elements in the worship.

(i) Inability to address the spiritual and social issues[367] of the youths and the migrant community at large. There is an urgent need to equip the youths to face the challenges of the religious pluralism and the globalized culture.

---

[365] Kuruvila, *An Indian Fruit From Palestinian Roots*, 78-79.
[366] Thomas Thazhayil, "The Church at Crossroads," *Mar Thoma Messenger* 32, no.3 (July 2013): 32.
[367] Gay marriage, cohabitation, pre-marital sex, homosexuality, discrimination in the name of colour and sex, injustice and inequality in the place of worship, bullying, racial discrimination.

Mission and Liturgy

(j) Communication gap between clergy and the young. Lacking is an ecclesial ambience in which the young can feel at ease in expressing their spiritual problems.

(k) Inability or indifference to integrating with the local culture because of fear of cultural erosion and of losing identity. Needed correspondingly is a general attitude of increased understanding and acceptance of inter-cultural and inter-religious marriages.

These are some of the pertinent issues that the Mar Thoma diaspora community faces.

2 Liturgical Challenges in the Mission centers

Plurality is a unique nature in the mission field context of the MTC since each state of India is totally different in culture, language, lifestyle, food, traditions, practices, ethos and customs. Even though Hinduism is a predominant religion in society,[368] the constitution of the country assures religious freedom and affirms the secular ideologies in the country. Religious tolerance is the distinctiveness of Indian secular identity and unity in diversity is the hallmark of Indian society. But at present there are incidents of religious intolerance and riots in different parts of Indian society. Politicisation of religion is a major threat to the secular character of the country. Very often political parties exploit religion to achieve power. At present, government-sponsored religious terrorism creates fear in the minds of religious minorities. Very often, the members of the Church in the mission fields are converted Christians. Now conversion from one religion to another religion is banned in many states of India such as

---

[368] As per the religious census data of 2011, released by the Registrar General and Census Commissioner, the total population in the country in 2011 was 121.09 crore. (Crore-10 Million) Hindu population is 96.63 crore (79.8 percent); Muslim 17.22 crore (14.2 percent); Christian 2.78 crore (2.3 percent); Sikh 2.08 crore (1.7 percent); Buddhist 0.84 crore (0.7 percent); Jain 0.45 crore (0.4 percent), other religions and persuasions (ORP) 0.79 crore (0.7 percent) and religion not stated 0.29 crore (0.2 percent). http://www.firstpost.com/india/india-has-79-8-percent-hindus-14-2-percent-muslims-2011-census-data-on-religion-2407708.html (accessed December 27, 2015).

Maharashtra, Chhattisgarh, Gujarat, and Rajasthan. Many fundamental religious groups like Rashtrivya Sowyam Sevak, (RSS), Vishwa Hindu Parishad (VHP), Hindu Maha Sabha etc., perceive the activities of the Christian missionaries with an eye of suspicion.

While considering the strategies for the success of the mission field, there is a need for studying and reflecting on the Church's accomplishments in different parts of India. in this matter, it is worth listening to the experiences of sister churches ranging from the Roman Catholic Church to the Evangelical Church. Developing an appropriate mission strategy for each mission field is vital. In the face of rising fundamentalism the Church has to design suitable mission strategies and appropriate new initiatives to relate to the struggles of local communities. Desirable is a comprehensive review of each mission field to evaluate whether the programmes are addressing the significant needs of the local community. The review programme should also feature some sort of positive methodology for energizing missionaries. It should also help the missionaries to experience support from the Church in the many challenges they face in the field. People working in the mission fields require great commitment, passion for evangelisation, training and skill to deal with the needs of each field. Their vocation demands greater creativity. To this end, thorough and effective training should be given to missionaries, whereas at present more attention is given to the training of clergy than to the training of missionaries proper.

Worship within the new faith communities is a matter of urgent attention. The context of a particular mission field could prove quite different from the general matters affecting migrant youth within and outside India. Therefore, the liturgies for the mission fields, including Dalit communities in Kerala, could be different from that for traditional parishes in Kerala and for urban migrant youths. In the mission fields there is an extensive reservation about different versions of the Mar Thoma liturgy since it is translated from the Malayalam liturgy. Forms of worship which are contextually relevant, biblical and meaningful to the local culture is needed. Conscious and deliberate effort is also needed to manifest the signs of the Kingdom of God in the local context.

While considering the liturgy, two great difficulties or dangers arise for the Church in mission fields. The first is the difficulty which people in mission lands experience when they transfer from the old social structures to a new culture. Special care must be taken that they do not lose all the good there is of their own culture and tradition. The second danger is that of falling victim to materialism when one can become dazzled by Western technological progress. Integration of social and liturgical action is indispensable for any mature Christian life in this contemporary world.[369] All new cultures in the mission field must needs be subsumed into Christianity. Adaptation rightly understood is always relevant to missionary endeavour.

Effective missionary work means effective engagement with the community. Mutual respect in the community engenders religious tolerance and harmony. Very often the work of the missionaries from Kerala in many mission fields of India outside Kerala seems ineffective because of language barriers and cultural differences. It must be admitted that the effectiveness of missionaries sent to various fields is often questionable. One problem is that the Church is not getting sufficient native missionaries from the local area as co-workers. The Church should simply be recruiting young people from these groups to co-shoulder responsibility as ministers, deacons and deaconesses.[370] Of course, lack of adequate financial support to carry out these various projects always remains a problem.

There is no actual orientation towards mission within the liturgy. Indeed, there is at present a call to impose uniformity in some of the liturgical practices. This jars, however, with the Church's affirmation that unity is not univocal in meaning with uniformity. Capacity for some degree of diversity has always been a hallmark of the Church. Neither the New Testament nor the Orthodox traditions call for an imposed uniformity. Christians are encouraged to participate in a rich and inclusive harmony, not a flat, dull and exclusive unison.[371]

---

[369] Hofinger, *Liturgy and The Missions*, 41.
[370] Alexander, *The Mar Thoma Church: Tradition and Modernity*, 70.
[371] David Stancliffe, "The Making of the Church of England's Common Worship," *Studia Liturgica* 31, no.1 (2001): 17.

Chapter. 6

Scope of Liturgical Renewal in the Mar Thoma Church

The liturgy is a school where the faithful members learn to live their faith. If people are unable to participate in the liturgy, or if the liturgy has no influence on their life, all which is left is lifeless irrelevance. Since the liturgy is the celebration of faith, a continued renewal of this celebration is an essential task of Christian communities. Liturgical renewal means renewal of the liturgy as a public and representative work of the people of God. This requires, as the Constitution on the Sacred Liturgy of the Second Vatican Council says, the "full, conscious participation" of the people.[372] If liturgy reveals the identity of the Church, the Church has to renew and revise its liturgy by considering the changing image and the role of the Church in the society. Any liturgical revision depends on the interest in the subject among the members of the Church.[373] The image of the Church changes by healthily accommodating the ripples of the post-modern culture. If liturgy is not open enough to accept the changes, it will be static and drain the Church of its dynamism and vibrancy. The purpose of liturgical renewal is to strengthen the spiritual life of the worshipper and to enable them to actively participate in the worship. The renewal of worship is therefore an ongoing process, but it is only possible under

---

[372] The Constitution on the Sacred Liturgy, *Sacrosanctum Concilium* No.24, Promulgated in December 4, 1963. http://www.stolivers.com/ReligiousEd/constitution.pdf (accessed September 10, 2015).

[373] "For a confessional Church, standardized liturgical forms are necessary because they ensure the consistency of the theology enshrined in its doctrinal standards with that expressed in its worship. Worship practices in many congregations are fragmented and incoherent, which resulted in ignorance of their doctrines and confusion about the liturgical heritage of their reformed traditions." Christopher Dorn, "Lord's Supper in the Reformed Church in America," in *Tradition in Transformation American University Studies VII: Theology and Religion*, vol. 264 (New York: Peter Lang, 2007), 108.

conditions of constant attention and readiness to change. Liturgical renewal is not an instant act, but rather an intentional and creative move initiated by the Holy Spirit to make worship more meaningful to the participants.

As mentioned above, the purpose behind all liturgical renewal is the active involvement and participation[374] of the faithful in the Holy Mystery. In the words of Pope Pius XII, who first made the statement and the Second Vatican Council (1962-1965) which reaffirmed it, "liturgical renewal is a sign of the providential disposition of God in our time, a movement of the Holy Spirit..."[375] Since liturgy is particularly associated with the very understanding of Church, the renewal of the Church through Scripture and Tradition necessarily brought with it a corresponding renewal of liturgy through reassessment of its original sources. According to the Constitution of the Sacred Liturgy, "the liturgy is the summit towards which the activity of the Church is directed; it is also the fountain from which all her power flows."[376] Here, the Eucharist in particular is emphasised as the source, summit, and climax of the life of the Christian community (LG.11:26).[377] Vatican II calls for an active participation of the whole people of God in Christian worship. The concept of liturgical renewal cannot be limited to ceremonies, rites, texts etc., it does not consist only in external activity but, above all, in interior and fruitful participation in the paschal mystery of Jesus Christ."[378]

1 Liturgical Adaptation and Inculturation

Liturgical adaptation is an integral aspect of Christian tradition and that has been a constant feature of the history of Christian liturgy. It is a theological

---

[374] The term "active participation" was first used by the Pope Pius X. This term was almost a throwaway line within a 1903 document on Gregorian chant and other Church music: "the primary and indispensable source" from which the faithful derive "the true Christian spirit is active participation in the sacred mysteries and in the public and solemn prayer of the Church." Frederick R. McManus, *Liturgical Participation: An Ongoing Assessment* (Washington: The Pastoral, 1988), 4.
[375] *The Assisi Papers* (Collegeville, MN: Liturgical, 1957), 223-236.
[376] *Sacrosanctum Concilium*, 10.
[377] Figura, "The Works of Communion: Christian Community in Act," 226-227.
[378] *Sacrosanctum Concilium*, 11.

imperative arising from the event of the incarnation.[379] The term adaptation is the official word used by the Constitution on the Liturgy, especially in articles 37-40 to refer the general programme of Church renewal or updating. The Constitution on the Liturgy proposes two ways to achieve this: revision of the existing rites and adaptation to the needs of the time.[380] The term inculturation[381] signifies presenting the Gospel and fashioning Christian life in a way adapted to the culture of the people. Prior to the Second Vatican Council terms like culture adaptation, accommodation, indigenization etc., were used to denote the idea of relating the gospel to

---

[379] Chupungco points out that, "from a theological point of view inculturation is a consequence of the mystery of the incarnation. The incarnation of Jesus is the paradigm or model of inculturation. Just as Christ became human in all things, the Church has the mission to make the mystery of Christ's incarnation a continuing reality in the world. The community of the faithful accomplishes this by integrating suitable components of human culture into its preaching, worship, and works of service to humankind. The incarnation of the Church means that, in imitation of Christ, it shares the history, culture and traditions of its people." Anscar J.Chupungco, "Mission and Inculturation: East Asia and the Pacific," in *The Oxford History of Christian Worship*, eds. Geoffrey Wainwright, Karen B. Westerfield Tucker (Oxford: Oxford University, 2006), 662-663.

[380] Anscar J. Chupungco, *Liturgical Inculturation, Sacramentals, Religiosity, and Catechesis.* (Collegeville, MN: Liturgical, 1992), 24.

[381] The incarnation of Christ is the theological basis of inculturation. Inculturation is the incarnation of the Christian life and message in a concrete cultural situation. Concerning incarnation there are two aspects that need special attention; that is, the eternal truth that contains the Word of God becoming man and the circumstance of time and space accompanying this mystery. Koodapuzha, *Eastern Theological Reflection in India*, 14. It pertains to the incarnation of Christian liturgical experience in a local worshipping community. According to G. De Napoli, this term was coined in 1973 by G. I. Barney, a protestant missionary, who used the term in the context of frontier missions. Chupungco, *Liturgical Inculturation Sacramentals*, 25. "It is made up of three elements. The first is interaction or dialogue between the Church's liturgical worship and the local culture with its components of values, rites, symbols, patterns and institutions. The second is the integration into the liturgy of such cultural elements as are pertinent and suitable. The third is the dynamic whereby the Christian form of worship is enriched by culture without prejudice to its nature as a divine-human institution." Bradshaw, *The New SCM Dictionary of Liturgy and Worship*, 244-245. The concern of inculturation has occupied a major share of the theological reflection of Asian theologians, particularly Indian theologians. Samuel Ryan, "An Indian Christology: A Discussion of Method," *Jeevadhara* 1/3, (1971): 212-227, Michael Amaladoss, "Inculturation: Theological Perspective," *Jeevadhara* 6 (1976): 293-302, D.S. Amalorpavadass, Theological Reflections on Inculturation," *Studia Liturgica* 20/1, (1990): 36-54. Subash Anand, "Inculturation in India: Yesterday, Today and Tomorrow," *Indian Missiological Review* 19/1 (1992): 19-45. Felix Wilfred, *From the Dusty Soil: Contextual Reinterpretation of Christianity* (Madras: University of Madras, 1995), 20-70.

the cultural context of the hearers. This term appeared for the first time in an official document of the Church in 1977 in the "Message to the People of God" issued at the end of the synod of Bishops. Adaptation denotes peripheral and external changes, whereas inculturation has a deeper and more radical significance. Inculturation concerns the faith of the Church, not excluding the fundamental teachings and the whole life of the Church.[382] A good number of liturgists interchange the terms "adaptation" and "inculturation" or else combine them to form the hybrid expression "cultural adaptation." According to Chupungo, adaptation and inculturation refer to the updating of Church institutions. Adaptation denotes the general programme of updating, while inculturation is one of the ways to achieve it.[383] Inculturation is much more than purely adaptation. By the process of adaptation two things are achieved. Firstly, all the authentic values and noble elements of the culture of the people integrate into Christianity. Secondly, the gospel values are transmitted to the culture, thus purifying the culture.[384] An adaptation of the liturgy to various forms of native genius and tradition is not a novelty, but fidelity to tradition.[385]

To understand and express the relationship between liturgy and culture, many technical terms have been used in liturgical circles. The most popular among them are 'indigenization,[386] incarnation, contextualization,[387] revision, adaptation,[388] acculturation[389] and inculturation.[390] Liturgical inculturation in itself is a branch of liturgical study. One can define it as

---

[382] Koodapuzha, *Eastern Theological Reflection in India*, 10-11.

[383] Chupungco, *Liturgical Inculturation Sacramentals*, 25.

[384] Koodapuzha, *Eastern Theological Reflection in India*, 12.

[385] Chupungco. *Cultural Adaptation of the Liturgy*, 3.

[386] Indigenization was intended to indicate the process of conferring on liturgy a cultural form native to the local church. Bradshaw, *The New SCM Dictionary of Liturgy and Worship*, 244.

[387] Contextualization was introduced into ecclesiastical vocabulary by the World Council of Churches in 1972 to express the need for the church to be relevant to contemporary society. Bradshaw, *The New SCM Dictionary of Liturgy and Worship*, 244.

[388] Adaptation is the word used by the Constitution of Sacred Liturgy of the Second Vatican Council

[389] Acculturation describes the juxtaposition of two cultures, which interact but without mutual integration. Bradshaw, *The New SCM Dictionary of Liturgy and Worship*, 244.

[390] Chupungco, *Liturgical Inculturation: Sacramentals*, 13.

"the creative and dynamic relationship between the Christian message and a culture of cultures."[391] There are mainly three notable traits for this: firstly, inculturation is an ongoing process and is relevant to every country or region where the faith has been sown. Secondly, Christian faith cannot exist except in a cultural form and, thirdly, between Christian faith and culture there should be some interaction and reciprocal assimilation.[392] The term, contextualization represents the Church's continuing concern to be relevant to the contemporary world. It suggests that worship should not be disassociated from the actual context of human life. Context is a vibrant expression of human culture. If the liturgy is to be inculturated, it must also be contextualized. Contextualization is a part of the process of acculturation.[393]

Regarding the theological principles of adaptation, Chupungco explains that "expedience is not the sole nor the principal reason for adaptation. The main reason must be sought in the nature of the Church as the prolongation in time and space of the incarnation of the Word of God. In the final analysis, the mystery of the incarnation is the theological principle of adaptation. The Word of God, bound himself to the history, culture, traditions, and religion of his own people."[394] The Word of God, in other words, assumed not only what pertained to the human race, but also what was proper to the Jewish race. He inherited its natural traits, its genius, its spiritual endowments and its peculiar mode of self-expression. The historicity of the incarnation demanded that Jesus be identified with his own people with heart and mind, in flesh and blood.

The liturgical renewal and adaptation can be understood only with the historical data. History teaches how to take risks with creativity and how to be prudent with novelty. If sound tradition is to be retained, while legitimate progress is encouraged, a knowledge of historical facts becomes

---

[391] Chupungco, *Liturgical Inculturation: Sacramentals*, 28.
[392] Aylward Shorter, *Toward a Theology of Inculturation* (London: Geoffrey Chapman, 1988), 5-6.
[393] Chupungco, *Liturgical Inculturation: Sacramentals*, 21.
[394] Chupungco, *Cultural Adaptation of the Liturgy*, 58-59.

imperative. History of liturgical adaptation is a part of the Church's history. Interpretation of historical data is important for finding new ways of liturgical renewal.[395] Adaptation is a need to adjust to a new situation, not some abstract theological reflection. Adapting liturgical celebrations to the present day living conditions and local culture is a notable thing in the present context. Special care has to be taken, with a discernment based on the continuity of the tradition and the deep understanding of the history and theology of the liturgy and its traditions. In modifying ancient liturgical practices, it must be determined if the element to be introduced is coherent with the contextual meaning in which it is placed. The context should be understood by referring to scripture, interpretation of the holy fathers, traditions, liturgical reforms previously made and mystagogical catechesis. Here it must be verified that the new changes are homogeneous with the symbolic language, with the images and style specific on the liturgy of the particular church.

2   Inculturation of Liturgy

Liturgical inculturation may be defined as the process of inserting the texts and rites of the liturgy into the framework of the local culture. As a result, the text and rites assimilate the language, values, rituals, symbolism and artistic patterns of the people. The liturgy is inserted into the culture, history

---

[395] In the apostolic period, Christianity was a religious movement within Judaism. The Christian liturgy rooted in Jewish settings and liturgy. For instance, the "Last Supper" was a reinterpretation of the paschal meal; no longer a memorial of the exodus, but his passing over from this world to the Father for the salvation of humankind. (1 Cor.11:26). Even the apostolic Church was a convergence of many strong currents. Mainly, it was a pervasive movement to imbue the Jewish cult with the mystery of Christ. The traditional form, especially the synagogue, was not rejected, but centred on the person of Christ. This attitude of not destroying but of rectifying, and reorienting the traditions of the chosen people characterized early Christianity's approach to adaptation. At the age of Christian persecution, an adaptation of the liturgy means instilling Christian worship with salvation history. Liturgical celebration was in the mainstream of salvation history. It was during the time of persecution that the apostolic practice of breaking of the bread in private homes was institutionalized. The rich families offered their house for the liturgical celebrations. Another feature of this period was to express the apostolic tradition in the language and rituals of a pagan culture, the Greco-Roman culture. Chupungco, *Cultural Adaptation of the Liturgy*, 7-14.

and tradition of the people among whom the Church dwells. It begins to think, speak, and ritualize according to the local cultural pattern. [396]

Liturgical inculturation calls for a long reciprocal adjustment between the proclamation of the Gospel on the one hand and the religious sensibility of the celebrating assemblies on the other.[397] It operates according to basic principles emerging from the nature of Christian worship, which are: (a) Trinitarian in nature and orientation. (b) Biblically grounded in a doxological action in the power of the Holy Spirit. (c) Anamnesis of the mystery of Jesus Christ. (d) A community gathered in the name of One, Holy, Catholic and Apostolic faith. (e) The faith is that God is present in the proclaimed Word, in the sacraments, prayers as well as in the gathered assembly of worshippers. (f) Hope of the future glory and dedication to the work of building the Kingdom of God.

The Commission of Faith and Order of the WCC observes that there are certain theological, liturgical and cultural criteria for the inculturation of liturgy. The theological criteria are mainly based on the *Lex orandi* of biblical and apostolic tradition. This tradition refers to the Word of God consisting of reading and preaching in the power of the Holy Spirit; baptism with water in the name of the Trinity; Eucharist as ritual "breaking of bread" in memory of the Christ event; the community of believers and its ministries and social concerns flowing from the Eucharist. These theological criteria are rooted in the mystery of the incarnation of Christ which is the model of liturgical inculturation.[398] Liturgical criteria refers to the elements that constitute the shape of the liturgy. These elements refer to baptism, Eucharist,[399] and the other forms of public worship such

---

[396] Chupungco, *Liturgical Inculturation: Sacramentals*, 30.

[397] Joseph Gelineau, "New Models for the Eucharistic Prayer as Praise of All the Assembly," *Studia Liturgica*, 27, no.1 (1997): 79.

[398] Commission of Faith and Order, WCC, "Towards Koinonia in Worship: Consultation on the Role of Worship within the Search of Unity," *Studia Liturgica* 25, no.1 (1995): 17.

[399] The usual liturgical components of the Eucharist are: the reading and preaching of the word, intercession for the whole church and the world and in accord with the actions of the Lord at last Supper: anamneses, words of institution, communion of saints. The basic liturgical components of baptism that emerge from tradition are: proclamation of Scripture, invocation of the Holy Spirit, renunciation of evil, profession of faith in the

as the service of the Word, and the prayer of the hours. Cultural criteria of liturgical inculturation are based on the components of culture and human values such as family, hospitality, and leadership, the people's pattern of language, rite, and the arts, and institutions such as rites of passage and festivals. The Church should respect what is honest, noble and beautiful in every culture, but not everything good in culture is necessarily suited for the liturgy.[400] Furthermore, cultural elements should not remain as tokens or as alien bodies that do not relate to Christian worship.

In the modern world, because of the rapid advancement of facilities for communication and technological development, there is a marked interaction between cultures taking place. The mass media has globalized the cultures. Almost every culture has come into contact with other cultures and has been influenced by them. In this process of interplay of cultures, one culture absorbs elements from other cultures.[401] The cultural adaptation is a part of the missionary experience of the Church.[402] There are two methods of adaptation. One is substitution and the other is assimilation. The former was carried out by replacing pagan cultic elements with Christian ones. The process of substitution had its rationale, for there was a similarity of themes or analogy between the one and the other. By the method of assimilation, the Church adopted pagan rituals and gestures into which she could infuse a Christian meaning.[403]

There are three ways of handling the question of inculturating liturgical texts. The first is by translation. The second is by the revision of existing

---

Trinity, and the use of the water in the name of the Father, and of the Son and of the Holy Spirit. Commission of Faith and Order, "Towards Koinonia in Worship," 17.

[400] Commission of Faith and Order, "Towards Koinonia in Worship," 18.
[401] Koodapuzha, *Eastern Theological Reflection in India,* 11.
[402] Chupungco, *Cultural Adaptation of the Liturgy,* 14.
[403] Chupungco, *Cultural Adaptation of the Liturgy,* 23-24. For example, the celebration of Christmas is derived from the substitution process of the celebration related to the birth of the true sun of Justice, replacing the feast of the birth of the sun-God in Mithraic religion. Facing the East during prayer, was a Mediterranean custom inspired by solar cults. The Arabic and Ethiopian versions of the apostolic tradition of Hippolytus instruct the baptized and to face the east as they profess faith in the Holy Trinity. The Christian custom of praying towards the east and of orienting churches toward it is a vestige of a similar custom in solar religions

texts, and the third is by original composition. To define translation, it is useful to review its chief elements. Translation consists of re-expressing in the receptor language the message of the source language. The source language of the liturgy contains the original message. The receptor language is the language currently employed by the liturgy for a particular assembly. The message is the doctrine that the church intended to convey to the assembly through the text that had been originally prepared for it. Liturgical text can also mirror the traditions and culture of the people they address. The purpose of liturgical translation is to communicate the message of salvation to believers and express the prayer of the Church to the Lord. Liturgical translation has become the voice of the Church. It is not sufficient that a liturgical translation merely reproduces the expressions and ideas of the original text, rather it must faithfully communicate to a given people, and in their own language, that which the Church, by means of this given text, originally intended to communicate to another people in another time.[404]

Inculturation does not justify the mutilation of the message of the gospel or any kind of syncretism. The content of the Gospel remains unchanged, only the modes of its presentation can change. Without compromising the integrity of Christian faith, inculturation should embrace all aspects of Christianity and the whole life of the Church including theology, liturgy and the structures of the Church. There are mainly two guiding principles for incorporation that are compatible with the Gospel and communion with the universal Church. Inculturation is primarily for those who have accepted the faith, that they may live the faith in the context of their culture, in a way more congenial to them. The purpose of inculturation is the transformation or purification of every culture in the light of the Gospel.

2.1 Liturgical Inculturation in the Malankara Church

In the account of the Malankara Church, inculturation is a historic process because of its interaction with various ecclesiastical groups as mentioned

---

[404] Bradshaw, *The New SCM Dictionary of Liturgy and Worship,* 245-246.

in the previous chapter. Very often in the past there was limited success among the Indian churches in experimenting with liturgical adaptation; this might have been due to a historical situation wherein to non-Indian Christians used to forms of worship wrapped in Western garb Indian external modalities almost seemed like a foreign religion. Interestingly, another curious factor might sometimes come into play: the caste identity and usage of caste-based terminologies in the liturgy often emerge as a kind of stumbling block to the process of adaptation. For instance, the usage of the term "OM" in Christian worship. This word is a Hindu-Aryan expression literally signifying what is related to God. However, in its more practical usage, it is a purely high-caste Hindu symbolic expression of Deity. This, of course, can understandably be off-putting to those of the so-called low-caste populace who are embracing Christianity. The expression "OM" has now come to be used in practice among Hindus to denote their own belief in a manner similar to our customary use of the sign of the cross.[405] Generally, the term "Indian" is not to be identified with Hindu religion; Indianisation is not Hinduisation. In the Indian culture, Indianisation of the liturgy means being understood in the contemporary context by incorporating cultural elements.

The formation of the MTC and the translation of the Eucharistic liturgy into Malayalam is a visible expression of inculturation in Malankara Church. The reformation ideals motivated the leaders to find the necessity of more translated prayers and accommodation of local cultural elements in the liturgy. They took the initiative to shorten the liturgy without compromising the content, simplified and altered it for the active participation of the people. The reforms of the liturgy was in essence translations and adaptations of earlier texts, not new compositions or wholly innovative rites. They tended toward simplification of what had been very complex material.[406] In their move to a vernacular liturgy, they did indeed introduce changes. It was not for the sake of changes; rather, it

---

[405] Podipara. *Reflections on Liturgy,* 292.
[406] J. Barrington Bates, "Expressing What Christians Believe: Anglican Principles for Liturgical Revision," *Anglican Theological Review,* (March, 1992): 455.

was a result of gradual and systematic study. When we analyse the whole scene of liturgical inculturation and translations, the following aspects are very clearly employed in its process: Simplicity of the liturgical prayers for the active involvement of the common mass, Conformity with the year old traditions of the Church, Language of the liturgy made simple in sanction with Scripture, avoiding over dramatization of rituals and finally endorsed by mutual consent through the administrative bodies of the Church. Of the basic nature, Liturgy is "of the People." However, it is further rendered both significant and authoritative through common agreement on the liturgy by the relevant ecclesiastical administrative bodies.[407] The MTC further translated its liturgy into various languages to accommodate members from other ethnic and linguistic background. Critically speaking, however, the Church has considerably to move forward in the whole area of inculturation.[408]

2.2 Liturgical Adaptation in the Mar Thoma Church

The liturgy must be consistent with the Gospel message and Christian traditions while also remaining relevant to the life of the people. In the quest for authenticity, the relationship between worship and culture is of particular importance. For a sound liturgical adaptation and revision, a theological, historical, and pastoral investigation into each aspect of the liturgy is essential. As already seen, the reformation in the Malankara Church launched a renewed awareness of Scripture, liturgy (worship), mission and culture. While retaining the essential structure and character of the West Syrian liturgical traditions, the pioneers of reformation introduced changes in the liturgy conforming to the ideals of reformation. A major concern for the reformation in this whole process was that participation in, and understanding of, the liturgy should rest solidly on

---

[407] www.anglicantheologicalreview.org/static/pdf/articles/bates.pdf (accessed December 08, 2015).
[408] An attempt of changes in the liturgy always caused disturbance in the Church in the history. There is a tension between the views of traditionalist and liberal wing in the Church. Interview with Joseph Mar Barnabas on July 10, 2013.

the foundation of Scripture and patristic sources. In due course, as a result of evangelistic work, people from different cultural and linguistic regions such as Dalits (Tamil Nadu, Karnataka, Andhra Pradesh) and Tribal regions (Orissa, Madhya Pradesh, Chhattisgarh) became members of the Church. Accordingly, in order to meet the spiritual and liturgical needs of these new members, the Eucharistic liturgy of the Church is translated and simplified.

The liturgical adaptation is not an option, but a theological imperative arising from incarnational exigency. Inculturation is a long process which requires discernment and a balanced approach. It is not the prerogative of a few experts, but must involve the whole people. It must come from the faith experience of the community of the faithful. The Church must incarnate itself in every race, as Christ incarnated himself in the Jewish race.[409] The Church cannot remain as an alien to the people with whom it lives. The MTC through its incarnational model of mission[410] enters into the sphere of people with the Gospel but from other cultures. The Church becomes incarnated in her socio-cultural settings. Even though the Church adapted many Hindu cultural features into its liturgy[411] she often remains hesitant to incorporate more cultural elements in the mission centres, especially those existing among newly converted Dalits and aboriginal Adivasi. Still, the converted Christians from the regions of Andhra, Orissa, Madhya Pradesh, and Karnataka use the same Syrian liturgy in translated form; this is the agreed procedure arising from fear that if the liturgy were to be revised, it would shake Church discipline.[412] The liturgy not only involves texts and rites, but also music, liturgical space and cycles of time. All of

---

[409] Chupungco, *Cultural Adaptation of the Liturgy*, 59.
[410] Christ became a human in all things, in order to set an example for the Church to which he gave the mission to extend the mystery of his incarnation in time and space. The incarnation is a paradigm of mission for the Church.
[411] Tying of the minnu in the marriage ceremony.
[412] One of the reasons of the split in the Mar Thoma Church in 1961 and the formation of the St. Thomas Evangelical Church of India was mainly in connection with liturgical revision on the basis of liturgy and doctrines.

these mentioned should be shaped according to both liturgical criteria[413] and the requirements of local culture.[414] It is, after all, in worship that the Church experiences and expresses the deepest source of its life. Indeed, it is in worship that the Church is whole and is one.[415]

As an important element of a reformed and reforming Church, the liturgical movement within the Church must logically form part of ongoing general reform. This means a necessity to reform preaching and its underlying theology along with ministries. The liturgical renewal should aim to help the congregation fully and consciously to participate in worship. A pluralistic view of culture and openness to the traditions and rituals of other people foster the universality of the Church. In the MTC, because of its long existence in the land, a certain degree of inculturation of worship has already taken place. But the search for a more authentic and contextual liturgy should be continued. This is essential, especially for the people who embrace Christianity from other faiths. The Church uses both indigenous and western hymns in worship. They are non-liturgical songs, but are quite often used during worship.[416] In view of liturgical renewal and enrichment of the common worship of the Church, the first necessary step is that of gathering all that data relative to the need for revision. Then there is needed an educational programme to deepen liturgical understanding, which, among other things, calls for the development of material. Producing liturgically rich language is one aspect of this revision, but the revision should also respond to the Church's common needs by keeping ever in sight its multi-cultural, multi-ethnic, multi-lingual and multi-generational nature.

---

[413] Commission of Faith and Order, WCC, "Towards Koinonia in Worship: Consultation on the Role of Worship within the Search of Unity," *Studia Liturgica* 25, no.1 (1995): 17.
[414] Cultural criteria based on the components of culture are human values such as family, hospitality, and leadership, the language pattern of the people, rite, arts, architecture and institutions such as rites of feast and festivals. The Church should respect what is honest, noble and beautiful in every culture, but not everything good in culture is necessarily suited for the liturgy. Furthermore, cultural elements should not remain as tokens that do not relate to Christian worship. Commission of Faith and Order, "Towards Koinonia in Worship," 18.
[415] Commission of Faith and Order, "Towards Koinonia in Worship," 19.
[416] Bradshaw, *The New SCM Dictionary of Liturgy and Worship,* 296.

Mission and Liturgy

Lastly, therefore, liturgical reform can only fulfil its ultimate purpose by accepting that there must be ongoing need for reform in both Church and community. "Liturgy expresses what Christians believe. To change the liturgy therefore runs the risk of changing doctrine - or at least those doctrines which worshippers regularly hear and absorb and which become part of their Christian identity."[417] Liturgy is a component of community formation, and therefore the Church should consider the following things when it revises its liturgy. Firstly, it has to enhance the celebration of Christian life. Christian life is nurtured by participation in the Holy Table, the reception of the Word of God as well as the strengthening fellowship of the people of God; liturgical renewal helps worshippers to live life to its fullness. Secondly, it has to reflect the varieties of cultures and traditions within the Church. An ancient liturgy is primarily a tradition of the Church. While retaining the richness of the traditional liturgy, there should also be space to accommodate the various cultural elements of a region. The criteria for adaptation is biblical and cultural. The scope of a new liturgy is a matter of study. The easiest procedure would be to formulate, in a liturgical spirit, new rites for the sacraments by Christianizing the cultural or even religious rites of the people among whom a given liturgy functions. Adaptation in music, architecture, etc. should be encouraged in the Church. The Church has to appreciate the wealth of the diversity and the common vocation of the Church to build up the body of Christ and enhance fellowship and relationship.

The MTC needs more flexibility to admit variations according to different cultures. Without sacrificing the essential theological content and message of the liturgy, the Church should provide cultural expressions, reinterpretations, modifications, and variations to its liturgy.[418] The

---

[417] John R. K. Fenwick and Bryan D. Spinks, *Worship in Transition: The Liturgical Movement in the Twentieth Century* (New York: Continuum, 1995), 169.
[418] The Dioceses of North American and Europe published a shorter version of the Eucharistic liturgy for the use of churches in the diaspora region. There is an openness to liturgical renewal and adaptation of the new elements in the liturgy. It is a sign of progress towards the reforming tradition of the Church. With the consent of the Diocesan Bishop, women assisted the celebrant in the Eucharistic service. It is a novel practice in

essential message of the reformation and the programme of reform have a universal and lasting value. The revision of the liturgical rites should be distinguished by noble simplicity, brevity, clarity, sobriety and practicality. One of the difficulties encountered when working on inculturating the liturgical ordo is how to distinguish between what is immutable in the liturgy and what is subject to change. All liturgical rites are celebrated in a particular culture; no liturgy can be celebrated in a cultural vacuum. Such a void would lead people to miss the theological meaning and consequence of Christ's Incarnation. Therefore there is an underlying principle of liturgical unity, which might be formulated as "unity in essentials and diversity in cultural form." Since the MTC is a widespread Church, there is an urgent need for addressing matters of liturgical renewal with increased seriousness.

3   Contextual Liturgies and its Relevance

Even though Christ was born in Jewish culture, the mystery of His incarnation is the model and the mandate for the contextualization of Christian worship. God can be, and is, encountered in the local cultures of the world. A given culture's values and patterns, insofar as they are consonant with the values of the Gospel, can be used to express the meaning and purpose of Christian worship. Contextualization is a necessary task for the mission of the Church in the world, so that the Gospel can be ever more deeply rooted in diverse local cultures.[419] Among the various methods of contextualization, that of dynamic equivalence is particularly useful. It involves re-expressing components of Christian worship with something from a local culture that has an equal meaning, value and function. Dynamic equivalence goes far beyond mere translation; it involves understanding

---

the MTC since women are not allowed to enter into *madbaha* (sanctuary). Interview with the Diocesan Bishop Mar Theodosius on August 28, 2015. According to his opinion, the Church is open enough to accept new practices which is not contradictory to the biblical truths and constitution of the Church. He further said that the democratic constitutional nature of the Church gives enough space for adapting contextual and relevant practices.

[419] Lutheran World Federation, "Nairobi Statement on Worship and Culture: Contemporary Challenges and Opportunities," *Studia Liturgica* 27, no.1 (1997): 90.

Mission and Liturgy

the fundamental meanings both of the elements of worship and of the local culture, and enabling the meanings and actions of worship to be 'encoded' and re-expressed in the language of local culture.[420] In applying the method of dynamic equivalence, the following procedure may be followed. First, the liturgical ordo (basic shape) should be examined, its theology, history, basic elements, and cultural background. Second, those elements of the ordo that can be subjected to dynamic equivalence without prejudice to their meaning should be determined. Third, those components of culture that are able to re-express the Gospel and the liturgical ordo in an adequate manner should be studied. Fourth, the spiritual and pastoral benefits the people will derive from the changes should be considered.[421]

The method of creative assimilation is another aspect of contextualization. This consists of adding pertinent components of local culture to the liturgical ordo in order to enrich its original core. Unlike dynamic equivalence, creative assimilation enriches the liturgical ordo - not by culturally re-expressing its elements, but by adding to its new elements from local culture. In contextualization, the fundamental values and meanings of both Christianity and of local culture must be respected. An important criterion for dynamic equivalence and creative assimilation is that sound or accepted liturgical traditions are preserved in order to keep unity with the universal Church's tradition of worship, while progress inspired by pastoral needs is encouraged. On the side of culture, it is understood that not everything can be integrated with Christian worship, but only those elements, that are connatural to the liturgical ordo. Elements borrowed from local culture should always undergo critique and purification, which can be achieved through the use of biblical typology.[422] In considering the scope of alternative liturgies, its aim is to give expression to different facets of liturgical tradition or modern life that are not considered as common. Culture, technology, and ideology influence the shape of creative liturgies.

---

[420] Lutheran World Federation, "Nairobi Statement on Worship and Culture," 90-91.
[421] Chupungco, *Cultural Adaptation of the Liturgy, 83-84.* Pecklers, *Dynamic Equivalence,* 128-129.
[422] Lutheran World Federation, "Nairobi Statement on Worship and Culture," 91.

Creative liturgies are very often associated with contextualization. Culture and ideology affect creative texts. Symbolic dance is an art form able to convey the spirit of joy, sorrow or gratitude present in the liturgical rite. The mimetic interpretation of a biblical passage can have a catechetical value. Audio visuals can engrave the message more deeply in the memory of the assembly.[423]

---

[423] Chupungco, *Liturgical Inculturation Sacramentals,* 52-53.

Chapter. 7

Scripture and Liturgy: Convergence and Congruence for Mission

Even though, the geographical and cultural landscape of the MTC widens consistently through the migration and evangelisation process, the reformed Eucharistic liturgy is the centre of its liturgical life and mission. The Church communicates its theology and proclaims its faith through the liturgy, especially by liturgical prayers, preaching, teaching, singing, using signs and symbols. The reformed liturgy is rich in theological content, simple and easy to follow, which helps the believers to actively participate in the liturgical celebrations. As mentioned in the earlier chapter, an integration of liturgy and Scripture in the life and mission of the Church mark it as a bridging Church in between the Orthodox and Protestant traditions. The liturgical celebration binds the Mar Thoma community together irrespective of its ethnic plurality and cultural differences and it motivates the Church to discover new avenues for mission. An awareness of the uniqueness of the liturgy encourages the faithful to participate in it actively. The signs and symbols, the dramatic way of presenting the salvific act of Christ and entire liturgical settings enable the faithful to experience the presence of God. It calls for a life pleasing to God and beneficial to all by being the children of peace in the name of the Trinity.[424]

The liturgy cannot be comprehended fully without a clear understanding of the Bible. It is essential for a meaningful liturgical celebration and for

---

[424] In the final benediction, in the name of Trinity, the celebrant dismiss the faithful with an assurance of the presence of God in their life and reminds them of their spiritual responsibility to be ambassadors of peace and reconciliation. "My beloved brothers and sisters, I commend you the grace and blessings of the Holy and glorious Trinity depart in peace with gifts and blessings that you have received in the atoning sacrifice of the Lord…" Titus II, *Qurbana Thaksa,* 40.

an active participation. Since the MTC holds the position of a bridging Church in between the Oriental Orthodox and Protestant Churches, it is important to understand how these two traditions hold Scripture in its very life. Hence, this chapter studies the integration of Scripture and liturgy and also the lectionary of the Church. Further, it critically analysis the various characteristics' of the reformed liturgy of the Church.

1 Scripture and Liturgy in the Mar Thoma Church

The proclamation of the Bible and the administration of the sacraments are the foundations of the Christian Church. The Bible and liturgy are intrinsically related to each other and both are mutually complementary.[425] A liturgy is a Patristic synthesis on the basis of valued traditions and sacred scriptures. It is difficult to understand unless one is familiar with Scripture. For a thorough understanding of the liturgy, it is essential to know the biblical world, sacred history, historical context, content of the books, the metaphors and symbols of the biblical world and the biblical ethics.[426] The Constitution on the Sacred Liturgy, *Sacrosanctum Concilium* teaches: "sacred scripture is of greatest importance in the celebration of the liturgy. For it is from Scripture that lessons are read and explained in the homily, and psalms are sung; the prayers, collects, and liturgical songs are scriptural in their inspiration and their force; and it is from the Scriptures that actions and signs derive their meaning."[427] In the liturgy, the symbolic importance of Scripture is very evident. For instance, when the celebrant reads the gospel in the liturgical celebration, it is believed that the person of Jesus himself speaks through the celebrant.[428] It is the revelation of Jesus as Christ that makes Scripture the inspiring and empowering source of

---

[425] Bradshaw and Johnson, *The Eucharistic Liturgies*, 28-29,
[426] Podipara, *Reflections on Liturgy,* 19.
[427] *Sacrosanctum Concilium* No.24.
[428] "Through the readings the Church's belief is that Christ is truly speaking in the present moment amidst his assembled body: Christ is present in his word, since it is he himself who speaks when the holy Scriptures are read in the Church" (CS.7). In liturgy, the scriptural passages are not merely read, studied, or personally reflected upon but, rather, the Word comes alive amidst a people, making present a living encounter with the Lord Jesus. Christ is present in the liturgy, through the power of the Holy Spirit, because of the

meaning in liturgy's symbolic words and actions. The Bible inspires the content of the texts of the liturgy and the meaning of its symbolic actions.

Scripture has influenced the formation of the liturgy. It is noted that the Jewish liturgy is the womb from which the Christian liturgy is born.[429] The original setting of Scripture was in the liturgy, the ritual worship of the community. It is on the basis of the Old Testament that Christian liturgy is derived initially. The place in which Israel most directly experienced and received its identity was in the liturgical setting.[430] Later, by following the tradition of worships at synagogues, the Christian Church began to read out Scripture portions in the midst of the liturgical gatherings. Most of the early Christian believers were from the Jewish background. They went to the Jewish temple or to the Synagogue in order to pray and hear the Word of God spoken through the law and the prophets (Acts.3:1-2). They gathered in the house to break the bread (Acts.2:46-47). Gradually they gathered together in the Christian Church for the ministry of the word and the administration of the sacraments. In the early Christian communities, faith was transmitted through the liturgy.[431] By a thorough examination, one can understand that Scripture itself is a liturgy or creedal statements of the people of God.

1.1 The Orthodox and Protestant Approaches to Scripture

Since the MTC stands in between the Oriental Orthodox and Protestant Churches, it is essential to understand how these two traditions hold Scripture in their very life. It is to be noticed that in the Eastern churches'

Paschal Mystery that every celebration of the rites enacts, affording all the opportunity to recognize that mystery as "present and active within us" (CS.35.2).
[429] Bradshaw and Johnson, *The Eucharistic Liturgies*, 1-24.
[430] The formation of the scriptures of Israel really only received its impetus with the destruction of the temple that had been the centre and focus of Israel's spiritual life and identity. But even before that we can see the liturgical origins of many texts: the psalms; the first chapter of Genesis; the importance of sanctuaries and high places; festivals. It was in the narration and recounting of its greatest founding events that Israel reaffirmed its identity. Damien Casey, "Liturgy Matters: Liturgy and Scripture as the Mirrors of Catholicity," *Australian e Journal of Theology* 4 (February 2005): 1.
[431] Kuttiyil, *Liturgy for our Times*, 16.

more importance was given to the liturgy than to Scripture. In fact the liturgy and Scripture are inseparable, so equal importance should be given to the liturgy and to Scripture. In fact, these two are inseparable in the understanding of the Eastern tradition.[432] The early Fathers of the West Syrian tradition[433] had played a great part in the development of liturgies. The Eastern Church considered the Bible as a part of the apostolic tradition, which had a living continuity with their faith experiences. For them, the liturgy and the writings of the Church Fathers were the basis for the understanding of Scripture.[434] In the Orthodox tradition, Scripture is part of the living tradition. A tradition means the whole teaching of the Church, whether in the Church Councils, official dogmas, the Bible, or the liturgy. A tradition is not merely an aggregate of the dogmas, rites and institutions of the Church. It is dynamic and living, unchanging and constant, the revelation of the Holy Spirit in the Church.[435] As Timothy Ware put it, tradition has a broad, comprehensive meaning: "to an Orthodox tradition means the books of the Bible; it means the Creed, it means the decrees of the Ecumenical Councils and the writings of the Church Fathers; it means the Canons, the Service Books, the Holy icons- in fact, the whole system of doctrine, the Church government, worship and art which Orthodoxy has articulated over the ages."[436] The Orthodox Christians of today visualise themselves as heirs and guardians to a great inheritance received from the past, and they believe that it was their duty to transmit their inheritance

---

[432] Tradition means a dynamic movement of God in history. For which liturgy is the principal means of transmission. It is the possession of the Church, and lived out in the Church, which can create competing visions of what tradition is or who is to interpret it. From the perspective of the Church, "tradition is a continued engagement and interpretation of Scripture in light of the Church's worship, experience of living God and practice of the Christian life." Yves Congar, *Tradition and Traditions: An Historical and Theological Essay*, trans. Michael Naseby and Thomas Rainborough (New York: McMillian, 1967), 434. A. N. Williams, "Tradition." in *Oxford Handbook of Systematic Theology*, eds. John Webster, Kathryn Tanner, and Iain Torrance (London: Oxford University, 2007), 363.
[433] Ephraim the Syrian, Aphrahat, Isaac of Nineveh and Isaac of Antioch.
[434] J. Mayendorff, *Byzantine Theology: Historical Trends and Doctrinal Themes* (New York: Fordham University, 1979), 8.
[435] Robert Letham, *Through Western Eyes- Eastern Orthodoxy: A Reformed Perspective* (Wales: Mentor, 2007), 177.
[436] Timothy Ware, *The Orthodox Church* (London: Penguin, 1969), 204.

Mission and Liturgy

unimpaired to the future generations. The Orthodox Christian accepts the Bible as the word of God, a record of Divine will. As Stylianopoulos says, "an Orthodox approach has to do with a comprehensive and balanced appreciation of the Holy Scripture in its own nature, authority and witness as the Word of God, while committed to the standards of critical study and freedom of research."[437] The Eastern Church places theology in the context of the Church, since the Bible was given to the Church in the first place.[438] The Orthodox consider the Church has the authority to interpret the Bible since she is the only authentic depository of apostolic *kerygma*.[439]

Among Protestants, Scripture and tradition are viewed as competitive. The traditions of the Church are considered as inconsequential. Protestants view the Bible as the standard by which all Christian behaviour must be measured. This belief is commonly referred to as "*Sola Scriptura*."[440] The Protestants consider the Bible as the only authority for the Christian faith. Traditions are valid only when they are based on Scripture and are in full agreement with Scripture. They believe that the Bible alone is the source of God's special revelation to humankind and necessary for our salvation from sin. The Bible is the supreme authority in all matters of faith and conduct, and the highest court of appeal when controversial questions were

---

[437] T.G Stylianopoulos, *The New Testament: An Orthodox Perspective. Vol. One: Scripture, Tradition, Hermeneutics* (Brookline: Massachusetts: Holy Cross Orthodox, 1997), 7.

[438] He argues that the Orthodox view of Scripture is dynamic. "God's revelation dealt with persons, patriarchs, prophets, priests, and ultimately with Jesus Christ. An authority was not usually accorded to the biblical books at the time they were composed, but came gradually over the course of centuries. Thus behind the books of the Bible lies a dynamic history of oral tradition." Stylianopoulos, *The New Testament: An Orthodox Perspective*, 7-13.

[439] Clendenin, *Eastern Orthodox Theology*, 112.

[440] The phrase *sola scriptura* is from the Latin. The term *sola* means alone, ground, base, and the word *scriptura* means writings which often refers to Scriptures. This phrase denotes that Scripture alone is authoritative for the faith and practice of the Christian and the Bible is complete, authoritative, and true. *Sola scriptura* was the rallying cry of the Protestant Reformation. This is not as much of an argument against tradition as argument against unbiblical, extra-biblical and/or anti-biblical doctrines. *Sola scriptura* does not nullify the concept of Church traditions. Rather, it gives a solid foundation on which to base Church traditions. For Protestants, traditions to be valid, that must not be in disagreement with God's Word. Norman L. Geisler and Ralph MacKenzie, *Roman Catholics and Evangelicals: Agreements and Differences* (Grand Rapids, MI: Baker Books, 1995), 177-202.

raised. The Protestants believe that the Holy Spirit is the primary author of Scripture, who does not and cannot err. The Word of God has priority and all human opinion must submit to the voice of the Holy Spirit speaking through Scripture. The "Westminster Confession of Faith"[441] affirms that the sixty six books in the Bible are an "inspiration of God to be the rule of faith and Life."[442] Protestants hold the view that the authority of the Church comes not solely from apostolic succession but from the Bible. Spiritual power and authority do not rest in the hands of a mere man but in the very Word of God.[443]

1.2 Integration of Scripture and the Liturgy

The liturgy of the MTC is a combination of Scripture and tradition. The liturgy of the word and the liturgy of the Eucharist are inseparably united. The Bible illuminates the mystery of the Eucharist, just as the Eucharist is what actualizes and fulfils the saving truth of Scripture. As mentioned earlier, the translation of the Bible into Malayalam language and its availability to the common people made a revival in the Malankara Church. Openness of the CMS missionaries in interpreting the Bible and its exposition led to a renewed understanding of the Church and its mission. The pioneers of reformation reviewed the faith and practice of the Malankara Church in the light of a renewed understanding of Scripture.[444]

---

[441] The Westminster Assembly was a council of divines, called by Parliament to reform the government, worship and discipline of the Church of England, Wales and Ireland, initially to defend "The Thirty Nine Articles of religion of the Church of England" against false aspersions and calumnies. It is instituted as a part of the covenanted uniformity in religion between the churches of Christ in the Kingdoms of Scotland, England, and Ireland. It is approved by the General Assembly in 1647, and ratified and established by acts of parliament 1649 and 1690. This assembly considered the Trinitarian and Christological pronouncements of the first six ecumenical councils to be in harmony with the Bible.

[442] Thirty-nine books in the Old Testament and Twenty-seven books in the New Testament. *The Westminster Confession of Faith*, Chapter.1, http://www.pcaac.org/wp-content/uploads/2012/11/WCFScriptureProofs.pdf (accessed September 07, 2015).

[443] Geisler *Roman Catholics and Evangelicals: Agreements and Differences,* 177-202.

[444] A detailed examination on the liturgical renewal of the Church in the light of reformation is dealt in the Second Chapter.

Mission and Liturgy

The Church maintains an intrinsic relationship and unity between the liturgy and Scripture in its spiritual life. It is the Word of God that gives authority for any sacrament; therefore, in the Church, readings from Scripture are done with great devotion and solemnity. The Psalms, Pauline Epistles, and gospel are read and the congregation is asked to listen to the proclamation of the living Word of God with reverence.[445] The Church keeps a balance between Scripture and tradition in its very life and ministry. The liturgical traditions of the Church as per the scriptural interpretation is a unique character of the MTC. The Church gratefully remembers the contributions of the Syrian Church Fathers and values their liturgical contributions to the spiritual growth of the community. The Church always gives importance to the teachings of the Church Fathers like Aphrem, Mar Bala and uses their prayers and petitions in its liturgical worship. The early Eastern Fathers who composed the prayers of the liturgy were soaked in Scripture. And the congregation, both literate and illiterate, listened to these meditations year after year throughout the liturgical cycle and in repeated prayers. The words of the Bible became engrafted in the consciousness of the ordinary believer more than any formal teaching. Here chants and liturgical hymns play a major role. Through the liturgical songs believers memorize scriptural truth and handed it over to the subsequent generations. There is a liturgical conditioning that happens in worship. This liturgical conditioning of the mind helps the Bible achieve a more profound effectiveness so as to touch deeper levels of consciousness in the believers.[446] The Bible is the base of the liturgy of the Church and the liturgy is redolent with biblical passages. Hence one can say that the liturgy reiterates Scripture. Without Scripture, liturgy is nothing or in a vacuum. The Bible is an indispensable source of the language of the liturgy, of its signs, and of its prayers, especially in the psalms. The liturgy is of crucial importance because it touches upon the source and sustenance of Christian belief. The liturgy is, however, the mirror of the faith that the individual

---

[445] Mathew, "The Baptismal Liturgy of the Mar Thoma Syrian Church of Malabar," 118.
[446] Geevarghese Mar Theodosius, "Mar Thoma Church," in *The Mar Thoma Church: Tradition and Modernity,* 101.

holds in the community. It transcends the limits of space and time not in a historical and disembodied sense, but in the faith of this person, and this community remains in communion with the Church as a whole. As mentioned earlier, the Eastern liturgies are dramatic in form. Prayerful preparation and an active participation are essential for the effectiveness of liturgical celebration. One could understand the spiritual richness in worship only by full and repeated participation along with a community nurtured in the same liturgical tradition. No true liturgy can be performed with words alone, for words are only one of the elements in liturgical worship. The gestures of the priest and the laity, Kiss of Peace, bowing of the heads, signing of the cross, and reverence paid to the Eucharistic elements etc., are part of the rich liturgical act of the worship in the Mar Thoma community which is rooted in the biblical teachings.

The reading of Scripture takes up a significant part of the worship. It is surrounded with a certain reverence and ceremony. It shapes the language of prayer. The reading and interpretation of Scripture form a part of the ongoing conversation between the worshipping community and God.[447] The Church considers the Bible as a sacramental word. The Bible is the Word of God in a sacramental sense, uniting the faithful to Christ, the one true Word of God. It brings Christ to believers.[448] As a sacramental word, "it draws the faithful into Christ's presence and invites them to be transformed into his image. It opens the possibility of relationship between the divine and the human."[449] The Bible is born in the Church and for the Church and tradition bears from the very beginning the seal of the Church. It is in the Church that Scripture and tradition appear and are contained. Thus Scripture, tradition and the Church are linked through an inner relationship, a harmonious co-existence, a mutual supplementation and agreement.[450] The teaching of tradition is part of ecclesiology; indeed the

---

[447] Stephen Conway, *Living the Eucharist: Affirming Catholism and the Liturgy* (London: Darton, Longman and Todd, 2001), 29.
[448] Dyk, "Proclamation: Revelation, Christology," 66-67.
[449] Dyk, "Proclamation: Revelation, Christology," 65-66.
[450] Alexander, *The Mar Thoma Church: Tradition and Modernity,* 125.

very heart of ecclesiology of the Church. The Church has the obligation to see that Orthodoxy is maintained in the worship and liturgy corresponds to the faith. In the liturgy the faith of the Church is expressed in a symbolic form. The Church has to be sensitive that legitimate variations and adaptations must provide a substantial unity of the liturgy.

1.3 The Lectionary of the Mar Thoma Church

A lectionary is a table of readings from the Bible authorized for use in public worship. It helps the faithful to have a systematic pattern of understanding and meditating the Word of God. This liturgical calendar is developed as a theological tool to educate believers in the liturgical context. Through the lectionary, the Church commemorates the salvific act of Christ - birth, life, ministry, passion, death, resurrection, ascension - and awaits his second coming, thereby affirming the celebration of life in its fullness through Christ. The Christian year is far more significant than a mere calendar. The life of Christ is envisioned within a year. Hence the liturgical year is an attempt to provide ample resources to grow unto Christ through liturgical activities. It is a means for grace, whereby the faithful can understand time in its fullness and immerses oneself into the mystery of redemption. It is also an instrument of living the fullness of faith and holds the life of the Church and faith community together.[451] According to Kevin Irvin, the lectionary is very important in Christian nurturing because "it structures the hearing of the faithful and help them to discover continually in different ways and contexts who God is for them."[452] The variety of Scripture reading from the lectionary disclose various images and likenesses of God to the faithful in their contemporary life. When taken together, the readings make a concrete theological statement about the observance of the liturgical season. In short, through the lectionary, the Church reveals the mystery of incarnation and the redemption of Christ

---

[451] Clergy Conference, *Self-formation through Worship and Sacraments* (Thiruvalla, Christava Sahitya Samithi, 2008), 35.
[452] Irwin, *Models of the Eucharist,* 104-105.

by the power of the Holy Spirit and helps the faithful to experience it systematically in the settings of the liturgy.

The MTC gives space for reading and interpreting the Bible in its liturgical celebration. There are mainly four readings during the celebration of the Eucharistic service. The first reading is from the Old Testament and second reading is from the New Testament,[453] which are usually read by laity from the congregation. The third reading is from the letters of St. Paul or from any other apostle, which is read by the deacon or lay ministrant at the left side of the Altar. The Gospel reading is taken in a solemn way by the celebrant, which is considered as the most important part of the worship. When the Gospel is read out from the centre of the madbaho, the congregation stands in reverence and awe. The lectionary which is being used in the Church is a common lectionary prepared by the Commission on Worship and Mission of the Communion of Churches in India (CCI).[454] From the year 2000 onwards, this lectionary is being systematically arranged as a three year cycle reading programme in which more than five million people are participating. This lectionary is arranged in the background of reformed and West Syrian liturgical traditions[455] of Christendom, which is a visible sign of unity and common mission.

---

[453] The Old Testament draws the plan of God for the redemption of His people in history, and the New Testaments reveals the redemptive action of God in Christ through the Church for the redemption of the whole world. The Church accepts the sixty six books of the Old and New Testament which is the basis of all theological subjects and proclaims the essentials for salvation.

[454] Communion of Churches in India is an ecumenical body comprised of three major reformed Churches in India: the Mar Thoma Church, the Church of South India and the Church of North India.

[455] The Syrian Orthodox Church lectionary system is a cycle of biblical readings for the church year. In the Syrian Orthodox Church these readings are for a calendar year beginning with the *Qudosh 'Idto* (Sanctification of the Church) that falls on the eighth Sunday before Christmas. Both the Old and the New Testament books are read, including the Apocrypha, except the books of Revelation, Song of Solomon, and I and II Maccabees. (For Roman Catholics: deuteron canonical (as) "apocrypha" cf. *The Jerome Biblical Commentary*, Raymond R. Brown, Joseph A. Fitzmyer, Roland E. Murphy, and O. Carm, eds (London: Geoffrey Chapman, 1970), 518-536. Scripture readings are assigned for Sundays and feast days, for each day of Lent and the Holy Weeks, for consecrating laymen and clergy to various offices of the Church, for the blessing of Holy Oil and various services such as baptisms and funerals. Generally, three Old Testament lessons, a selection from the prophets, and three readings from the New Testament are prescribed for each

Mission and Liturgy

The MTC uses the lectionary of the West Syrian tradition with certain adaptations,[456] and a theme is provided for preaching and for meditation on each Sunday. This lectionary is arranged on the basis of the salvific act of Christ's event. The liturgical year begins with the celebration of *Koodash eatho* - purification of the Church),[457] which falls on Sunday the 30th of October or on the following Sunday. After this celebration, during the following seven weeks, the Church commemorates the era of the annunciation and the birth of Christ. The ministry, miracles, and life of Christ are the themes of devotion and reading for meditation till the *Penticosta*. The *Penticosta* is followed by twenty four weeks, during which the Church contemplates various theological and biblical themes related to the doctrines, faith, mission and ministry the Church which includes fruits and gift of the Holy Spirit, commissioning of disciples, Trinity, Sacraments, Christian unity, awaiting the second coming of Christ, Christian social commitment, Christian mission, Witnessing, the ecological concerns etc., which are systematically arranged. The Church arranges the lectionary with a view that the Christian faith is given for the sustenance of Christian community, building up of the Christian Church and for the glory of the Holy Trinity. The Christian lentern days are very specifically arranged in the lectionary. These themes and readings are arranged to meditate and celebrate once in three years. In conclusion, the lectionary of the Church helps the faithful to nourish in Christian faith. The Church calendar is an instrument for the believers for studying and meditating the life of Christ,

---

Sunday and Feast day. The New Testament readings include a reading from Acts, another from the General Epistles or the Pauline Epistles, and a third reading from one of the Gospels. Varghese, West *Syrian Liturgical Theology*, 155, Rouwhorst, "Jewish Liturgical Traditions in Early Syriac Christianity," 72-93. Romeny, *Jacob of Edessa and the Syriac Culture of His Day*, 104, Dale A. Johnson, "Lectionary", Syriac Orthodox Resources, http://sor.cua.edu/Lectionary/ (accessed February 12, 2016).

[456] The Church incorporated various socially relevant themes in the liturgy such as the Ecumenical Sunday, the Mission Sunday, the Medical Mission Day, the Environmental Sunday, Diaspora Sunday, Reformation Day, Education Day, Sevika Sangham Day, Senior Citizens Day, Youth Sunday, Christian Family Dedication Day etc.

[457] Bradshaw, *The New SCM Dictionary of Liturgy and Worship*, 295-296.

which strengthens them to face the challenges of everyday life and to equip themselves for partaking in the mission of God.[458]

2   Characteristics of the Eucharistic Liturgy of the Mar Thoma Church

The current Eucharistic liturgy of the MTC has several unique features. Following are some of the characteristics of that Eucharistic liturgy.

Trinitarian in nature - The Eucharistic liturgy of the MTC is reformed in nature so as to be centred on the doctrine of Trinity.[459] Since Trinity is a paradigm of community formation and community living, it is very much emphasized in the Eucharistic liturgy. The role of the Trinity in divine salvation is profoundly presented in the ante- communion and communion service of the liturgy. Praising and glorifying the Trinity is very common in the liturgy. All the liturgical prayers are concluded with the glorification of the Father, the Son and the Holy Spirit. The blessings which are given by the celebrant during Holy Communion are mainly Trinitarian in nature. This Trinitarian emphasis in the liturgy calls for unity in the Church and thus proclaims the Church which ever endures as community for the fulfilment of Christ's salvific mission. The gathered community experiences the spirit of unity and fellowship under the inspiration of the model of that august Trinitarian community life. A Trinitarian emphasis in the Eucharistic liturgy motivates the Church to affirm plurality in the Church and calls for openness to distinctions in the world; it summons the Church to launch a mission of unity in the midst of differences and divisions.[460]

---

[458] Interview with Joseph Mar Barnabas Episcopa the Chairman of the Liturgical Commission of the MTC on 08th September 2015.

[459] In Trinity, there is only the fellowship and community of equals. "In the divine community there is no above or below, superior and inferior, but only the society of equals who are different from one another, but live together in mutual respect and self-giving love." Shirley C. Guthrie Jr, *Always Being Reforming* (London: Westminster John Knox, 2008), 37-38.

[460] During the fourth and fifth centuries when there were lot of controversies about the "person of Christ" in the Church, the doctrine of Trinity gained strength in the order of worship and teaching of the Church. Baby Varghese, "West Syrian Anaphora as an Expression of Trinitarian Doctrine," *Harp* IV, no.12 (1999): 2-3.

This liturgy is rich in theological content - As one of the Oriental Orthodox Churches, the faith, practices and theology of the Church are not documented but are embedded in the liturgy. Theology is by definition talk of God, God's words spoken, and transposed into talk about God.[461] The Church, through its liturgy talks and reveals the theology. The liturgy has an authority as a source of theology. Theology should be evolved by interpreting liturgical texts along with scriptures. An interpretation of liturgy will contribute to the Church a sound theology and an authentic liturgical life. The liturgy has a very important role in the formation of the faith of its members. This liturgy has been seen as a privileged witness of the apostolic tradition. [462]

The liturgy is Scripture oriented - An emphasis on Scripture is clearly evident in the Mar Thoma liturgy. The main thrust of reformation in the Church was an amendment or correction of the liturgy on the basis of Scripture. The Mar Thoma liturgy is built on the foundation of Scripture. Biblical imagery, Biblical echoes, allusions and parallelisms, paraphrase of Biblical passages, woven into the text abound in the prayers of the liturgy and thus the original flavour of revelation as expressed in the Bible is preserved intact.[463] The Bible, which is the basis for the formation of the liturgy, subsequently also becomes the parameter for the renewal of the liturgy in the Church. The "ministry of the Word" is a significant aspect in the Mar Thoma liturgy.[464] The Bible and the liturgy equip the faithful to participate in the mission of the Church.

The Christological nature of the liturgy - One of the most significant characteristics of the liturgy is its recurrent Christological thread emanating out of the Trinitarian theme. The liturgy is the celebration of the salvific act of Christ. Jesus Christ is the centre of the celebration of the liturgy and

---

[461] David Noel Power, *Love Without Calculation: A Reflection on Divine Kenosis* (New York: The Crossroad, 2005), 1.

[462] George Mathew, "Liturgy for the 21st Century," in *The Mar Thoma Church: Tradition and Modernity*, 118.

[463] Geevarghese Panicker and John Vellian, *A Historical Introduction to the Syriac Liturgy* (Kottayam: SEERI, 2010), 33.

[464] Alexander, *The Mar Thoma Church; Tradition and Modernity*, 113-115.

the faithful experience the living presence of Christ through their active participation in it. Majority of the prayers taken from the Bible constitute a mighty Christological affirmation.[465] Through the liturgy one can experience a living God the Father who reveals His intimate relationship with Jesus Christ. The liturgy unfolds God's plan for redemption, not only for the members of the Church, but also for the whole of humanity.

The liturgy reveals the "salvation plan of God" in a dramatic way - Every Sunday through the Eucharistic liturgy, the Church demonstrates the birth, life, ministry, passion, death, resurrection and ascension of Jesus Christ in a dramatic and systematic way. The dramatic expression of the salvific act of Christ enables the faithful to experience and participate in it subjectively. This dramatic expression is not a mere ritualistic presentation of the Christ event, rather it unfolds the divine plan of salvation in a simple and meaningful manner. The Church is very cautious about the metaphorical languages of the liturgy employed and the over dramatization of the liturgy. The Church lives in virtue of her liturgical celebration of the economy of salvation.

Active participation of the people in the liturgy - The liturgy gives emphasis to the active participation of the worshipping community. The prayers are arranged in a dialogue model. Worshippers participate in the richness of the liturgy through their active involvement in the rituals, signs and non-verbal communications. By their response to the prayers in the liturgy through the recitals and singing they make the worship quite lively. In the MTC, an ordained person does not celebrate the Holy Communion without the presence of the worshippers.[466] The Church considers the celebration of the Eucharist as a spiritual matter of the believing community rather than an isolated, individual affair.

An **Eschatological dimension of the liturgy** - An eschatological dimension of salvation is another emphasis of the present liturgy which

---

[465] For instance, the first blessings: "The love of God the Father, the grace of the only begotten Son and the communion and abiding presence of the Holy Spirit be with you all, dearly beloved forever," which is taken from 2 Cor.13:14. Titus II, *Qurbana Thaksa,* 23.
[466] Kuttiyil, *The Faith and Sacraments of the Mar Thoma Church,* 61.

Mission and Liturgy

drives her toward mission. Along with the doctrinal emphasis, soteriological themes are well reflected in the Eucharistic liturgy, especially in the anaphora of St. James. God's future for the cosmos becomes present in the Church through the liturgy. This is "heaven on earth"-the future is now.

Liturgy is rich in signs and symbols - The faith and practices of the Church are communicated through signs and symbols. The presence of God has been portrayed through symbolic representation in the action of worship. The most important feature of symbols lies in its richness of expression.[467] Signs and symbols motivate people to become involved in the worship in its fullness. It is necessary to reinterpret the existing signs and symbols for a meaningful translation of faith. Through the vehicle of sight, smell, sound, words, taste and gestures, the community at prayer experiences the richness of worship and the presence of God. The gestures and symbolic actions in the liturgy are fundamentally oriental. Since, the liturgy maintains an ongoing dialogue between the celebrant and the worshippers through its symbolic interchange, it can be designated the "liturgy of the people."

The liturgy is penitential in nature - The liturgy acknowledges the need for confession. The Holy Communion is celebrated by a community that consists of individuals who have become reconciled to each other and to God by confession and repentance. An active participation in the liturgy inspires the participants to confess and seek forgiveness from God through the redeeming act of Christ. By confessing their sins the faithful receive divine forgiveness. There is no auricular confession in the MTC. A public confession is conducted before the anaphora of the liturgy, usually after the sermon. This is a significant aspect of Protestant theology. It is by the power of the Holy Spirit that the Word of God challenges a person to confess his/her sins. Without confession, one cannot partake in the Holy Qurbana. Only after the Sacrament of Confession, even the celebrant is allowed to enter in the darga (step of the *thronos*) for the celebration of *anaphora*. The Church affirms that the mediation of Christ is significant

---

[467] Fawcett, *The Symbolic Language of Religion,* 28.

in the life of the faithful. Confession is made to God and God forgives the sins. The minister representing the Church makes the declaration of absolution.[468] The absolution confirms the truthfulness of the confessor, in which clearly says "Those who have truly confessed their sins…"[469] The absolution confirms a complete deliverance from sin.

The pedagogic aspect of liturgy - The liturgy is a tool for Christian education. Christian values are communicated and transmitted through its liturgy. The purpose of the liturgy is to equip the people to live according to the knowledge and grace they receive from God. The whole act of worship and prayers is a means of Christian education. It is said that liturgy forms the Church, informs the Church and transforms the Church. The liturgy provides explicit teaching: introductions, Scripture readings, commentaries, sermons, exhortations, and the teachings are for inculcating moral and doctrinal truths.

The Mar Thoma liturgy is missiological - one of the main aspects of the liturgy is its emphasis on evangelisation. The very purpose is to lead the faithful to experience the salvific act of Christ, and at the same time it calls on them to participate in the mission of God. Participation in the liturgy involves a missionary mandate for the faithful. The missiological themes in the liturgy are a motivation for mission. In the benediction one is exhorted to engage in ongoing mission; that is, one is sent out into the world so as to cooperate with God in his own Divine mission.[470]

2.1   A Critical Reading on the Prospects of the Liturgy

The renewed liturgy of the MTC is the product of the socio-religious and doctrinal reforms of the believers. The present liturgy is formulated to meet the spiritual needs of the reformed community. If so, how can the literal translation of the reformed liturgy of the Syrian community be relevant

---

[468] Kuttiyil, *The Faith and Sacraments of the Mar Thoma Church,* 50-52.
[469] Titus II, *Qurbana Thaksa, 28-29.*
[470] Kuttiyil, Liturgy *for Our Times,* 102. George Mathew. *An Introduction to Liturgy in Theological Thinking* (Thiruvalla: Mar Thoma Yuvajana Sakhyam, 1995), 14-15. Baby Varghese, *In Spirit and Truth: A Study of Eastern Worship* (Kottayam: OTC, 1987), 34-36.

to the newly converted people who are totally different from the people of Kerala in culture, language, customs and traditions? Could it not happen that the translated liturgy might actually turn out to become, unfortunately and ironically, a tool for dampening the spiritual energy of the converted people? In other words, is the MTC taking into sufficient consideration indigenous people and their freedom to worship according to their own cultural style? Should they not have also Scripture and the liturgy in their own tongue? Is the present liturgy relevant or contextual to their own settings; is it meaningful to them in their spiritual journey? Is the liturgy just turning out to serve as a tool for transforming a people or community? These are hard but honest questions, but they are quite pertinent when dealing with the matter of liturgical renewal and adaptation. Since the Malayalam Eucharistic liturgy serves as basis for other translations, there is a need for its scrutiny. The following are some suggestions for reflection on the revision of the Malayalam liturgy.

The order of worship should be simple, relevant and easy to follow. A new liturgy needs to be developed in considering the new situation and need, without changing the structure of the order of the Holy Qurbana. The language of the liturgy should be simple, indigenous and easy to follow. The Church should give space for liturgical innovations in considering the context, region, culture and traditions of the local people especially people from another region and who speak another language. Instead of preserving the liturgy in a lengthy form, it has to reduce. In addition, rubrics have to be kept to a minimum, which will assist the worship leader to develop styles appropriate to situation.

The Eucharist is the celebration of the victory of Christ over sin and death. It is a thankful remembrance of his gift of salvation. However, the notions of sin and salvation are often very shallow in the liturgy. A social dimension of sin is not seriously or adequately reflected in the way reflected in the present mode of Church worship; this is particularly so in the way the Church celebrate the Eucharist.[471] The prime confrontation of Jesus in his earthly ministry arose from his confronting the Jews about the validity of their assumptions regarding attitude to the sinners, the Samaritans, the non-Jews and the way they observe the Sabbath. The call of Jesus is to transcend the inherited definitions of truth and to seek righteousness within the framework of the Kingdom of God and not within the framework of the local culture. These aspects are not sufficiently expressed in the liturgy. Since the Eucharistic liturgy forms the spiritual mind set of the faith community, it is important that a holistic understanding of sin and salvation be reflected in the Eucharistic liturgy.[472]

At present, the prayer for the Holy Spirit in the liturgy is for the sanctification of the bread and wine and all believers. This is now prayed silently by the priest. This has been omitted in the English order of worship, and this should be changed to a public prayer for the participation of the whole congregation. A clear emphasis should be given to the biblical faith that Church is the community of creation in its entirety. The idea that all creation comes in for divine redemption through the instrumentality of the Church is conveyed in the liturgy of St. James. More emphasis should be given to this teaching.

There is need for shorter liturgy. Since modern life is fast-moving there is urgent need to shorten the liturgy without changing its fundamental content and structure. Even though Eucharistic liturgy remains the basis for the mission of the Church, there seems to be no really explicit emphasis in it for the mission calling. Therefore missional aspects of the liturgy should be

---

[471] All human beings are born into an existing society with a specific world view, belief system, and ethics. To a large extend these are internalized by members of a human community as they grow up in that community. Very often the prevailing world view and belief system achieve true value for the members of that society. Ways of living in accordance with the received world view, belief system and construction of faith will be approved by the society. Moreover departures are likely to be vehemently opposed. This is how the feudal system, the slave trade, the caste system, racism, apartheid and the practice of *sathi* (It is an abolished Hindu religious practice which demanded the death of the widow in the pyre of her departed husband) all survived with social approval or Church approval. Kuruvila. *Indian Eucharistic Liturgy*, 80-81.

[472] Kuruvila, *Indian Eucharistic Liturgy*, 81-82.

Mission and Liturgy

quite strongly heightened. In addition to, and related to, what has just been stated, duties like the preservation of the environment are also ultimately a Christian missionary responsibility to be proclaimed in liturgy.

It is appreciable that the ancient practices of bringing the bread and wine as offertory by the people during the Holy Communion should be re-introduced. Liturgical hymns need more attention.[473]

In the Church there is no emphasis on the concept of con-celebration. The celebrant is the leader of the celebration of the liturgy. There is no active role for other priests who are participating in the liturgy. It is appreciable to keep the liturgical format of con-celebration in the liturgical celebration of the Church. The liturgical actions should be in conformity with established rubrics.

The Eucharist is granted as a gift to the Church which is entrusted with a mission. Therefore, the believers should see the larger plan of God to preserve creation from the power of sin. The notion of personal and corporate dimension of Christian witnessing guided by the power of the Holy Spirit deserves its appropriate place in the liturgy's section dedicated to benefits of communion.[474]

While keeping the liturgical format, it is desirable to have more liturgical prayers like *sedro* and *promeion* reflecting the need and realities of the Church in different contexts. In the existing liturgies the content of the *sedro* is dominated by the potential theme. The rubrics for the celebration of the liturgy should be at its minimum level. There should be an option for appropriate symbols, ritual gestures, postures etc., taking into account the geographical and cultural diversity of the Church. The thrust has to generate a liturgical text relevant to the Church rooted in the liturgical tradition of the Church of the |East.

---

[473] Abraham Kuruvila, *Revision of Liturgy and Renewal of People* (Thiruvalla: Mar Thoma Church Publication Board, 1988), 24-33.
[474] Kuruvila, *Indian Eucharistic Liturgy*, 83.

Chapter. 8

Liturgical Proposals for Mission in the Mar Thoma Church

In the ongoing institution of dialogue on the Eucharistic liturgy and other liturgies of the MTC, it is essential to explore ever more possibilities for the continuance of mission. The mission of the Church is mainly to cooperate with God in His redemptive action. An active participation in the liturgy motivates the believers to cooperate with God in His mission. As mentioned earlier, the liturgy is the celebration of the salvific act of Christ; consequently active participation in the liturgy enables the faithful to experience this salvific act on a personal level. In this sense, the liturgy of the Church is precisely designed to reflect the life of Christ to His people, restoring His image in them. As a reformed Church in the Malankara tradition, with a renewed understanding of Scripture and mission, the MTC plays a significant role in carrying out the mission of God extensively through it various ministries. All the while, the Eucharistic liturgy is the liturgical foundation stone for this mission. Following are some liturgical suggestions for the furtherance of the mission of the Church. These proposals or suggestions are formulated in consultation with the bishops, clerics, laity and the youngsters from the urban India and diaspora regions. The opinion and comments of missionaries who minister in the mission fields of the Church in India is also considered. If the Hon. Episcopal Synod, clergy, evangelists and the whole members of the Church would seriously consider and implement these proposals, that will aid in reinforcing its missional identity and will provide an impetus in its ongoing Church reforming process.

(a) The MTC should give special attention to enhancing a spirituality based on the Sacrament of Eucharist. The Eucharist is the centre of the whole life and mission of the Church. This aspect should be strongly and repeatedly inculcated among the believers. This liturgical spirituality[475] must find itself situated in a decidedly Eucharistic ecclesiology.[476] The Eucharistic ecclesiology, places the Eucharist at the heart and essence of the very life of the Church. The nature of the Church is seen and experienced through the Eucharist and it is the meeting point of God and humanity. The liturgy confirms that the mission of the Church is centred on the paradigm of the Eucharist. The Church is a Eucharistic community and all activities of the Church must gravitate towards the goal of communion with Christ and thereby communion with others. Since the liturgy is the source of spirituality, an expression of faith and theology, the Church has to give utmost attention to a liturgy-oriented life. It ought to nourish Christian life by participation in the received liturgy, wherever it is celebrated. Consciousness of both the clergy and laity should be awakened to the traditional spiritual treasury, i.e. the sacred liturgy of the Church. This spirituality is centred on the liturgical seasons and feasts of the Church and the Church should encourage the observance of feasts and fasting among its members. Going back to the roots of the spiritual source of the Church such as teaching of the Church

---

[475] According to Pfatteicher, liturgical spirituality "refers to that distinctive interior life of the spirit that is formed and nurtured by the liturgy of the Church." Philip H. Pfatteicher, *Liturgical Spirituality* (Pennsylvania, Trinity International, 1997), ix. It is the official spirituality of the Church because it flows from the public worship or liturgy of the Church. Xaviour Koodapuzha, ed., *Liturgical Spiritualties in the Eastern Theological Reflection in India* (Kottayam: OIRSI, 1999), 222.

[476] It is from the Eucharist that grace of God is channelled to the faithful. It is the sanctification of the faithful in Christ and the glorification of God, to which all activities of the Church are directed as towards their goal. James Aerthayil, "The Liturgical Spirituality of the Syro-Malabar Church in the Spirituality," in *The Syro-Malabar Church*, ed. Sebastian Naduthadam (Kochi: Liturgical Research Center, 2009), 69-70. Christoph Bottigheimer, "Unity, Yes, But which Unity?" *Theology Digest* 52, no. 2 (Summer 2005): 119-126.

Fathers, noble traditions and practices and spiritual heritage of the Malankara Christians, which will help the members to understand the renewed liturgy and the mission of the Church.

(b) The MTC should retrieve and restore its original liturgical songs and prayers which are rich in theological content. Such a re-awakening is of great value in nurturing the spiritual needs of the people. The Church should go back into its traditional roots and reinstate meaningful prayers, liturgical hymns, signs and symbols. The loss of the original content occurred firstly because of the Latinization of the liturgy by the Portuguese Catholic invasion and, later, in consequence of omissions during the process of renewal carried out under the influence of CMS missionaries. True reformation (that is, re-formation) means to form once again that which once existed.[477] The traditional liturgical prayers must be recovered and reinstated before it can be renewed. The seeds of liturgical renewal will flourish within the original liturgical settings of a community. A distinction should be made between restoration (which is retrieving a tradition that has been lost) and renewal (which is making the tradition meaningful and practicable to worshipping communities.) The retrieval of older liturgical forms might sometimes prove relevant in certain occasions if it also meets the needs of contemporary worshippers.

(c) The Church should give special attention to the spiritual needs and challenges of the diaspora community, especially the youth. In the diaspora context, the second and subsequent generations of youth in migrant lands struggle to establish their identity in two worlds: the world of their parents and the world they inhabit. One of their important needs is to belong to the land of migration and not be alien there. The Church is responsible to serve them in three

---

[477] John R K. Fenwick, *Liturgy for Identity and Spirituality* (Kottayam: Thomas Mar Athanasius Memorial Research and Orientation Centre, 2008), 28. The practice of using of the baptismal crown and marriage solemnization crown faded away from the practice of the Church in its course of development.

important ways. Firstly, they need theological tools to critique the assumptions behind the local culture and local spiritual traditions so as to discern between the appropriate and the inappropriate in their tradition as well as in their context. This is important in particular because versions of Christian spirituality which uncritically accept the assumptions of globalisation and the market economy are being aggressively propagated. Building a substantial catechetical literature is therefore an urgent need. Secondly, they need literature to understand the heritage of the Church from within their context. Thirdly, they need contemporary expressions of Eastern worship which are culturally and contextually appropriate. A large number of migrant youth have deserted the Church because of insufficient attention to the above. In this context the Church should bring special focus to bear on the spiritual needs of the diaspora youth. Here it is vital to build up a team of competent lay leaders drawn from the ranks of the young themselves who can help their peers to draw authentically from their roots and then to adapt their findings to the land of migration. Young people today have great trust in leaders emerging from their own peer group cohorts. It is, therefore, this writer's conviction that a systematic liturgical orientation and leadership training for sacramental living and channelization of the young towards the heritage and richness of the liturgical traditions of the Church will exert noticeable impact on the future of the Church. In this youthful catechetical cadre, the Church will have a seedbed which generates elements to take on major ministry in the community. In this connection it might also be desirable to set apart one day as "Diaspora Sunday" in order to propagate the diaspora mission and to address the various challenges the Church is facing today.

(d) A concrete and systematic liturgical education, then, is essential in the MTC. A clear understanding of the liturgy is indispensable for its spiritual growth and effective witnessing. A new liturgical movement has to be initiated in the Church, which should focus on the liturgical orientation, teaching, explanation, training and liturgical life. An ongoing liturgical education will make the members conscientious and will increase their awareness of their vocation as a missional community. Liturgical upbringing is indispensable for discovering all the riches contained in the liturgy, especially the signs, symbols, prayers and practices. Such a programme will help the faithful to participate in the liturgy more actively and intelligently. Liturgical education must be provided within the Eucharistic celebration through the harbouring of all its best aspects - word, song, gestures, silent meditation and reflection, homily and dignified conducting of liturgical action. It is essential to underline the need for a periodic and regular education in different languages that are employed in the liturgy - biblical, laudatory, ritual, symbolic, gestures, iconic etc. This education should be in place before the Eucharistic celebration. There is a need to generate literature for the education of the laity. A new text book outlining the basic doctrines of the Church, including sections on sacraments and sacramental theology, needs to be brought out. A continual liturgical course should be initiated for the laity of the parish. A curriculum for the training of lay leaders should be prepared. All parishes should have a team of competent lay leaders. This training programme should be flexible so as to address the needs of the various parishes, be they in Kerala, in other areas of India, or in parishes outside India. Of great value also is to have well in place an ongoing and systematic liturgical orientation and refresher courses for the clergy as well. At present there are no such systematic refresher courses for the clergy. Opportunities for cross-cultural ministry, refresher courses and advanced theological education for all ministers of the Church, both lay and ordained, is another area which needs attention.

(e) In concordance with the traditions of the Oriental Orthodox Church, the lectionary requires some revision. The Church should revive and educate the significance of the liturgical year in the liturgical life of

Mission and Liturgy

the community. The lectionary of the Church must incorporate both traditional and contemporary themes for contextual relevance. The Eucharistic liturgy is arranged sequentially through the seasons of the liturgical calendar, providing forms of Advent, Christmas, Epiphany, Ash Wednesday, Lent, Easter, and Pentecost. The period of Lent should be observed as a period of comprehensive renunciation of affluent and irresponsible living. The Church should encourage the observance of fasting and feasting among its members. Both celebrations and penitential seasons should be observed. Along with that, the Church should give more emphasis in educating the meaning of liturgical colour, season, chants, since these factors could inspire and lead the members forward towards a liturgy-oriented life.

(f) There is a persistent need for liturgical revisions in the Church. Apart from the present Liturgical Commission of the Church, it is desirable to have in each diocese a liturgical committee entrusted with the responsibility of making proposals for the revision of the liturgies relevant to its own context. The working groups must include persons from the respective communities in addition to experts in liturgy. The liturgy must have sufficient shared elements to preserve the unity of the Church and at the same time it should be relevant for the populace for whom these liturgies are created. There should be adequate freedom for liturgical explorations, contextual liturgies and creative liturgical experiments. The Episcopal Synod should give permission to each diocese to initiate contextual liturgies focusing on the needs of the region. Inculturated Eucharistic prayers must be subjected to critical, doctrinal and stylistic evolution. The concept "liturgy as the action of the people" should get recognition. These initiative will increase the corporate participation in the liturgical celebration.

(g) The Church should give importance to the use of "daily office" among its members. Currently, due to the lack of attention to the liturgy, there is a danger that individuals, who are isolated from the faith community could belong to any Church. This is where the "daily office" can be of great value. It has an objective content and value, for it links the believers with others availing of the same format, both contemporaries and those to come in successive generations. The liturgy has the power to bind people together to a particular community or tradition. It guides and support the newly joined members in their faith. The "daily office" will help a member of the Church to connect with others in the community. It can help them to affirm their identity in the Church. Therefore, the Church should keep a liturgical link based on their reformed tradition with its members.[478]

(h) The Church needs a shift in its liturgical provision. There should be a space for popular devotions and spiritual expressions of the local people in the liturgy. As contemporary liturgical theologian David Power remarks that, the people are "rarely invited to express their faith on their own in the public worship. Rather, they are given models of doctrinal belief to follow, instead of being expected to generate their own expressions."[479] The liturgy should not be only "the work of the elite." He calls for the incorporation of indigenous traditions of popular devotions into corporate celebrations.[480] In the liturgy, there should be more space, openness and freedom to incorporate the cultural element of a particular region. The Church should give immediate attention to formulate new liturgies for an active participation of the faithful from the non-Syrian liturgical background such as Dalits and Adivasis. It is unfortunate to state that there is a big gap between the converted Christians and the Syrian Christians in the MTC. The Church should be flexible enough to accommodate changes in the liturgy in connection with the adaptation of the liturgy and inculturation. Liturgical freedom

---

[478] Fenwick, *Liturgy for Identity and Spirituality,* 25-26.
[479] David N. Power, *Worship: Culture and Theology* (Washington DC: Pastoral, 1990), 67-68.
[480] Power, *Worship,* 83.

Mission and Liturgy

should be given to the newly converted Christians to incorporate some of their own old customs and traditions, if any, in the liturgy, and that must be a channel to enhance their spiritual experience and liturgical life. There should be a space for different patterns of worship that helps the people to relate to their particular local culture.

(i) The liturgy has an authority as a source of theology. As has already been noted, however, it is not properly used for the articulation of the doctrine of the Church. Biblical interpretation played a major role in establishing the foundation of the Church and nurturing faith in the people. Theology should be evolved by interpreting the liturgical text, along with Scripture. Such an interpretation of the liturgy will endow the Church with a sound theology and authentic liturgical life. It is appreciable to have biblical hermeneutics on the basis of liturgical texts and the Church has to discourage the misinterpretation of Sacred Writ. Liturgical preaching should get special attention. According to Mar Theodosius, history, theology, worship, liturgy and mission of the MTC emerges from the text. Text texture the daily life of the people.[481] The bible-centred religious living of the people brought in the question of hospitality and the attitude of welcoming stranger with an open mind-set to embrace particularly the last, lost and the least. The Church shall become relevant when it ministers to the people by bringing the centrality of Text (Scripture) for their faith life and enabling them to understand Christian mission and identity of all. Preaching in the context of worship can be a great blessing if it is contextual and integrates with the realities of life. The preacher should connect the message of Scripture to the liturgical ceremonies. Very often the Church seems to divorce two important realities -the liturgical life on one hand and the life of Christian activity and witness on the other. In contrast, she should be giving equal weight to all aspects

---

[481] Theodosius, "Shifting Meaning in Public, Religion and Domestic Spaces,"17-18.

of life; life and mission spring from liturgy. The very purpose, peace and wellbeing of humankind should flow from worship.

(j) In the present media-tech world, new modes of communication are a blessing. Accordingly, in guiding members towards active participation, the Church should avail of the new modes of media and technology to teach more effectively its doctrines, faith and practices. Since the function of the liturgy is to communicate the Christian faith and values, the Church should use the blessings of modern media for its effective communication. For this purpose, the mode of communication and content of the liturgy should be contextualized for the modern period. It is very beneficial to use media in an effective way in the proclamation of the Gospel and integrate the Gospel values with the culture created by modern communications. The Church has to make use of the possibilities of internet and multimedia for the faith formation and communication. Network all the dioceses, parishes and mission stations and the institutions which will enhance the effective coordination in the mission work.

(k) Very often, the liturgical worship in the Church seems to be focused only on elders in the Church. The children are very often mere spectators in the worship. The Church should not exclude children from the mainstream worship. In the MTC, children are confirmed at the age of 12 to 14, and they are formally admitted to Holy Communion. Here, the Church has moved away from the traditional practice of giving Holy Communion to the children. It is important that the Church should take care of the children and should give them a role in conducting the worship and Holy Communion service. Introducing children' to Eucharistic prayers will make a great difference. It is desirable that the Church offer holy elements to children, as in either the Orthodox tradition[482]

---

[482] In the Orthodox tradition, where a baptized and Christianised infant is a full member of the Eucharistic community and grows up nurtured in the community of faith, with in the

or reformed traditions. Along with children, the involvement of women in worship also needs special attention. They also deserve sufficient role and recognition in the celebration of the Eucharist. Traditionally, women are not even allowed to enter the madbaho. There is no theological or pastoral justification for this practice. It is high time to think about the possibility of the ordination of women in the Church. Further, it is appreciable to have an all age worship[483] in the Church.

(l) The usage of inclusive language[484] has to be considered in the revision and translation of the liturgy. The linguistic style of the Mar Thoma liturgy is generally patriarchal in nature. The use of inclusive language in the liturgy will do justice to all the worshippers. The New Revised Standard Version of the Bible, which uses gender-inclusive language when referring to the human community, has become a primary version for public reading in congregations especially in the migrant contexts. In short, there is also need to redefine "Reformed" measured against the context of migration communities. After all, the core of reformation is not changing practices of the Church, but in the renewal of believers in a contextually vibrant Christian life. Such vibrant life needs to be seen as of the very identity of the Church through ongoing reformation. Here it is helpful to recall that the 19th century Reformation went quite beyond simply modifications in liturgy; it aimed at instituting ethical renewal of mind geared for energized Christian living.

---

threatening "hurdles" to jump in adolescence. In some parts of the Anglican Communion children of five or under are receiving the sacrament now.

[483] Phillip Tovey, "Two Models of Inculturation and Eucharistic Prayers with Children," in *The Serious Business of Worship: Essays in Honour of Bryan D.* Spinks, eds. Melanie Ross and Simon Jones (London: T and T Clark International, 2010), 130-142.

[484] Inclusive language means a language in which all the worshippers find themselves, and their religious experience of God as revealed in Christ, more completely reflected. It calls for a "balanced language" that is, avoiding 'an over-reliance on metaphors and attributes generally perceived as masculine and seeking 'images which describe God in feminine and other scripturally based terms. Ruth A. Meyers, "Ongoing Liturgical Revision in the Episcopal Church USA," *Studia Liturgica* 31, no.1 (2001): 63.

(m) The Church should acknowledge and consider the ecumenical liturgical development. The Church has to develop an ecumenical Eucharistic order of worship for promoting the ecumenical spirit among the people, specifically in the local context at the micro-levels. Finding common ground for the celebration of the Eucharist and to enhance fellowship in Christ for Christian witnessing is the need of the hour. The formation of an ecumenical liturgy will foster relationship among various denominations and it could motivate them to find out a common space for mission. Local parishes should be encouraged to enter into experimental programmes which promote contact with the local community. Ecumenical worship can be true to confessional origins.[485] To put it in almost slogan form, "universality and particularity without detriment to one another." The formation of a liturgy aware of and reflecting *"oikoumene ge"* (the inhabited earth) is only re-proclamation of that heartfelt desire for universal embrace first issued by Our Lord. At the same time, the liturgy remains relevant to its own context through particularized modes of expression tied to time and space: this takes in language, art, music, architecture, ethical norms and cultural customs.

General guidelines should be prepared for enhancing creative forms of Christian living and witnessing in the local community and in sustaining ecumenical contacts. This would contribute to rendering the mission of the local parish more meaningful. This would also promote ecumenism and communal harmony. There is need for a liturgy which summons everyone to wider unity irrespective of legitimate differences. Along with it, the Church has to find ways to develop new mission models like mission as eco-justice, mission as transformation, mission as human empowerment, etc., for keeping mission more appealing and creative.

---

[485] Siobhan Garrigan, "A New Model for Ecumenical Worship," *Studia Liturgica* 43, no.1 (2013): 43.

Mission and Liturgy

(n) There must be a call to all parishes and mission fields to submit proposals to deepen their involvement in the life of the local community and to strengthen the mission in the local community. As an Episcopal Church with democratic values and ethos, it is always important to consider the views of the members. The more creative proposals should be published in the various publications for the consideration of other parishes. A selected number from parishes and mission fields should be encouraged to enter into experimental programs to deepen their witness within the local community. A series of workshops should be arranged for priests, and for those who are interested in innovative forms of pastoral ministry and liturgical worship.

(o) There is an urgent need for a shorter liturgy in the Church, especially in the urban and diaspora context. The monastic nature of the liturgy is very long. Long liturgical services should be shortened without the erosion of the theological content. The liturgy must be contextual which reflects the realities of life. The present liturgy is penitential in nature and more concerned with the idea of sin and salvation of the soul. The liturgy should reflect the day to day affairs of the community, their problems, hopes and frustrations, etc. It should also address the issues of poverty, injustice, inequality, exploitation, discrimination etc.

(p) Very often, the Mar Thoma liturgy is clergy-centred. The laity is not getting enough opportunity for participation and assuming leadership roles in the services. It would be a welcome move to introduce an option of "secular clergy"[486] or voluntary deacon service in the Church. Thereby an ordained person can be assisted by a deacon in his ministry, in particular for administering the cup at Holy Communion, in general assistance during the service, and in

---

[486] This term is used not in the popular understanding of the Catholic Church (clergy under the obedience to the local bishop) rather, I talk about the parsons who are ordained and not engage with the full time ministries of the Church. This geographically permanent clergy can take up secular responsibilities along with the parish ministry and their service is voluntary in nature.

reading the prayers, etc. The clergy ministrants should be appointed for administering the sacraments of the Church. Presently, spiritual care of the parish is mostly vested in the parish priest who is often over burdened with administration and liturgical responsibilities. There is underutilization of the lay resources of the parishes. There has consequently been a decline in competent lay leadership and a progressive clericalisation of the Church. In the urban parishes, many young people have left the Church since their leadership potential has not been harnessed by the Church. There is a need for voluntary pastoral care team (PCT) in each and every parish to provide a partnership in mission with the clergy. In the urban context and in the diaspora settings of the Church, with a membership of more than 200 families, it is an enormous task to take care of the spiritual needs of the people by the service of a single clergyman. In addition, there is an urgent need in the diaspora context because of the discontinuity of pastoral care arising from the three year cycle of ministry[487] of parish priests. Therefore, the Church should think about the possibility of ordaining part-time (secular) clergy[488] or appointing deacons. Pastoral care is all about understanding with a sense of compassion and love. It is all about understanding the hidden needs of others and tackling those needs with a high level of sensitivity and confidentiality.

(q) The Church should undertake more efforts related to the transcultural, contextual, counter-cultural and cross-cultural nature of the Christian worship. For this, the Church should recover the centrality of Scripture, and the practice of celebrating the Eucharist every Sunday. The liturgy is the principal transcultural element of Christian worship and the signs of Christian unity, which constitutes a strong centre of all Congregational life and the authentic basis for contextualization and mission. More

---

[487] Usually the term of service of a clergyman in a particular parish is three years. After three years of service, he is transferred to other parishes in the Church anywhere in India by the Episcopal Synod of the Church.

[488] Same like NSM in the Catholic tradition (Non-stipendiary auxiliary).

Mission and Liturgy

serious attention needs to be dedicated to the exploration of local or contextual elements in liturgy, such as language, posture and gesture, hymnody along with other forms of music even attended by forms of instrumentalization, art and architecture. In this way worship should become more truly rooted in the local culture.

(r) If the Church is indeed multi-cultural and multi-racial, then it has to open enough to redefine its liturgical identity as "Syrian Christians." The new believers in the mission fields and those born and brought up outside Kerala are challenging the MTC to redefine its identity. Traditionally, this Church has defined itself as an oriental, Eastern, Reformed Church. These characteristics in the identity of the Church should be redefined in the context of the expansion of the Church through migration and evangelistic mission. A certain exclusivism is implied in the designation of the Church as "Syrian Christian," and therefore such appellation must needs be forfeited in favour of an openness and inclusiveness which can accommodate the linguistic, cultural and ethnic plurality within the Church. "Eastern" and "Reformed" need to be clearly defined in liturgical and theological terms. The migrant youths and the new faith communities in the mission fields can hardly benefit from a casteist description of the Church as "Syrian Christian." In the diaspora and mission centres, Malayalam is no longer the mother tongue of many and hence they are no more an exclusively Malayalee Church. The Church now includes people who speak English, Hindi, Kannada, Tamil, Telugu, and Oriya, as their mother tongue. The resultant plurality demands a plurality in liturgy, ministerial forms and in the composition of the ordained ministry. It is important to develop culturally and linguistically homely type liturgies for the different linguistic and cultural groups. The liturgies need to preserve the genius of Eastern worship with contextually relevant forms and content. The trend to use more of Syriac and revive archaic practices is anachronistic. It is also important to equip the clergy and the other missionaries of the Church to serve people in a cross-cultural context. This applies equally to evangelists from Kerala who serve outside, clergy born in Kerala but serving outside, and to clergy born outside Kerala but serving in Kerala.

(s) There is a need of contextual liturgies in the Church to affirm and celebrate various aspects of life on this planet. Ecological Sunday offers a classic example. The liturgy should be affirming the theology of ecology, which would be reminding everyone of the responsibility of preserving and protecting God-given planetary life. An "eco-theology" emphasis within liturgy constitutes just such a reminder to assume a responsible human stewardship of creation. As things now stand, ecology is inadequately highlighted; therefore it, too, has a claim for greater relief in the overall composition of liturgy because it is one very important derivative of multi-faceted justice. It holds its place alongside the other social, economic, cultural and political problems like hunger, poverty, discrimination, inequality, child labour, slavery, prostitution, unemployment, denial of rights to food, clothing and shelter, violence, torture, child abuse, addictions, disease, war, rivalry, religious fundamentalism, terrorism etc. Liturgical revision is to be a continuous process.

(t) I would propose new liturgies based on the needs of the people, including Eucharistic rites. It should be more inclusive in nature and reflect the issues of the present generation. Instead of using the old prayers it is meaningful to employ the new terminologies, signs and symbols. It has to do justice to the inclusive mission of the Church and consider the ecological theme along with the voice of oppressed and neglected communities. Liturgy is meaningful when it reflects realities; only then can it motivate all to the greater glory of God. It is then that it has the effect of what might be called "reciprocal approach."[489]

---

[489] It means a reciprocity between the transcendent and the imminent or between the vertical and horizontal.

6 Conclusion

A major manifestation of the missionary activity of the Orthodox Church lies in its celebration of the liturgy. The mission of the Church is to be itself, especially in its worship. As part of the Oriental Orthodox tradition, which upholds the St. Thomas spiritual heritage and antiquity, the reformed liturgy stands as foundation of the MTC in its mission and identity. As expression of a reformed and reforming Church, its liturgy is to reflect a theological simplicity and lucidity of style which motivate the faithful to participate actively in the mission of God. The liturgical celebration helps the faithful to experience a sense of belonging, a sense of community, and a sense of God's presence.[490]

The MTC is no longer monolithic in nature. As has been already demonstrated, there are multiple cultural contexts in existence in the community. While reflecting on its now multicultural and multi-ethnic nature, the Church has the obligation to take care of all its members, especially those in the diaspora and mission fields. There is the need first of all to study the various emerging identities and the local cultures with their values, patterns and institutions; then to facilitate how they can be suitably integrated into the liturgy. This calls for adaptation and attendant contextual revision. The aim of renewal and revision of liturgy in the Church should not be simply revision of liturgical books, but part of a deeper spiritual renewal of community consistent with the reformed spirit and tradition of the Church. The aim is to achieve a spiritual awakening through liturgical renewal and revision; to help people in active liturgical participation and in their personal quest for the realization of truth. Participation in the liturgy is not an isolated phenomenon; it consciously relates to the very life of the Church. An active involvement in liturgy involves as well an active participation in the sacrificial death of Christ for the forgiveness of sins, the glorification of God, purification of the community and the participation in

---

[490] Kim Aldi Wanner, *Preparing the Assembly to Celebrate* (Collegeville, MN: Liturgical, 1997), 7-9.

the mission of God. It should motivate and challenge the believers to take their part in the mission of God in this world.

The celebration of the Eucharist is not just the proclamation, but it is the Gospel itself. It is through the Eucharist that the Church witnesses the mission of God. Mission means sharing the faith through Christ, sharing his life. An emphasis on Eucharist-centred ecclesiology guides and motivates the faithful to enliven a mission-oriented life.[491] Awareness of liturgy is essential for participating in the mission of God through the Church. Therefore, liturgical education is an essential component in making the Church a mission-based community. A serious and systematic edification is essential to discover the richness contained in the liturgy. To realize this task of enlivening the liturgy there are required preparation, humility, dedication, faith and profound appreciation of the tradition and heritage of the Church.

At present, one quite serious challenge to the Church, one which sets up a major obstacle to experiencing the reconciling power of Christ, is discrimination based on caste and colour. As a missionary community, then, the Church must shine forth in the world as a mighty reality defined by unity in Christ, a unity which irradiates powerfully among its members. The mission of the Church is not a mere reflection mirrored from one location to another. It is charged with creating something new, by incarnating the gospel among the peoples and cultures of the world. The way of mission then, must be the way of inculturation and dialogue following the example of Christ.[492] To this end, the Church should be open enough to accept its diverse ethical and social setup and willing to accept and adapt the relevant cultural elements and traditions of the people whom she serves.

---

[491] Putting Eucharist at the centre of life motivates the believer to acknowledge its formative power. The believer allows Eucharist to work not only in him as an individual, but also as an energizing organ of Christian community. The individual surrenders the self and embraces the challenges and implications of this unique and revolutionary event which is none other than Christ's Passover thrust into, and extended throughout, all human history. Meisner, "Eucharist and Evangelization," 25-27.

[492] Billy Swan, *The Eucharist, Communion and Formation: Proceedings of the International Symposium of Theology* (Dublin: Veritas, 2013), 577.

General Conclusion

The MTC is a "bridging Church" connecting Protestantism and Orthodoxy. The theological and liturgical position of the Church marked it as a "special family of Church" among the global Churches, which means this new ecclesial group is rooted in the spiritual heritage of the St. Thomas Christians, its liturgical footings in the Oriental Eastern tradition and theological underpinnings in the European Protestant doctrines. In the Oriental Eastern tradition, a theology of the Church is not articulated in "articles of faith" but is embedded in the liturgy. But in the reformed tradition, Scripture is central to the life, order and mission of the Church. The spoken Word is built around Scripture and the embodied Word is centered on the celebration of the Eucharist. This is the basis of the MTC and its mission. In considering the unique nature of this Church, it is recognised as a "hybrid Church" in the ecumenical circle.

The Eucharist is not only the source and nourishment of the mission of the Church, but also it determines its content and method. The Eucharist is the central expression and celebration of the Church's identity as the sacrament of God's universal and unconditional love, manifested in Christ.[493] Mission is not only the conclusion of the Eucharist, but a concrete living out of that mystery of divine love that it symbolizes and celebrates. Hence the ministry of the Church must be appropriate and designed as per the need of a particular region and context. While the MTC moved out as a mission oriented faith community, it is imperative to understand how the concept of mission is historically developed and being practiced in the Church. The Church is commissioned to be a "Community of Witness" through its very liturgical celebrations in its varied cultural and geographical contexts. The MTC in line with the Oriental Orthodox tradition goes along with the concept of worship as offering glory to God.

---

[493] Michael McCabe, "Mission: Climax and Consummation of the Eucharist," in *The Eucharist, Communion and Formation*, 575-581.

The gathered community experiences the life and love of Christ mystically through the liturgy and moves out into the world to share this abundant life through their interactions with fellow human beings. The Church shares the glory of God through its transformative actions by its various ministries. As stated in the previous chapter, the various mission models employed in the Church give witness to this fact.

The Church is a Eucharistic community and its mission and identity derives from the celebration of the Eucharist. Generally, the Church wants its members to have an evangelical fervour, but within the framework of corporate life and liturgical devotion of an Eastern Church. Currently, there is no cultural homogeneity among the members in the Church. The mass media and the modern technologies affect the attitude and life style of the people at large and also traditional cultures and values undergo tremendous changes. At this juncture, the Church has to reaffirm its reformed ideas for its ongoing renewal by considering its multicultural and multi ethnic identity. In this Church, the diverse culture is accepted and identified as a means of the mission and that leads to unity and communion. No culture retains its identity in isolation. An identity is attained in relationship, in preserving essential cultural differences while respecting other cultures, in breaking barriers and remaining open to synthesis. The Church is a community which is called out to affirm the cultural differences and to transform the culture by the power of the Gospel. Here the liturgy stands as a means for community formation and that calls for a sacramental living. Where there is genuine worship and holiness (sanctification) in life, the mission will be a natural outcome. The heart of the priestly ministry of the Church is the Holy Qurbana. Therefore, every baptized member of the Church is ordained into this Eucharistic priesthood. The Church is a sacramental presence of Christ in the world.

The engagement with the liturgical community, liturgical space, liturgical actions, observance of liturgical time and rituals and the participation in the sacraments empowers the members to strengthen their relationship with God and their fellowship with the faith community for a relevant mission. Generally, the mission is an invitation of God to

Mission and Liturgy

participate in His redeeming act. The Church internalises it through an active participation in the liturgy. The participation in the liturgy enables the faithful to experience the renewing, rejuvenating and re-energising power of God. The Sacrament of Baptism is positioned as an entrance into the community of mission. It incorporates a person into the body of Christ. There is an inexpressible link between the Sacrament of Baptism and the Eucharist in the MTC. Both Baptism and Eucharist lead believers into a communion with the Triune God and into communion with one another. In baptism and in the Lord's Supper, the Church encounters the risen Christ to whom Scriptures bears witness. The baptism is an entry point into the communion of saints and the Eucharist is an ongoing means to nurture and strengthen by the presence of God for His mission. When we connect baptism and the Eucharist, one can say that there is a trajectory of font before the table. The Eucharist as a recapitulation of baptism, both deepens and sustains the baptismal journey into a new life.[494]

Since the MTC has expanded extensively beyond the culture of Kerala and its geographical background as a result of the migration and the evangelisation process, it encounters immense possibilities and innumerable challenges in its course of growth. The influence of liturgy among the members in the diaspora and the mission centres in the Church varies in accordance with its cultural and social setting. A strong liturgical and scriptural texturing has to happen in the Church especially in the diaspora and mission field context. The Church has to take serious attention to make the liturgy more contextual and relevant by adopting various cultural aspects. Liturgical adaptation and inculturation does not mean a mere embracing of a particular cultural context and thrusting it into the act of worship; it means rather familiarising the people with the deep spirit of liturgy through the vehicle of certain local cultural symbols. To put it somewhat differently, it is not for the mere sake of inculturation but for one particular promising and convenient mode of integrating liturgy and the teachings of the Church with the life of the local people. Very often in the

---

[494] Westerfield, "Baptism and Ecumenism," 12.

context of the diaspora and mission fields, youth find it difficult to actively engage in the liturgical celebrations, because of its cultural and linguistic differences. If Church is not giving appropriate attention to keep the liturgy convenient to its members, its relevance as a missionary community may change in the near future. The liturgy is a solemn space which unifies its members under an umbrella. As a reformed and reforming Church, it has to be more open to accommodate the necessary trends of the time for making the liturgy a relevant experience. Then only the liturgy can be a tool for mission in the MTC.

The Bible is the foundation of the liturgical revision in the Church. The mission understanding of the Church is dual in nature, which is based on the liturgy and Scripture. It is not contradictory, but complementing each other for relevant mission. The MTC holds Scripture and liturgy together in its spiritual journey and mission. The authority of the liturgy is based on its scriptural footing. The scriptural emphasis in the liturgy makes it more authentic and unique. Without a scriptural base, liturgy is like a balloon without air in it. The influence of Scripture and the integration of Scripture and liturgy in the formation and the sustenance of community living is analysed. In considering the lectionary of the Church, it helps the faithful to internalise their spiritual experience on the basis of their relationship with Scripture contextually. The reformed liturgy of the Church helps the believers to a certain extent to be involved in the worship positively and to engage subjectively. But at present, it seeks more space for the participation of people, subjectivity and for the expression of local culture, ethos, and set of values.

The liturgy should be a subjective component of worship rather than an abstract set of doctrines and set of principles. The worshipping community could freely engage with it since the liturgy is the "work of the people." The liturgy should address the pain and pathos of the people and the realities of the society. It should be a solemn space in which they can find solace, comfort and a means to ease their worries, anxieties and tensions. The response of the members of the Church from the diaspora and the mission centres restate the fact that there should be more liturgical flexibility to

Mission and Liturgy

adapt and incorporate the cultural and contextual aspects in the everyday liturgy. Instead of upholding the one time revised liturgical format the Church has to be more open to experiment with new forms of worship by keeping its traditional rooting and biblical emphasis.

There is an urgent need in the Church to have a liturgical reformation. It has to consider the needs of the time by inculcating the cultural elements of the worshipping community, adapting new ways of liturgical format, incorporating relevant contextual prayers, signs and symbols. Through a systematic liturgical orientation, liturgical affirmation and a Eucharistic centred life style, the Church can exist as a true missionary community. In order to keep the concept of mission relevant, the Church has to develop a liturgical Eucharistic spirituality and to practice it through its very life. Eucharistic centred spirituality always seeks the "other" and invites others to the heavenly banquet of God and the communion of saints. An active participation in the Eucharistic celebration motivates the faithful to lead a Eucharistic living, which means a life grounded on the Eucharistic values. It is an enactment of the Eucharistic life style which is more self-transcending and self-giving. In the words of Irvin, "Eucharist is integral and integrating of the Christian life."[495] The Eucharist should shape our perception, and evaluation on life.

Redefining the concept of worship is important in the present context. Worship is not just a gathering of the assembled community rather it has to help the participants to experience the fellowship with God and others. Reformation in the MTC was a process of redefining the definition of worship from ritual to experience. It helped the faithful to experience the abiding presence of Christ in their lives which motivated them to cooperate with God in His mission. Worship is not a mere ritualistic act rather it is an expression of one's dynamic relationship with the Risen Lord. It is an experience of being empowered by the Holy Spirit to ascribe praise and glory to the Triune God in every moment of one's life. The concept of liturgy after liturgy is most important in this juncture. Every encounter

---

[495] Irwin, *Models of the Eucharist*, 294.

that Jesus had with the people helped them to have new understanding about life, existence, and one's calling. It is this new understanding of life that helps a person to have the concept of mission in life. But this concept of mission comes only when we redefine worship and participate in the Paschal Mystery actively. In the MTC, the reformation process ignited the people with new understanding of worship and thereby new awareness of its mission in the society. At present, the Church has to redefine the concept of worship to remain as an inclusive community in its emerging contexts. The liturgy of the Church has to help the members to encounter Christ in their lives in order to bring change and transformation. Liturgy should always be understood as the axis and anchor that gives the Christian life its purpose, shape and meaning. The real object of liturgy is not only getting the rituals right; the real object of liturgy is that it puts our very lives in the perspective. The celebration of the Eucharist should help the faithful to see the world from the perspective of the gospel and enable them to lead a sacramental life in the midst of the challenges of living in the world.[496] In the words of Mar Theodosius, in the MTC, the "reformation keeps challenging the Church and the people to view the world sacramentally and to live sacramentally. Reformation today is to address all issues arising from the geographical spread of the Church to almost all continents, including the issues of migration and the consequent plurality. It is necessary for the Church to become inter-racial and multicultural. This kind of reformation can only happen in a Church that practices sacramental living."[497] In order to guide the people for a sacramental living, the Eucharist centred approach of mission is the need of the time and it is crucial for accomplishing a relevant mission.

---

[496] Irwin, *Models of the Eucharist,* 295.
[497] Geevarghese Mar Theodosius, *Churching the Diaspora. Disciplining the Families* (Thiruvalla: Diocese of North America and Europe, 2015), 25.

Bibliography

BOOKS AND JOURNALS

Abbot, Walter M. ed. *The Document of Vatican II, Sacrosanctum Concelium.10.* New York: The America Free, 1966.

Abraham, K.C. "Mission and Ministry of the Church: A Liberative Perspective." *Bangalore Theological Forum* 29, no.3 (September 1989): 41-46.

Abraham, T.P. *Malankara Mar Thoma Syrian Church: Journey Through Centuries.* Thiruvalla: Christava Sahitya Samithi, 2012.

Adam Adolf. *The Eucharistic Celebration: The Source and Summit of Faith.* Collegeville, MN: Liturgical, 1994.

Amalados, Michael. "Challenges of Mission in the 21st Century." *Theology Digest* 47, no.1 (Spring 2000): 15-20.

Amalados, Michael. "Our Mission in India Today." *Vaigarai* 6, no. 2 (September 2001): 18-23.

Amalorpavadass, D.S. "Approaches, Meaning and Horizon of Evangelization." In *Light and Life We Seek to Share.* Patna: All India Consultation on Evangelization, 1973. 54-57.

Amalorpavadass, D.S. "Indigenization and the Liturgy of the Church." *International Review of Mission* 65 (1976): 164-167.

Amalorpavadass, D.S. "Theological Reflections on Inculturation." *Studia Liturgica* 20 (1990): 35-53.

Anastasios of Tirana. "Cultural and Gospel. Some Observations From the Orthodox Tradition and Experience." *International Review of Mission* 74 (1985): 185-198.

Anastasios, Archbishop. *Mission in Christ's Way.* Geneva, World Council of Churches, 2010.

Anderson, Gerald H., and Thomas F. Stransky, eds. *Mission Trends No.1: Crucial Issues in Mission Today.* New York: Paulist, 1974.

Anderson, William. *Towards a Theology of Mission*. London: SCM, 1955.

Aram, I. "The Incarnation of the Gospel in Cultures: A Missionary Event." *Ecumenical Review* 48 (1996):

Baldovin, J.F. *Liturgy in Ancient Jerusalem*. Nottingham: Grove Liturgical Study, 1989.

Baptism, Eucharist, and Ministry. Faith and Order Paper No. III, Geneva: WCC, 1982.

Barker, Chris. *Cultural Studies, Theory and Practice*. New Delhi: Sage, 2000.

Barsoum, Ignatius Aprem I. *History of Syriac Literature and Sciences*. Pueblo: Passeggiata, 2000.

Bates, Barrington J. "Expressing What Christians Believe: Anglican Principles for Liturgical Revision." Anglican Theological Review ATR/92:3, 455. www.anglicantheologicalreview.org/static/pdf/articles/bates.pdf (accessed December 08, 2015).

Baumstark, A and West F. *On the Historical Development of the Liturgy*. Collegeville, MN: Liturgical, 2011.

Bevans, Stephen B, and Roger P. Schroeder. *Constants in Context: A Theology of Mission for Today*. New York, Maryknoll: Orbis, 2004.

Bevans, Stephen B, and Roger P. Schroeder. *Prophetic Dialogue: Reflections on Christian Mission Today*. New York, Maryknoll: Orbis, 2011.

Blumhofer, Edith L., and Randall Balmer, eds. *Modern Christian Revivals*. Chicago: University of Illinois, 1993.

Bordeyne, Philippe, and Bruce T. Morrill. "Baptism and Identity Formation: Convergence in Ritual and Ethical Perspectives: A Dialogue." *Studia Liturgica* 42 (2012): 154-175.

Borght, Eduardus Van der. *Studies in Reformed Theology, Vol.18: Unity of the Church: A Theological State of the Art and Beyond*. Boston: Brill, 2010.

Bosch, David J. *Transforming Missions: Paradigm Shifts in Theology of Missions.* New York: Orbis, 1992.

Bouyer, Louis. *Eucharist: Theology and Spirituality of the Eucharistic Prayer.* trans. *Charles Underhill Quinn.* Notre Dame, Indiana: University of Notre Dame, 1968.

Braaten, Carl E., and Robert W. Jenson, eds. *Reclaiming the Bible for the Church.* Grand Rapids, MI: William B Eerdmans, 1995.

Bradley, C. Randall. *From Memory to Imagination: Reforming the Church's Music* Cambridge: Grand Rapids, 2012.

Bradshaw, Paul F., and Maxwell E. Johnson. *The Eucharistic Liturgies: Their Evolution and Interpretation.* Collegeville, MN: Liturgical, 2012.

Bradshaw, Paul F. "Patterns of Ministry." *Studia Liturgica* 15, no.1 (1982): 55-58.

Bradshaw, Paul F. ed. *Essays in Early Eastern Eucharistic Prayers.* Collegeville, MN: Liturgical, 1997.

Bradshaw, Paul. *The New SCM Dictionary of Liturgy and Worship.* London: SCM, 2002.

Bria, Ion. "Unity and Mission from the Perspective of the Local Church: An Orthodox View." *The Ecumenical Review* 39 (1987): 265-270.

Bria, Ion. ed. *Go Forth in Peace: Orthodox Perspectives on Mission.* Geneva: WCC, 1986.

Bria, Ion. *The Liturgy after the Liturgy: Mission and Witness from an Orthodox Perspective.* Geneva: WCC, 1996.

Brink, Laurie. "In Search of the Biblical Foundations of Prophetic Dialogue: Engaging a Hermeneutics of Otherness." *Missiology: An International Review* 41, no.1 (January 2013): 9-21.

Broadley, George and Howard. *The Christians of St. Thomas and their Liturgies.* London, John Henry and James Parker, 1864.

Brock, Sebastian P. *Fire from Heaven: Studies in Syriac Theology and Liturgy.* Aldershot: Ashgate, 2006.

Brock, Sebastian P. *The Bible in the Syriac Tradition.* Kottayam: SEERI, 1988.

Brock, Sebastian P. *The Luminous Eye, the Spiritual World Vision of St. Ephrem.* Kalamazoo: Cistercian, 1985.

Brock, Sebastian. P. "An Early Syriac Commentary on the Liturgy." *Journal of Theological Studies* 37 (1986), 387-403.

Buchanan, Claudius. *Christian Researches in Asia with Notices of the Translation of the Scriptures into the Oriental Language.* London: T. Caddell and W. Davide, 1814.

Buchanon, Collin. ed. *Anglican Eucharistic Liturgies 1985-2010.* London: Canterbury, 2011.

Burns, Stephen. *The SCM Study Guide to Liturgy.* London: SCM, 1996.

Callaghan, Paul O. *Christ Our Hope: An Introduction to Eschatology.* Washington D.C: The Catholic University of America, 2011.

Carino, Feliciano V., and Marina True, eds. *Faith and Life in Contemporary Asian Realities.* Hong Kong: Christian Conference of Asia, 2000.

Carson, D.A. *Christ and Culture Revisited.* Nottingham: Inter-Varsity, 2008.

Casey, Damien. "Liturgy Matters: Liturgy and Scripture as the Mirrors of Catholicity." *Australian eJournal of Theology* 4 (2005): 1-7.

Chacko, M.C. *Thaksa Committee Report.* Thiruvalla: R.V. 1925.

Chacko, T. C. *The Concise History of the Mar Thoma Church.* 5th ed. Thiruvalla: Episcopal Jubilee Institute, 2001.

Cherian P, *The Malabar Syrians and the Church Mission Society: 1816-1840.* Kottayam: Church Missionary Press, 1935.

Chupungco, Anscar J. *Handbook for Liturgical Studies,* Collegeville, MN: Liturgical, 2000.

Chupungco, Anscar J. *Cultural Adaptation of the Liturgy.* New York: Paulist, 1992.

Chupungco, Anscar J. *Liturgical Inculturation, Sacramentals, Religiosity, and Catechesis.* Collegeville, MN: Liturgical, 1992.

Clarke, Sathianathan. *Dalits and Christianity: Subaltern Religions and Liberation Theology in India.* Calcutta: Oxford University Press, 1998.

Clavairoly, Francois. "Protestantism and Theology of Ministries: Ecumenical Perspective." *Theology Digest* 49, no. 1 (Spring 2002): 51-56.

Clendenin, Daniel B. ed. *Eastern Orthodox Theology: A Contemporary Reader.* Grand Rapids, MI: Baker Book, 1995.

Clifford, Greets. *The Interpretations of Cultures.* New York: Basic Books, 1973.

Cohen, Robin. *Global Diasporas: An Introduction.* London: Routledge, 2008.

Commission of Faith and Order, World Council of Churches. "Towards Koinonia in Worship: Consultation on the Role of Worship within the Search of Unity." *Studia Liturgica* 25, no.1 (1995): 1-31.

Commission on World Mission and Evangelism. *Together Towards Life: Mission and Evangelism in Changing Landscapes.* Geneva: World Council of Churches, 2013.

Congar, Yves. *Tradition and Traditions: An Historical and Theological Essay.* New York: Macmillan, 1967.

Crawford, David S. "Christian Community and the States of Life." *Communio-International Catholic Review* XXIX (2002): 337-365.

Crockett, William R. "Christianity and Culture in Modern Secular Society." *Studia Liturgica* 20 (1990): 28-35.

Cullman, Oscar. *Baptism in the New Testament.* London: SCM, 1950.

Daniel, Joseph. *Ecumenism in Praxis: A Historical Critique of the Malankara Mar Thoma Syrian Church.* Frankfurt: Peter Lang, 2014.

Daniel, K. N. *Malankara Sabhayum Naveekaranavum.* Vol. I. Thiruvalla: K. N. Daniel, 1949.

Daniel, W. Harrison. "The Young John Wesley as Cross-Cultural Witness; Investigations into Wesley's American Mission Experience and

Implications for Today's Mission." *Missiology: An International Review* 28/4 (October 2000): 443-458.

Danielou, Jean. *The Bible and the Liturgy.* Notre Dame: University of Notre Dame, 1973.

Darragh, Neil. "Hazardous Missions and Shifting Frameworks." *Missiology: An International Review* XXXVIII, no.3 (July 2010): 271-280.

Davies, John Gordon. "The Missionary Dimension of Worship." *Studia Liturgica* 6, 2 (1969): 79-84.

Davies, John Gordon. *Worship and Mission.* London: SCM, 1966.

Davis, Charles. *Sacraments of Initiation, Baptism, and Confirmation.* New York: Sheed and Ward, 1964.

Day, Peter D. *The Liturgical Dictionary of Eastern Christianity.* Kent: Burns and Oates, 1993.

Dimock, Giles. *The Eucharist.* New York: Paulist, 2006.

Doe, Michael. *Saving Power: The Mission of God and Anglican Communion.* London: SPCK, 2011.

Dorn, Christopher. "Lord's Supper in the Reformed Church in America: Tradition in Transformation." *American University Studies VII: Theology and Religion.* Vol. 264. New York: Peter Lang, 2007.

Draper, Jonathan A. "The Apostolic Fathers: The Didache." *Expository Times* 117:5 (Feb. 2006): 177-181.

Egan, Joe., and Brendan McConvery, eds. *Faithful Witness: Glimpses of the Kingdom.* Dublin: Milltown Institute of Theology and Philosophy, 2005.

Elavathingal, Sebastian. *Inculturation and Christian Art: An Indian Perspective.* Rome: Urbiana University, 1990.

Eliade, Mircea. ed. T*he Encyclopaedia of Religion.* Vol.14. London: Mac Millan, 1997.

Engineer, Asghar Ali. *On Developing Theory of Communal Riots.* Bombay: Institute of Islamic Studies, 1984.

Ernest Falardeau. *A Holy and Living Sacrifice: The Eucharist in Christian Perspective*. Collegeville, MN: Liturgical, 1996.

Ervvine, Roberta R. *Some Distinctive Features in Syriac Liturgical Texts*. New York: St. Nersess Armenian Seminary, 2006.

Faith and Order Paper No.210. *One Baptism: Towards Mutual Recognition-A Study Text*. Geneva: World Council of Churches, 2011.

Federov, Vladimir. "Orthodox Mission Today." *Together in Mission: Orthodox Churches Consult with the Church Mission Society*. Mosco (April 2001): 13-14.

Fenwick, John R K. "The Missing Oblation." *The Contents of the Early Antichene Anaphora* Grove Liturgical Study 59. Nottingham: Grove Books, 1989.

Fenwick, John R. K, and Bryan D. Spinks. *Worship in Transition: The Liturgical Movement in the Twentieth Century*. New York: Continuum, 1995.

Fenwick, John R. K. *The Forgotten Bishops: The Malabar Independent Syrian Church and its Place in the Story of the St. Thomas Christians of South India*. Piscataway, New Jersey: Gorgias, 2009.

Fenwick, John R.K. *Liturgy for Identity and Spirituality*. Kottayam: Thomas Mar Athanasius Memorial Research and Orientation Centre, 2008.

Ferguson, Everett. ed. *Encyclopedia of Early Christianity*. London: St. James, 1990.

Figura, Michael. "The Works of communion: Christian Community in Act." *Communio-International Catholic Review* XXIX (2002): 220-238.

Fink, Peter. ed. *The New Dictionary of Sacramental Worship*. Collegeville, MN: Liturgical, 1990.

Flannery, Austin. ed. *Sacrosanctum Concilium* 14, Vatican Council II: Conciliar and Post –Conciliar Documents. New York:.Costello, 1975.

Francis, Mark R. *Liturgy in a Multicultural Community*. Collegeville, MN: Liturgical, 1991.

Garrett, T.S. *Christian Worship: An Introductory Outline*. Oxford: Oxford University, 1961.

Garrigan, Siobhan. "A New Model for Ecumenical Worship." *Studia Liturgica* 43, no.1 (2013): 32-53.

Geevarghese, K.E., and Mathew T. Thomas, eds. *Beyond the Diaspora*. Thiruvalla: Mar Thoma Church Diocese of North America and Europe, 2014.

Gelder, Craig Van, and Dwight J. Zscheile. *The Missional Church in Perspective: Mapping Trends and Shaping the Conversation*. Grand Rapids: Baker Academie, 2011.

Gelineau, *Joseph*. "New Models for the Eucharistic Prayer as Praise of All the Assembly." *Studia Liturgica 27 (1997): 79-87.*

Gelston, A. "The East Syrian Eucharistic Prayers." In *The Serious Business of Worship: Essays in Honour of Bryan D. Spinks*, edited by Ross M. and Jones, S. London: T and T. Clark, 2010. 55-64.

George, Alexander. ed. *Maramon Convention Sathabdhi Valyam*. Thiruvalla: Mar Thoma Evangelistic Association, 1995.

George, Sam. "Diaspora: A Hidden Link to 'from Everywhere to Everywhere." *Missiology: An International Review* XXXIX, no.1 (January, 2011): 45-56.

Glasser, Arthur F, and Donal A. McGavran. *Contemporary Theologies of Mission*. Grand Rapids, MI: Baker Book, 1983.

Glover, Robert Hall. *The Bible Basis of Missions*. Chicago: MOODY. 1976.

Guder, Darrell L. "Missional Church." *International Catholic Review* XXIX (2002): 220-238.

Guder, Darrell L. ed. *Missional Church: A Vision for the Sending of the Church in North America*. Grand Rapids: Eerdmans, 1998.

Guthrie, Shirley C. *Always Being Reforming*. London: Westminster John Knox, 2008.

Guy, L. *Introducing Early Christianity: A Topical Survey of its Life, Beliefs, and Practices*. Illinois: Inter Varsity, 2004.

Hellwig, Monika K. *Encyclopedia of Religion.* Vol. V. Collegeville, MN: The Liturgical. 2004.

Hesselgrave, David J, and Edward Rommen. *Contextualization: Meanings, Methods and Models.* California: William Carey Library, 2000.

Hofinger, Johannes. ed. *Liturgy and the Missions: The Nijmegen Papers.* New York: P J. Kennedy and Sons, 1960.

Holeton, David R. ed. *Liturgical Inculturation in the Anglican Communion.* Liturgical Studies 15. Nottingham: Grove Books, 1990.

Hopko, Thomas. *The Orthodox Faith.* Vol 4. Crestwood, New York: Vladimir Seminary, 1984.

Irwin, Kevin W. *Models of the Eucharist.* New York: Paulist, 2005.

Jalmarson, Leonard E. "Trinitarian Spirituality of Mission." *Journal of Spiritual Formation and Soul Care* 6, 1 (2013), 93-109.

Jeffery, Peter. "The Meanings and Functions of Kyrie eleison." In *The Place of Christ in Liturgical Prayer: Trinity, Christology, and Liturgical Theology,* edited by Bryan D. Spinks and Martin Jean. Collegeville, MN: Liturgical, 2008. 127-194.

John, George. "Mar Thoma Syrian Church in the Arabia Gulf Context." In *In Search of Christian Identity in Global Community,* edited by M.J. Joseph. Thiruvalla: The Dioceses of North America and Europe, 2008. 63-67.

John, Zacharia. "*The Liturgy of the Mar Thoma Church of Malabar in the Light of its History.*" Master's thesis, University of Durham, 1994.

Johnson, Dale A. "Lectionary", Syriac Orthodox Resources, http://sor.cua.edu/Lectionary/ (accessed February 12, 2016).

Johnson, Maxwell E. "The Apostolic Tradition." In *The Oxford History of Christian Worship,* edited by Geoffrey Wainwright and Karen B. Westerfield Tucker. Oxford: Oxford University, 2006. 32-75.

Johnson, Maxwell E. *The Rites of the Christian Initiation: Their Evolution and Interpretation.* Collegeville, MN: Liturgical, 1999.

Joseph, M. J. ed. *In Search for Christian Identity in Global Community.* New York: Dioceses of North America and Europe, 2009.

Joseph, M. J. ed. *Malankara Mar Thoma Syrian Church: Sabha Directory 2015.* 4th ed. Thiruvalla: Mar Thoma Syrian Church, 2015.

Kane, Herbert J. *Understanding Christian Missions.* Grand Rapids, MI: Baker Book, 1983.

Kannookadan, Pauly. ed. *The Mission Theology of the Syro-Malabar Church.* Kochi: Liturgical Research Centre, 2008.

Kärkkäinen, Veli Matti. *An Introduction to Ecclesiology.* Downer's Grove: Intervarsity, 2002.

Karotemprel, Gregory., and Jacob Marangattu, eds. *Evangelizing In The Third Millennium.* Series No-1. Rajkot: Deepti Publication, 2006.

Kavanagh, Aidan. "Liturgical Inculturation: Looking to the Future." *Studia Liturgica* 20 (1990): 96-106.

Keay, F.E. *A History of the Syrian Church in India.* Delhi: ISPCK, 1960.

Kennedy, David J. *Eucharistic Sacramentality in an Ecumenical Context: The Anglican Epiclesis.* Aldershot: Ashgate, 2008.

Kennedy. Robert J. ed. *Reconciliation: The Continuing Agenda.* Collegeville, MN: Liturgical, 1987.

King, Archdale. *The Rites of the Eastern Christendom.* Rome: Catholic Book Agency, 1948.

Kirk, Andrew J. *The Mission of Theology and Theology as Mission-Christian Mission and Modern Culture.* Series, 6. Pennsylvania: Trinity Press International, 1997.

Kirk, Andrew J. *What Is Mission? Theological Explorations.* Minneapolis: Fortress, 2000.

Knight, Douglas H. ed. *The Theology of John Zizioulas.* Aldershot: Ashgate, 2007.

Koch, Kurt. "Principles for a Christian Theology of Baptism." *Theology Digest* 52 (2005): 231-242.

Kochuparampil, Jose. "The Missionary Dimension of the Liturgy in the Ananphora of the Apostles Addai and Mari." *Studia Liturgica* 36, 2 (2006): 129-137.

Kochuparampil, Xavier. "The Liturgical Dimension of Evangelisation." *Questions liturgique* 72 (1991): 218-230.

Koodapuzha, Xavier. ed. *Eastern Theological Reflection in India.* Kottayam: Oriental Institute of Religious Studies, 1999.

Kostarelos, Frances. "Short Term Missions in the Orthodox Church in North America." *Missiology: An International Review* 41, no.2 (April 2013): 179-185.

Kruisheer, Dirk, and Lucas Van Rompay. "A Bibliographical Clavis to the Works of Jacob of Edessa," *Hugoye: Journal of Syriac Studies* 1, no.1 (1998): 35-56

Kurian, Prema. "Denominationalism to Post-Denominationalism: Changes in American Christianity." *Mar Thoma Messenger 30*, no.2 (April 2011): 23-27.

Kuruvila, Abraham. "Revision of Liturgy and Renewal of People." In *Christheeyathayude Vishala Maanagal,* edited by *Abraham* Kuruvila. Thiruvalla: Mar Thoma Church Publication Board, 1988.

Kuttiyil, George Mathew. "Liturgy for the 21st Century." In *The Mar Thoma Church: Tradition and Modernity,* edited by P.J. Alexander. Thiruvalla: Mar Thoma Church, 2000.

Kuttiyil, George Mathew. "The Baptismal Liturgy of the Mar Thoma Syrian Church of Malabar." In *Baptism Today,* edited by Thomas F. Best. Geneva: World Council of Churches, 2008.

Kuttiyil, George Mathew. *Eucharist (Qurbana): The Celebration of the Economy of Salvation (Madabranutha) - A Theological Analysis of the Anaphora of St. James.* Kottayam: Oriental Institute of Religious Studies, 1999.

Kuttiyil, George Mathew. *Liturgy for Our Times.* Kerala: Christava Sahitya Samithi, 2006.

Lathrop, Gordon. *What are the Essentials of Christian Worship?* Minneapolis, MN: Augsburg Fortress, 1994.

Letham, Robert. *Through Western Eyes- Eastern Orthodoxy: A Reformed Perspective.* Wales: Mentor, 2007.

Liturgical Commission of the Church of England. *New Patterns for Worship.* London; Church House, 2002.

Lott, Eric J. ed. *Worship in an Indian Context.* Bangalore: United Theological College, 1986.

Lutheran World Federation. "Nairobi Statement on Worship and Culture: Contemporary Challenges and Opportunities." *Studia Liturgica* 27 (1997): 88-93.

Luzbetak, Louis J. *The Church and Cultures: New Perspectives in Missiological Anthropology.* Maryknoll, New York: Orbis, 1988.

Malipurathu, Thomas., and L. Stanislaus, eds. *A Vision of Mission in the New Millennium.* Mumbai: St Paul's, 2001.

Mannion, Francic M. *Masterworks of God: Essays in Liturgical Theory and Practice.* Illinois, Chicago: Hillenbrand Books, 2004.

Mannooparambil, Thomas. "Liturgical Spiritualty." In *Eastern Theological Reflection in India,* edited by Xaviour Koodapuzha. Kottayam: Oriental Institute of Religious Studies, 1999. 220-225.

Mar Athanasius, Thomas Suffragan, and T. P. Abraham. *Navvekaranavum Sabhayude Dwuthyavum* Thiruvalla: T. A. M, 1984.

Mar Makkarios, Mathews. "Mission of the Church: Contextual and Universal." *Mar Thoma Seminary Journal of Theology* 1, no.1 (June 2012): 58-61.

Mar Theodosius, Geevarghese. "Mar Thoma Church." In *Mar Thoma Church: Tradition and Modernity,* edited by P.J. Alexander. Thiruvalla: Mar Thoma Syrian Church, 2000. 98-102.

Mar Theodosius, Geevarghese. "Maramon Convention: Mission and Ministry." *Mar Thoma Messenger* (2009): 28-31

Mar Theodosius, Geevarghese. "Shifting meaning in Public, Religion and Domestic Spaces: Theological, Ministerial and Missional Challenges." *Mar Thoma Messenger* 34, no. 3 (July 2015): 14-17.

Mar Theodosius, Geevarghese. *Churching the Diaspora, Disciplining the Families.* Thiruvalla: Diocese of North America and Europe, 2015.

Mar Thoma, Alexander. *The Mar Thoma Church: Heritage and Mission.* Thiruvalla: Mar Thoma Publication, 1985.

Mar Thoma, Juhanon. *The History of the Mar Thoma Church and the Christian Church in India.* Thiruvalla: Christava Sahitya Samithi, 1973.

Mar Thoma, Titus II. *Malankara Mar Thoma Suriyani Sabhayude Qurbana Thaksa.* Thiruvalla: Mar Thoma, 1942.

Marsh, Thomas A. *Gift of the Community Baptism and Confirmation.* Collegeville: MN: The Liturgical, 1984.

Mathew, C.P, and M. M. Thomas. *The Indian Churches of St. Thomas.* Delhi: ISPCK, 1967.

Mathew, Geevarghese. "Mar Thoma Theological Seminary: A Retrospective Reading." Mar Thoma Seminary Journal of Theology 1, no. 1 (June 2012):9-12.

Mathew, N. M. *Malankara Mar Thoma Sabha Charithram.* Vol. I.II.III. Thiruvalla: Mar Thoma Episcopal Jubilee Institute of Evangelism, 2003.

Mathew. C.P. *Thaksa Nirupanam.* New Delhi: Dharma Jyothi Viddya Peeth, 2008

Mattackal, Abraham. "The Mar Thoma Church and its Diaspora Communities around the world." *Mar Thoma Messenger* 10 (2009): 12-13.

Mazza, Enrico. *The Origin of the Eucharistic Prayer.* Collegeville, MN: Liturgical, 1995.

Mc Guckin, John Anthony. T*he Orthodox Church: An Introduction to its History, Doctrine, and Spiritual Culture.* Sussex: Wiley-Blackwell, 2011.

Mcanus, Frederick R. *Liturgical Participation: An Ongoing Assessment.* Washington: The Pastoral, 1988.

McKenna, J. H. *The Eucharistic Epiclesis: A Detailed History from the Patristic to the Modern Era.* Chicago, Illinois: Hillenbrand, 2009.

McMillan, David W., and David M. Chavis. "Sense of Community: A Definition and Theory." *Journal of Community Psychology* 14 (1996): 7-10.

Meisner, Joachim. "Eucharist and Evangelization." *Christ Light of Nations.* Sherbrooke: Paulines, 1994.

Menacherry, George. ed. *Indian Church History Classics. The Nazranis.* Thrissur: SARAS, 1998.

Menachery, George. ed. *The St. Thomas Christian Encyclopaedia of India.* Vol.1, Thrissur: St. Thomas Christian Encyclopedia, 1982.

Meno. "Syrian Orthodox Church." In *The Encyclopedia of Christianity,* Vol. 5, edited by E. Fahlbusch. Grand Rapids, MI: Eerdmans, 2008. 281-284.

Metropolitan, Titus II. Mar Thoma. *Qurbana Thaksa of the Malankara Mar Thoma Syrian Church.* 6th ed. Thiruvalla: Mar Thoma Sabha, 2001.

Meyendorf, John. *Trinitarian Theology East and West.* Brookline: Holy Cross Orthodox, 1977.

Meyendorff, John. "Christ as Word: Gospel and Culture." *International Review of Missions* 74 (1985): 246-257.

Meyers, Ruth A. "Ongoing Liturgical Revision in the Episcopal Church USA." Studia Liturgica 31(2001): 61-69.

Michael, John Britto. "*The Church's Marian Profile and Evangelization in India: In the Light of the Federation of Asian Bishop's Conferences'*

Documentation on Evangelization." PhD diss., St. Patrick's College, 2014.

Moltmann, Jürgen, "The Mission of the Spirit: the Gospel of Life." In *Mission: An Invitation to God's Future,* edited by Timothy Yates. Sheffield: Cliff College Publishing, 2000. 19-34.

Moolaveetil, L. *A Study of the Anaphora of St. James.* Kottayam: St. Thomas Apostolic Seminary, 1976.

Moreau, Scott. ed. *Evangelical Dictionary of World Missions.* Grand Rapids: Baker, 2000.

Muller, Karl, Theo Sundermeier, Stephen B. Bevans, and Richard H. Bliese. eds. *Dictionary of Mission: Theology, History, Perspectives.* New York: Orbis, 1999.

Mundadan, Mathias A. *History of Christianity in India, From the Beginning up to the Middle of the Sixteenth Century.* Vol. I. Bangalore: Church History Association of India, 1989.

Mundadan, Mathias A. *Indian Christians: Search for Identity and Struggle for Autonomy.* Bangalore: Dharamaram Publications, 1982.

Naduthadam, Sebastian. ed. *The Spirituality of the Syro-Malabar Church.* Kochi: Liturgical Research Centre, 2009.

Neill, Stephen. *A History of Christian Missions.* 2nd ed. New York: Penguin, 1986.

Nessan, Craig L. *Beyond Maintenance to Mission: A Theology of the Congregation.* Minneapolis: Fortress, 2010.

Newbigin, Lesslie. *The Logic of Election' in the Gospel in a Pluralistic Society.* Grand Rapids, MI: Eerdmans, 1989.

Newbigin, Lesslie. *The Household of God.* New York: Friendship, 1954.

Newbigin, Lesslie. *The Open Secret: An Introduction to the Theology of Mission.* Grand Rapids, MI: Eerdmans, 1975.

Newbigin, Lesslie. *The Relevance of Trinitarian Doctrine for Todays Mission.* London: Edinburgh House, 1963.

Niebuhr, H. Richard. *Christ and Culture*. New York: Harper and Row, 1951.

Ninan, K. I. *Sabhacharithra Vichinthanagal: Anglican Kalaghattam*. Thiruvalla: Christava Sahitya Samithi, 1997.

Nugent, Vincent J. "Theological Foundation for Mission Animation: A Study of the Church's Essence." *World Mission* 24, no.1 (Spring 1943): 7-18.

Nussbaum, Stan. *A Reader's Guide to Transforming Mission*. Maryknoll, New York: Orbis, 2005.

Oborji, Francis Anekwe. *Concepts of Mission: The Evolution of Contemporary Missiology* Maryknoll, New York: Orbis, 2006.

Old, H.O. *Worship: Reformed According to Scripture*. Louisville, Kentucky: John Knox, 2002.

Pallikunnil, Jameson K. *The Eucharistic Liturgy: A Liturgical Foundation for Mission in the Malankara Mar Thoma Syrian Church*. Bloomington: AuthorHouse, 2017.

Panicker, Geevarghese and John Vellian. *A Historical Introduction to the Syriac Liturgy*. Kottayam: SEERI, 2010.

Pathil, Kuncheria. "A Response to Religious Pluralism." In *In Search of Christian Identity in Global Community,* edited by M. J. Joseph. Thiruvalla: Dioceses of North America and Europe, 2008. 89-92.

Paul, Kadavil P. *The Eucharist Service of the Syrian Jacobite Church of Malabar: The Meaning and the Interpretation*. 2nd ed. Piscataway: Gorgias, 2003.

Payton, James R. JR, *Light from the Christian East: An Introduction to the Orthodox Tradition*. Illinois: Inter-Varsity, 2007.

Pecklers, Keith F. *Dynamic Equivalence: The Living Language of Christian Worship*. Collegeville, MN: Liturgical, 2003.

Pecklers, Keith F. *Worship, New Century Theology*. London; Continuum, 2003.

Perera, Rienze. "Religion, Cultures and Peace: The Challenge of Religious Pluralism and the Common Life of Asia." In *Faith and Life in Contemporary Asian Realities,* edited by Feliciano V. Carino and Marina True. Hong Kong: Christian Conference of Asia, 2000. 112-116.

Pfatteieher, H. Philip. *Liturgical Spirituality,* Pennsylvania, Trinity International, 1997.

Philip, A. T. "Liturgical Imperatives of the Mar Thoma Church." In *A Study on the Malankara Mar Thoma Church Liturgy,* edited by M.V. Abraham and Abraham Philip. Manganam: Thomas Mar Athanasius Memorial Orientation Centre, 1993. 22-42.

Philip, T.V. *East of the Euphrates: Early Christianity in Asia.* New Delhi: ISPCK, 1998.

Pitre, Brant. *Jesus and the Jewish Roots of the Eucharist.* New York: Image, 2011.

Pocknee, Cyril E. *Liturgical Vesture: Its Origin and Development.* Alcuin: A. R. Mowbray, 1960.

Podipara, Placid J. *Reflections on Liturgy.* Kottayam: Oriental Institute of Religious Studies, 1983.

Poikail, George. *ST. Thomas Christians and their Eucharistic Liturgy.* Thiruvalla: Christava Sahitya Samithi, 2010.

Porter, Stanley E, and Anthony R. Cros. eds. *Dimensions of Baptism: Biblical and Theological Studies.* London: Sheffield Academic, 2002.

Power, David Noel. "Liturgy and Culture Revisited." *Worship* 69 (1995): 225-243.

Power, David Noel. *Worship: Culture and Theology.* Washington DC: Pastoral, 1990.

Price, Charles, and Ian Randall. *Transforming Keswick.* London: OM, 2000.

Provost, James H. ed. *The Church as Mission.* Washington D.C: Canon law Society of America, 1984.

Rathe, Mark Steven. *"The Keswick Movement its Origins and Teachings."* Master's thesis, San Francisco: Simpson College, 1987.

Ratizinger, J. *The Spirit of the Liturgy.* San Fransisco: Ignatius, 2004.

Rausch, Thomas P. *Eschatology, Liturgy, and Christology: Towards Recovering an Eschatological Imagination.* Collegeville, MN: Liturgical, 2012.

Redding, Graham. *Prayer and the Priesthood of Christ in the Reformed Tradition.* London: T and T Clark, 2003.

Safran, Willaim. "Deconstructing and Comparing Diasporas." In *Diaspora, Identity and Religion: New Directions in Theory and Research,* edited by Waltraud Kokot, Kachig Tololyan, and Carolin Alfonso. London: Routledge, 2004. 8-14.

Saldanha Ulian. *Attempts of Evangelization in Mission History.* Mumbai: St. Paul's, 2009.

Samarth, Stanley J. *One Christ Many religions.* Bangalore: SATHRI, 1992.

Samartha, Stanley. J. "Exegetical Preaching in a Pluralist Society." *Masihi Sevak* 16 (January 1994): 28-34.

Sanneh, Lamin. *Translating the Message: The Missionary Impact on Culture.* Maryknoll, New York: Orbis, 1989.

Scherer, James A, and Stephen B. Bevans. eds. *New Directions in Mission and Evangelization: Theological Foundations.* Maryknoll, New York: Orbis, 1994.

Schineller, Peter. *A Handbook on Inculturation.* New York: Paulist, 1990.

Schmemann, Alexander. *Church, World, Mission.* New York: St. Vladimir's Seminary, 1979.

Schmemann, Alexander. *For the Life of the World.* New York: St. Vladimir's Seminary, 1973.

Schmemann, Alexander. *Of Water and the Spirit: A Liturgical Study on Baptism.* Crestwood, New York: St. Vladimir's Seminary, 1974.

Searle, Mark. *Called to Participate: Theological, Ritual and Social Perspectives.* Collegeville, MN: Liturgical, 2006.

Senn, Frank C. "Ninety-Five Theses on the State of Liturgical Renewal in the Lutheran Churches in North America." *Liturgy* 26, no.4 (2011): 26-35.

Senn, Frank C. *Christian Liturgy: Catholic and Evangelic.* Minneapolis: Fortress, 1997.

Sharma, S. L, and T. K. Oommen. eds. *Nation and National Identity in South Asia.* New Delhi: Orient Longman, 2000.

Sheerin, D.J. ed. *The Eucharist, The Message of the Fathers.* Vol. 7. Delware: Michael Glazier, 1986.

Sheridan, M. *Ancient Christian Commentary on Scripture.* Downers Grove, Illinois: Intervarsity. 2002.

Shorter, Aylward. ed. *Evangelisation and Culture.* London: Geoffrey Chapman, 1994.

Shorter, Aylward. *Toward a Theology of Inculturation.* London: Geoffrey Chapman, 1988.

Smith, David. *Mission After Christendom.* London: Longman and Todd, 2003.

Soares, Prabhu George M. "Religion and Communalism: the Christian Dilemma." In *Responding to Communalism: The Task of Religions and Theology,* edited by S. Arokiasamy. Anand: Gujrat Sahitya Prakash, 1991. 138-142.

Sowell, Thomas. *Migrations and Cultures: A World View.* New York: Basic Books, 1996.

Spencer, Stephen. *SCM Study Guide to Christian Mission.* London: SCM, 2007.

Spindler, M. R, F. J. Verstraelen, A. Camps, and L.A. Hoedemaker. eds. *Missiology: An Ecumenical Introduction.* Grand Rapids, MI: Eerdmans, 1995.

Spinks, Bryan D. "Eastern Christian Liturgical Traditions: Oriental Orthodox." In *The Blackwell Companion to Eastern Christianity,* edited by Parry, K. Oxford: Blackwell, 2007. 339-367.

Spinks, Bryan D. *Do This in Remembrance of Me: The Eucharist From the Early Church to the Present D*ay. London: SCM, 2013.

Stamoolis, James. J. *Eastern Orthodox Mission Theology Today.* Eugene: Wipf and Stock, 2001.

Stancliffe, David. "The Making of the Church of England's Common Worship." *Studia Liturgica* 31 (2001):14-25.

Staniforth, M. "The Didache." In *Early Christian Writings: The Apostolic Fathers,* edited by A. Louth. London: Penguin, 1987. 191-199.

Stanislaus, L, and Thomas Malipurathu. eds. *A Vision of Mission in the New Millennium.* Mumbai: St Paul's, 2001.

Stanley, Brian. ed. *Christian Missions and the Enlightenment.* Cambridge: William B. Eerdmans, 2001.

Stansky, Thomas F, and Gerals H. Anderson. eds. *Mission Trends No. 1: Critical Issues in Mission Today.* New York: Paulist, 1974.

Stauffer, Anita S. ed. *Worship and Culture in Dialogue.* Geneva: Lutheran World Federation, 1994.

Stauffer, S. Anita, "Worship and Culture: Five Theses." *Studia Liturgica* 26 (1996): 323-332.

Stauffer, S. Anita. *Christian Worship: Unity in Cultural Diversity.* Geneva: Lutheran World Federation, 1996.

Stearns, Peter. *Cultures in Motion: Mapping Key Contacts their Imprints in World History* New Haven: Yale University, 2001.

Stephen Conway. *Living the Eucharist: Affirming Catholicism and the Liturgy.* London: Darton, Longmand and Todd, 2001.

Stern, S. *Calendar and Community: A History of the Jewish Calendar, Second Century BCE-Tenth Century CE.* Oxford: Oxford University, 2001.

Stringer, Martin. *Rethinking the Origins of the Eucharist.* London: SCM, 2011.

Stylianopoulos, T.G. *The New Testament: An Orthodox Perspective. Vol. One: Scripture, Tradition, Hermeneutics.* Brookline: Massachusetts: Holy Cross Orthodox, 1997.

Swan, Billy. *The Eucharist, Communion and Formation: Proceedings of the International Symposium of Theology: The Ecclesiology of Communion Fifty Years after the Opening of Vatican II.* Dublin: Veritas, 2013.

Taft, Robert F, H-J Feulner, and E Velkovska. eds. *Crossroad of Cultural Studies in Liturgy and Patristics in Honour of Gabriele Winkler.* Rome: Pontificio Istituto Orientale, 2000.

Taft, Robert. F. *The Liturgy of the Hours in East and West: The Origins of the Divine Office and Its Meaning for Today.* Collegeville, MN: Liturgical, 1986.

Taylor, William D. ed. *Global Missiology for the 21st Century.* Grand Rapids, MI: Baker Academic, 2000.

Thazhayil, Thomas. "The Church at Crossroads." *Mar Thoma Messenger 32, no 3 (*July 2013): 31-33.

The Constitution on the Sacred Liturgy, *Sacrosanctum Concilium* No.24, Promulgated in December 4, 1963. http://www.stolivers.com/ReligiousEd/constitution.pdf (accessed September 10, 2015).

Thomas, Alex. "The Mar Thoma Church: Then and Now." In *In Search of Christian Identity in Global Community,* edited by M.J. Joseph. Thiruvalla: Dioceses of North America and Europe, 2008. 43-46.

Thomas, Alex. *A History of the First Cross Cultural Mission of the Mar Thoma Church 1910 - 2000.* Delhi; ISPCK, 2007.

Thomas, George. *Christian Indians and Indian Nationalism 1885-1950.* Frankfurt: Peter D. Lang, 1979.

Thomas, K.T. "Mar Thoma Evangelistic Association: Outside of Kerala." *Malankara Sabha Tharaka* 70, no. (September, 1963):18-21.

Thomas, M.C. "Diaspora, Mar Thoma Church Identity and Mission: Theoretical Considerations" In *Beyond the Diaspora,* edited by K.E.

Geevargeshe and Mathew T. Thomas. Thiruvalla: Mar Thoma Church Diocese of North America and Europe, 2014. 51-73.

Thomas, M.M. *The Church's Mission and Post Modern Humanism: Collection of Essays and Talks 1992-1996.* New Delhi: ISPCK, 1996.

Thomas, Norman E. ed. Classic Texts in Mission and World Christianity. *American Society of Missiology.* Vol.20. Maryknoll, New York: Orbis, 1995.

Thurian, Max. ed. *Churches Respond to BEM: Official Response to the "Baptism, Eucharist and Ministry." Text,* Vol. IV, Faith and Order Paper No. 137.Geneva: World Council of Churches, 1987. 7-13.

Thurian, Max. ed. *Churches Response to BEM - Official Response to the Baptism, Eucharist, and Ministry Text.* Vol. IV. Geneva: WCC, 1987.

Tillich, Paul. "The Theology of Missions." *The Journal Christianity and Crisis* (March 1955): 27-34.

Tololyan, Kachig, and Carolin Alfonso. eds. *Diaspora, Identity and Religion: New Directions in Theory and Research.* London: Routledge, 2004.

Torre, L. Della. *Understanding the Liturgy.* Athlon: St. Paul's, 1967.

Tovey, Phillip. "The Reformed Qurbana." *The Harp* XIV (2009): 253-258.

Tovey, Phillip. "Two Models of Inculturation and Eucharistic Prayers with Children." In *The Serious Business of Worship: Essays in Honour of Bryan D. Spinks,* edited by Melanie Ross and Simon Jones. London: T and T Clark International, 2010. 130-142

Tovey, Phillip. *Essays in West- Syrian Liturgy.* Kottayam: Oriental Institute of Religious Studies, 1997.

Tovey, Phillip. *Inculturation of Christian Worship.* Basingstoke: Ashgate, 2004.

Tovey, Phillip. *Inculturation: The Eucharist in Africa.* Nottingham: Grove Books, 1988.

Trevor, George. *India: its Natives and Missions.* London: The Religious Tract Society, 1859.

Tylor, E.B. "Culture at the Service of Evangelization in India" In *The St. Thomas Christian Encyclopaedia of India.* Vol.1, edited by George Menachery. Thrissur: St. Thomas Christian Encyclopaedia, 1982. 196-200.

Ussbaum, Stan. *A Reader's Guide to Transforming Mission.* New York: Orbis, 2007.

Varghese, Baby. "Some Aspects of West Syrian Liturgical Theology." *Studia Liturgica* 31, no.2 (2001): 171-178.

Varghese, Baby. "Anaphora of St. James and Jacob of Edessa." In *Jacob of Edessa and the Syriac Culture of His Day,* edited by Bas ter Haar Romeny. Leiden: Brill, 2008, 239-264.

Varghese, Baby. "West Syriac Liturgy: One Hundred Years of Research." *The Harp* 27, (2011): 53-72.

Varghese, Baby. *The Syriac Version of the Liturgy of St James: A Brief History for Students.* London: Grove Books, 2001.

Varghese, Baby. *West Syrian Liturgical Theology.* Aldershot: Ashgate, 2004.

Varghese, Eapen. "New Historicism and Michelle Foucault: Historiographical Critique of British Protestant Missionary Account of India Christianity." *Mar Thoma Seminary Journal of Theology* 1, no. 1 (June 2012): 103-116.

Varghese, J. *Biography of Mathews Mar Athanasios.* Thiruvalla: Mar Thoma Publication Society, 2011.

Varghese, Ninan. "Mar Thoma Medical Mission." *Malankara Sabha Tharaka* (February 2003): 21-22.

Varghese, Zac, and Mathew A. Kallumpuram. *Glimpses of the Mar Thoma Church History.* New Delhi: Kalpana Printing, 2003.

Varghese, Zac. "Mission and Message of the Mar Thoma Diaspora." In *In Search of Christian Identity in Global Community,* edited by M.J. Joseph. Thiruvalla: Christava Sahitya Samithi, 2008. 49- 52.

Varghese, Zac. ed. *Christian Witness: Revisiting the Mission Mandate of the Church*. Prathinidhimandalam 2009 Study. Thiruvalla: Mar Thoma Syrian Church, 2009.

Varughese, Koshy P. ed. *Challenges and Prospects of Mission in the Emerging Context*. Faridabad: Dharma Jyoti Vidya Peeth, 2010.

Vellian, Jacob. *History of the Syro-Malabar Liturgy*. Kottayam: Powrasthya Vidhya Peeth, 1967.

Vinayaraj. Y.T. "Border Lives and Border God: Diaspora Reconfigures Heritage, Mission and Theology." *Mar Thoma Messenger* 30 (2011): 10-11.

Wainwright, Geoffrey. "Christian Worship: Scriptural Basis and Theological Frame." In *The Oxford History of Christian Worship*, edited by Wainwright, Geoffrey and Karen B. Westerfield Tucker. Oxford: Oxford University, 2006. 1-31.

Walls, Andrew F. *The Missionary Movement in Christian History: Studies in the Transmission of Faith*. Maryknoll, New York: Orbis, 1996.

Westerfield, Karen B. "Baptism and Ecumenism: Agreements and Problems on the Journey Towards Mutual Recognition." *Studia Liturgica* 42 (2012): 1-12.

Whelan, Thomas R. "Multicultural Worship: Theological Reflections on Experience." In *Mission and Migration,* edited by Stephen Spencer. Derbys: Cliff College, 2008. 173-187.

Williams, A. N. "Tradition." In *Oxford Handbook of Systematic Theology*, edited by John Webster, Kathryn Tanner, and Iain Torrance. London: Oxford University, 2007. 363-365

Williams, Raymond. *The Sociology of Culture*. New York: Schocken Books, 1982.

Witvliet, John D. "The Opening of Worship-Trinity." In *A More Profound Alleluia: Theology and Worship in Harmony*, edited by Leanne Van Dyk. Grand Rapids, MI: William B. Eerdmans, 2005. 5-23.

Wood, George S. Jr and Juan C. Judikis. *Conversations on Community Theory.* West Lafayette, Ind: Purdue University, 2002.

Wright, Christopher. *The Mission of God.* Nottingham: Inter-Varsity, 2006.

Yannoulatos, Anastasios. "Orthodox Spirituality and External Mission." *International Review of Mission* 52 (1963): 300-302.

Zachariah, George K. "Mission of the Church." *Mar Thoma Messenger.* (October 2004): 17-19.

Zachariah, George K. "Mission of the Mar Thoma Church in the Context of the Diaspora Community in the West." *Mar Thoma Messenger* XXVI, no.4 (October, 2007): 24-28.

Zetterholm, Magnus. *The Formation of Christianity in Antioch.* London: Routledge, 2003.

Zizioulas, John. *Being as Communion.* Crestwood, New York: St. Vladimir's Seminary, 1985.

REPORTS/ MINUTES/ LETTERS/ MANUSCRIPTS

Report of the Third Meeting of the MTEA- (M.E. Dhanu 27, 1064) February 7, 1889. Thiruvalla: Mar Thoma Evangelistic Association, 1889.

Letter of Thomas Walker to Mrs. Walker, dated 15th February 1900. Thiruvalla: Mar Thoma Evangelistic Association, 1900.

Annual Report of the Mar Thoma Evangelistic Association. (23rd) 1911. Thiruvalla: Mar Thoma Evangelistic Association, 1911.

The Malabar Mar Thoma Syrian Christian Evangelistic Association: Memorandum and Articles of Association, as Amended in 1106 M.E. Thiruvalla: Mar Thoma Evangelistic Association, 1931.

Mar Thoma Syrian Church Samudayalochana Sabha. Resolution of the Mar Thoma Syrian Samudayalochana Sabha, May 5-6, 1936. Thiruvalla: Mar Thoma, 1936.

The Malabar Mar Thoma Syrian Christian Evangelistic Association Memorandum and Articles of Association: as Amended in 1106. Thiruvalla: TAM, 1960.

Annual Report of the Mar Thoma Evangelistic Association. Thiruvalla: Mar Thoma Press, 2011.

Annual Report 2012-13, Malabar Mar Thoma Syrian Christian Evangelistic Association, Thiruvalla: MMTSCEA, 2013.

Annual Report of the Church Council of the Mar Thoma Church for the Years: 1945-2010. Mar Thoma Church Office. Thiruvalla, India.

Mar Thoma, Abraham. "Metropolitan's Letter". In: *Malankara Sabha Tharaka,* all issues from 1945-1975.

Mar Thoma, Alexander. Metropolitan's Letter". In: *Malankara Sabha Tharaka,* all issues from 1976- 2000.

Seminar Report of the Liturgical Committee on 16th November 1977. Kottayam: CPMM Ecumenical Study Centre, 1977.

Constitution of the Mar Thoma Syrian Church of Malabar. English Version. Thiruvalla: Mar Thoma, 2002.

Joint Working Group between the Roma Catholic Church and the World Council of Churches. Ecclesiological and Ecumenical Implications of Common Baptism: A JWG Study Eighth Report. Geneva: WCC, 2005.

Annual Reports of the CARD: 1980-2012. Thiruvalla: Christian Agency for Rural Development.

The Malankara Mar Thoma Syrian Church, Constitution. Thiruvalla: V.G.C, 1998.

Unpublished liturgy of the Mar Thoma Episcopal Consecration, *Amalogia.* Thiruvalla: Kerala.

Mar Chrysostom, Philipose. Metropolitan's Letter". In: *Malankara Sabha Tharaka,* all issues from 2000-2008.

Mar Thoma Sleehayude Edavakayakunna Malankara Suriyani Sabhayude Canon, 2nd edition. New Delhi: Dharma Jyothi Vidhya Peedh, 2008.

Minutes of the Sabha Prathinidhi Mandalam, Thiruvalla, *Mar Thoma Sabha,* 2009.

The Service Book of Holy Eucharist (Anaphora). Puthencruz: JSC, 2010

CBCI Inter-Ritual Committee. Baptism and Confirmation. Bangalore: Theological Publications in India, 2010.

Mission Report of the Mar Thoma Church, Diocese of North-America and Europe -2011. New York: North America Europe Dioceses of the Mar Thoma Church, 2011.

Letter to the Metropolitan Joseph Mar Thoma on 10th December 2013 by the Liturgical Commission of the Mar Thoma Church, Thiruvalla, Kerala.

Mar Thoma, Joseph. "Metropolitan's Letter." In: *Malankara Sabha Tharaka*, All issues from 2005-2015.

Annual Report of the Malankara Mar Thoma Syrian Church 2014-2015. Thiruvalla: Mar Thoma Sabha Council, 2015.

Annual Report of the Council of Mar Thoma Parishes in Europe. London: COMPE, 2015.

Report of the Liturgical Commission of the Mar Thoma Church: 2014-2015. Thiruvalla: Mar Thoma, 2015.

Circular No. DC/568/15, by Dr. Geevarghese Mar Theodosius Episcopa, Dioceses of North America and Europe on 20th September, 2015.

Printed in Germany
by Amazon Distribution
GmbH, Leipzig